"*The Heresy of Orthodoxy* will help many to make sense of what is happening in early Christian studies today. It explains, critiques, and provides an alternative to, the so-called Bauer thesis, an approach which undergirds a large segment of scholarship on early Christianity. That 'doctrine'—Christianity before the fourth century was but a seething mass of diverse and competing factions, with no theological center that could claim historical continuity with Jesus and his apostles—has become the new 'orthodoxy' for many. The authors of this book do more than expose the faults of this doctrine; they point the way to a better foundation for early Christian studies, focusing on the cornerstone issues of the canon and the text of the New Testament. Chapter 8, which demonstrates how one scholar's highly-publicized twist on New Testament textual criticism only tightens the tourniquet on his own views, is alone worth the price of the book. Köstenberger and Kruger have done the Christian reading public a real service."

Charles E. Hill, Professor of New Testament, Reformed Theological Seminary

"The Bauer thesis, taken up in many university circles and popularized by Bart Ehrman and through TV specials, has long needed a thorough examination. *The Heresy of Orthodoxy* is that work. Whether looking at Bauer's thesis of diversity, at contemporary use made of the theory to argue for the early origin of Gnosticism, at the process that led to the canon, or what our manuscript evidence is, this study shows that Bauer's theory, though long embraced, is full of problems that need to be faced. What emerges from this study is an appreciation that sometimes new theories are not better than what they seek to replace, despite the hype that often comes from being the new kid on the block. It is high time this kid be exposed as lacking the substance of a genuinely mature view. This book does that well, and also gives a fresh take on the alternative that has much better historical roots."

Darrell L. Bock, Research Professor of New Testament, Dallas Theological Seminary

"This is an admirably lucid and highly convincing rebuttal of the thesis that the earliest form of Christianity in many places was what would later be judged as 'heresy' and that earliest Christianity was so diverse that it should not be considered as a single movement—a thesis first presented by Walter Bauer but most recently advocated by Bart Ehrman. As Köstenberger and Kruger show with such clarity and compelling force, this still highly influential thesis simply does not stand up to scrutiny. By looking at a whole range of evidence—early Christian communities in different regions in the Roman Empire, the New Testament documents themselves, the emergence and boundaries of the canon and its connection to covenant, and the evidence for Christian scribes and the reliable transmission of the text of the New Testament—they show step by step that another view of early Christianity is much more in keeping with the evidence. They show that there is a unified doctrinal core in the New Testament, as well as a degree of legitimate diversity, and that the sense of orthodoxy among New Testament writers is widespread and pervasive. They also unmask the way contemporary culture has been mesmerized by diversity and the impact this has had on some readers of the New Testament. In this astute and highly readable book—a tour de force—Köstenberger and Kruger have done us all a great service. It is essential reading for all who want to understand the New Testament and recent controversies that have arisen in New Testament studies."

Paul Trebilco, Professor of New Testament Studies, Department of Theology and Religion, University of Otago, Dunedin, New Zealand.

"Köstenberger and Kruger have written a book which not only introduces the reader to the problematic Bauer thesis and its contemporary resurgence, but which, layer by layer, demonstrates its failure to account reliably for the history of communities, texts, and ideas that flourished in the era of early Christianity. In their arguments, the authors demonstrate their competence in the world of New Testament studies. But, additionally, they weave throughout the book insights into how fallacies within contemporary culture provide fuel for a thesis that long ago should have been buried. Believers will find in these pages inspiration to "contend earnestly for the faith once for all delivered to the saints."

D. Jeffrey Bingham, Department Chair and Professor of Theological Studies, Dallas Theological Seminary

"In recent times, certain media darlings have been telling us that earliest Christianity knew nothing of the 'narrowness' of orthodox belief. Now the authors of *The Heresy of Orthodoxy* have provided a scholarly yet highly accessible rebuttal, showing that what is actually 'narrow' here is the historical evidence on which this old thesis is based. In a culture which wants to recreate early Christianity after its own stultifying image, this book adds a much-needed breath of balance and sanity."

Nicholas Perrin, Associate Professor of New Testament, Wheaton College

"Köstenberger and Kruger have produced a volume that is oozing with common sense and is backed up with solid research and documentation. This work is a comprehensive critique of the Bauer-Ehrman thesis that the earliest form of Christianity was pluralistic, that there were multiple Christianities, and that heresy was prior to orthodoxy. Respectful yet without pulling any punches, *The Heresy of Orthodoxy* at every turn makes a convincing case that the Bauer-Ehrman thesis is dead wrong. All those who have surrendered to the siren song of postmodern relativism and tolerance, any who are flirting with it, and everyone concerned about what this seismic sociological-epistemological shift is doing to the Christian faith should read this book."

Daniel B. Wallace, Professor of New Testament Studies, Dallas Theological Seminary

"In the beginning was Diversity. And the Diversity was with God, and the Diversity was God. Without Diversity was nothing made that was made. And it came to pass that nasty old 'orthodox' people narrowed down diversity and finally squeezed it out, dismissing it as heresy. But in the fullness of time (which is, of course, our time), Diversity rose up and smote orthodoxy hip and thigh. Now, praise be, the only heresy is orthodoxy. As widely and as unthinkingly accepted as this reconstruction is, it is historical nonsense: the emperor has no clothes. I am grateful to Andreas Köstenberger and Michael Kruger for patiently, carefully, and politely exposing this shameful nakedness for what it is.

D. A. Carson, Research Professor of New Testament, Trinity Evangelical Divinity School

The HERESY OF
ORTHODOXY

The HERESY OF ORTHODOXY

HOW CONTEMPORARY CULTURE'S FASCINATION *with* DIVERSITY HAS RESHAPED OUR UNDERSTANDING *of* EARLY CHRISTIANITY

ANDREAS J. KÖSTENBERGER
AND MICHAEL J. KRUGER

Foreword by
I. Howard Marshall

WHEATON, ILLINOIS

Cover design: Studio Gearbox
First printing 2010
Printed in the United States of America

All emphases in Scripture quotations have been added by the authors.

Trade paperback ISBN: 978-1-4335-0143-2
PDF ISBN: 978-1-4335-1813-3
Mobipocket ISBN: 978-1-4335-1814-0
ePub ISBN: 978-1-4335-2179-9

Library of Congress Cataloging-in-Publication Data
Köstenberger, Andreas J., 1957-
  The heresy of orthodoxy : how contemporary culture's fascination with diversity has reshaped our understanding of early Christianity / Andreas J. Köstenberger and Michael J. Kruger; foreword by I. Howard Marshall.
    p. cm.
  Includes bibliographical references and index.
  ISBN 978-1-4335-0143-2 (tpb)—ISBN 978-1-4335-1813-3 (hbk)—ISBN 978-1-4335-1814-0 (mobipocket)—ISBN 978-1-4335-2179-9 (ebook) 1. Theology, Doctrinal—History—Early church, ca. 30-600. 2. Christian heresies—History—Early church, ca. 30-600. 3. Bible. N.T.—Criticism, interpretation, etc. 4. Church history—Primitive and early church, ca. 30-600. 5. Postmodern theology. 6. Bauer, Walter, 1877–1960. 7. Ehrman, Bart D. I. Kruger, Michael J. II. Title.

BT1317.K67 2010
273'.1—dc22
                2009047371

Crossway is a publishing ministry of Good News Publishers.

VP		21	20	19	18	17	16	15	14	13	12	11	10
14	13	12	11	10	9	8	7	6	5	4	3	2	1

For Lauren
as you head off to college
Romans 12:1–2
1 John 2:15–17

and

For Melissa
for all your encouragement and support

Contents

Foreword

Old heresies and arguments against Christianity have a habit of reappearing long after they have been thought dead. Somebody has commented that most objections to the faith were voiced by Celsus (who was relentlessly answered by Origen). Nevertheless, there is a sufficient appearance of plausibility in some of them to justify their being taken off the shelf, dusted down, and given a makeover. When this happens, they need fresh examination to save a new generation of readers from being taken in by them.

Such is the case with the thesis of the German lexicographer Walter Bauer, who single-handedly read the entire corpus of ancient Greek literature in order to produce his magnificent *Lexicon to the New Testament*. Its worth is entirely independent of the fact that its compiler was in some respects a radical critic who claimed on the basis of his researches into second-century Christianity that there was no common set of "orthodox" beliefs in the various Christian centers but rather a set of disparate theologies, out of which the strongest (associated with Rome) assumed the dominant position and portrayed itself as true, or "orthodox."

At first there were indeed no concepts of orthodoxy and heresy, and this division was late in being consciously developed. Bauer claimed (without much argument) that this situation could be traced back into the New Testament period. His 1934 monograph defending his case had little influence in the English-speaking world until its translation in 1971. Various writers showed it to be flawed in its analysis of the early churches and their theology and mistaken in assuming that the New Testament writers did not know the difference between orthodoxy and heresy. Now it has undergone resuscitation (if not resurrection) largely through the popular writings of Bart Ehrman, who brings in the new evidence for many varied forms of early Christianity in Gnostic documents and adds his own contribution by pointing to the many variations in the manuscripts of the New Testament that he sees as evidence of differences in doctrine.

The new presentation of the Bauer hypothesis needs a fresh dissection lest readers of it be tempted to think that it demands credence. The authors of this volume set out the arguments on both sides with fairness coupled with critical examination. They show that Bauer's original case has been demolished brick by brick by other competent scholars. They argue that the existence of various Christian splinter groups in no way shows that there was a farrago of different theologies from which people were at liberty to pick and choose. They re-present the incontrovertible evidence that the distinctions between truth and falsity and between orthodoxy and heresy were clearly made within the New Testament, and they argue that the New Testament writings are in basic agreement with one another in their theologies. They show how the concept of conformity to Scripture was an innate characteristic of a covenantal theology. And they rout the appeal to variations in New Testament manuscripts as evidence for theological differences in the early church.

The authors write as adherents of what would probably be identified as an evangelical Christianity that maintains a belief in the divine inspiration of Scripture, but, so far as I can see, their arguments are not dependent on this belief and rest on solid evidence and reasonable arguments, so that their case is one that should be compelling to those who may not share their theological position. They present their arguments clearly and simply, so that, although this book is based on wide and accurate scholarship, it should be widely accessible to readers who want to know about the themes they address.

I am grateful for this careful and courteous assessment of the issues at stake and commend it most warmly to all who want to know more about the origins of Christian practice and theology.

—I. Howard Marshall
Emeritus Professor of New Testament Exegesis,
University of Aberdeen, Scotland

Pauls Pharisee Religion is the same as the religion of Jesus according to this →

List of Abbreviations

ABD	*Anchor Bible Dictionary*
AJP	*American Journal of Philology*
ANRW	*Aufstieg und Niedergang der römischen Welt: Geschichte und Kultur Roms im Spiegel der neueren Forschung*
ATR	*Anglican Theological Review*
AUSS	*Andrews University Seminary Studies*
Bib	*Biblica*
Bijdr	*Bijdragen*
BBR	*Bulletin for Biblical Research*
BFCT	*Beiträge zur Förderung christlicher Theologie*
BJRL	*Bulletin of the John Rylands University Library of Manchester*
CBQ	*Catholic Biblical Quarterly*
CSNTM	Center for the Study of New Testament Manuscripts
DJG	*Dictionary of Jesus and the Gospels*
DLNT	*Dictionary of the Later New Testament and Its Developments*
DPL	*Dictionary of Paul and His Letters*
FRLANT	Forschungen zur Religion und Literatur des Alten und Neuen Testaments
HTR	*Harvard Theological Review*
ICC	International Critical Commentary
Int	*Interpretation*
JBL	*Journal of Biblical Literature*
JEA	*Journal of Egyptian Archaeology*

JECS	*Journal of Early Christian Studies*
JETS	*Journal of the Evangelical Theological Society*
JR	*Journal of Religion*
JSNT	*Journal for the Study of the New Testament*
JSNTSup	Journal for the Study of the New Testament: Supplement Series
JSOT	*Journal for the Study of the Old Testament*
JTS	*Journal of Theological Studies*
LCL	*Loeb Classical Library*
LNTS	Library of New Testament Studies
NAC	New American Commentary
NIB	*The New Interpreter's Bible*
NIBCNT	New International Biblical Commentary on the New Testament
NIGTC	New International Greek Testament Commentary
NovT	*Novum Testamentum*
NSBT	New Studies in Biblical Theology
NTS	*New Testament Studies*
ODCC	*The Oxford Dictionary of the Christian Church*
PNTC	Pillar New Testament Commentary
ProEccl	*Pro ecclesia*
RBL	*Review of Biblical Literature*
SBLSBS	Society of Biblical Literature Sources for Biblical Studies
SecCent	*Second Century*
SPap	*Studia papyrologica*
StPatr	Studia patristica
ST	*Studia theologica*
TDNT	*Theological Dictionary of the New Testament*
Them	*Themelios*
TS	*Theological Studies*
TNTC	Tyndale New Testament Commentaries
TJ	*Trinity Journal*
TynBul	*Tyndale Bulletin*
VC	*Vigiliae christianae*
WBC	Word Biblical Commentary
WTJ	*Westminster Theological Journal*
WUNT	Wissenschaftliche Untersuchungen zum Neuen Testament
ZAW	*Zeitschrift für die alttestamentliche Wissenschaft*
ZNW	*Zeitschrift für die neutestamentliche Wissenschaft und die Kunde der älteren Kirche*
ZPE	*Zeitschrift für Papyrologie und Epigraphik*

Introduction

The Contemporary Battle to Recast the Origins of the New Testament and Early Christianity

What is truth? In a world in which at times right seems wrong—or even worse, where the lines between right and wrong are blurred to the point that we are no longer sure if there even *is* such a thing as right and wrong—Pilate's question to Jesus takes on new urgency. Instead, all truth, including morality, becomes perspectival and subjective, a matter of nothing but personal preference and taste.[1] In such a world, like in the days of the judges, everyone does what is right in his or her own eyes, but *unlike* in the days of the judges, this is not meant as an indictment but celebrated as the ultimate expression of truly enlightened humanity. All is fluid, doctrine is dead, and diversity reigns. Not only in restaurants and shopping malls, but even in churches and houses of worship, what people are looking for is a variety of options, and if they don't like what they see, they take their business—or worship—elsewhere. Consumers control which products are made, children are catered to by parents, students determine what is taught in our schools and universities, and no one should tell anyone else what to do—or at least not acknowledge that they do. We live in an age that prides

---

[1]See Andreas J. Köstenberger, ed., *Whatever Happened to Truth?* (Wheaton, IL: Crossway, 2005).

itself on its independence, rejection of authority, and embrace of pluralism. Truth is dead; long live diversity!

In this topsy-turvy world of pluralism and postmodernity, where reason has been replaced as the arbiter of truth by perspectivalism and the unfettered and untouchable authority of personal experience, conventional notions are turned on their head. What used to be regarded as heresy is the new orthodoxy of the day, and the only heresy that remains is orthodoxy itself. "The Heresy of Orthodoxy" is more than a catchy title or a ploy concocted to entice potential readers to buy this book. It is an epithet that aptly captures the prevailing spirit of the age whose tentacles are currently engulfing the Christian faith in a deadly embrace, aiming to subvert the movement at its very core. The new orthodoxy—the "gospel" of diversity—challenges head-on the claim that Jesus and the early Christians taught a unified message that they thought was absolutely true and its denials absolutely false. Instead, advocates of religious diversity such as Walter Bauer and Bart Ehrman argue not only that contemporary diversity is good and historic Christianity unduly narrow, but that the very notion of orthodoxy is a later fabrication not true to the convictions of Jesus and the first Christians themselves.

In the first century, claim Bauer, Ehrman, and other adherents to the "diversity" doctrine, there was no such thing as "Christianity" (in the singular), but only *Christianities* (in the plural), different versions of belief, all of which claimed to be "Christian" with equal legitimacy. The traditional version of Christianity that later came to be known as orthodoxy is but the form of Christianity espoused by the church in Rome, which emerged as the ecclesiastical victor in the power struggles waged during the second through the fourth centuries. What this means for us today, then, is that we must try to get back to the more pristine notion of diversity that prevailed in the first century before ecclesiastical and political power squelched and brutally extinguished the fragile notion that diversity—previously known as "heresy"—is the only orthodoxy there is.

Indeed, the "new orthodoxy" has turned conventional thinking upside down. In this book, we endeavor to take you on a journey on which we will explore such questions as: Who picked the books of the Bible, and why? Did the ancient scribes who copied the biblical manuscripts change the Christian story? Was the New Testament changed along the way, so that we can no longer know what the original authors of Scripture wrote? In addressing these questions, we will take our point of departure from a German scholar whose name you may never have heard but who has perhaps done more to pave the way for the new orthodoxy than anyone else: Walter Bauer. In his work *Orthodoxy and Heresy in Earliest Christianity*, Bauer stated what is now commonly known as the "Bauer thesis": the view that close study of the major urban centers at the end of the first and early second centuries reveals that early Christianity was characterized by significant doctrinal diversity, so that there was no "orthodoxy" or "heresy" at the inception of Christianity but only diversity—heresy preceded orthodoxy.

The implications of Bauer's thesis, picked up by Bart Ehrman and others, are somewhat complex, which requires that we take up his argument in three separate but interrelated parts. Part 1 of this volume is devoted to the investigation of "The Heresy of Orthodoxy: Pluralism and the Origins of the New Testament." In chapter 1, we will look at the origin and influence of the Bauer-Ehrman thesis, including its appropriation and critique by others. Chapter 2 examines Bauer's geographical argument for the precedence of early diversity in the Christian movement and considers patristic evidence for early orthodoxy and heresy, and chapter 3 turns to an area of investigation that Bauer surprisingly neglected—the New Testament data itself. How diverse was early Christianity, and did heresy in fact precede orthodoxy? These are the questions that will occupy us in the first part of the book as we explore the larger paradigmatic questions raised by the Bauer-Ehrman proposal.

Part 2, "Picking the Books: Tracing the Development of the New Testament Canon," will take up the related question of the Christian canon, the collection of divinely inspired books. Ehrman and other advocates of the Bauer thesis claim that with regard to the canon, too, early diversity prevailed, and the canon likewise was but a late imposition of the Roman church's view onto the rest of Christendom. Is this an accurate representation of how the canon came to be? Or do Ehrman and other diversity advocates have their own ax to grind and seek to impose their agenda onto the larger culture? This will involve a discussion of other alleged candidates for inclusion in the Christian Scriptures such as apocryphal gospels, letters, and other writings. Are there indeed "lost Christianities" and "lost Scriptures" that, if rediscovered, could reveal to us "the faiths we never knew," as Ehrman contends?

Part 3, finally, "Changing the Story: Manuscripts, Scribes, and Textual Transmission," addresses another fascinating topic: whether the "keepers of the text," ancient scribes and copyists, actually "tampered with the text," that is, changed the New Testament to conform it to their own beliefs and preferences. Again, this is what Ehrman alleges, in an effort to show that even if we *wanted* to know what first-century orthodoxy was—though, of course, Ehrman himself, as a devoted follower of Walter Bauer, believes there was no such thing—we would not be able to do so because the original text is now irretrievably lost. After all, have not the autographs (the original copies of Scripture) perished? How, then, can Christians today claim that they have the inspired text? This, too, is a vital question that strikes at the very core of the Christian faith and must therefore command our utmost attention.

As the remainder of this volume will make clear, as scholars, we believe that Bauer, Ehrman, and others are profoundly mistaken in their reconstruction of early Christianity. But this is not the primary reason why we wrote this book. The main reason why we feel so strongly about this issue is that the scholarly squabbles about second-century geographical expressions of Christianity, the formation of the canon, and the preservation of the text of Scripture are part of a larger battle that is raging today over the nature and origins of Christianity. This battle, in turn, we are convinced, is driven by forces that seek to discredit the biblical message about Jesus, the Lord and Messiah and Son of God, and the absolute truth claims of Christianity. The stakes in this battle are high indeed.

Finally, for those who are interested in the history of thought and in the way in which paradigms serve as a controlling framework for how we view the world, this book has yet another intriguing contribution to make. The question addressed by the Bauer-Ehrman thesis serves as a case study for how an idea is born, how and why it is appropriated by some and rejected by others, and how a paradigm attains the compelling influence over people who are largely unacquainted with the specific issues it entails. As Darrell Bock has recently argued, and as even Bart Ehrman has conceded, Bauer's thesis has been largely discredited in the details, but, miraculously, the corpse still lives—in fact, it seems stronger than ever! What is the secret of this larger-than-life persona that transcends factual arguments based on the available evidence? We believe it is that diversity, the "gospel" of our culture, has now assumed the mantle of compelling truth—and this "truth" must not be bothered by the pesky, obstreperous details of patient, painstaking research, because in the end, the debate is not about the details but about the larger paradigm—diversity.

As in any such book, we are indebted to those who helped make it possible. In the first place, these are our wives, Marny and Melissa, and our children. We also want to acknowledge the support of our respective institutions, Southeastern Baptist Theological Seminary and Reformed

Theological Seminary, and express appreciation to the wonderful people at Crossway for their expert handling of the manuscript. Thanks are also due Keith Campbell for his competent research assistance in preparing chapters 1 through 3. Finally, we were grateful to be able to build on the capable work of others before us who have seen the many flaws in the Bauer-Ehrman thesis, including Darrell Bock, Paul Trebilco, Jeffrey Bingham, Craig Blaising, Thomas Robinson, and I. Howard Marshall. It is our sincere hope that this volume will make a small contribution toward a defense of the "faith once for all delivered to the saints" in our generation. *Soli Deo gloria.*

PART 1

THE HERESY
OF ORTHODOXY

Pluralism and the Origins of the New Testament

1

The Bauer-Ehrman Thesis

Its Origins and Influence

It is no exaggeration to say that the Bauer-Ehrman thesis is the prevailing paradigm with regard to the nature of early Christianity in popular American culture today. As mentioned in the Introduction, people who have never heard the name "Walter Bauer" have been impacted by this scholar's view of Jesus and the nature of early Christian beliefs. One main reason for Bauer's surprising impact is that his views have found a fertile soil in the contemporary cultural climate.

Specifically, in Bart Ehrman, Bauer has found a fervent and eloquent spokesman who has made Bauer's thesis his own and incorporated it in his populist campaign for a more inclusive, diverse brand of Christianity. It cannot be said too emphatically that the study of the Bauer thesis is not merely of antiquarian interest. Bauer's views have been adequately critiqued by others. What remains to be done here is to show that recent appropriations of Bauer's work by scholars such as Ehrman and the fellows of the Jesus Seminar can only be as viable as the validity of Bauer's original thesis itself.

In the present chapter, we set out to describe the Bauer-Ehrman thesis and to provide a representative survey of the reception of Bauer's work, both positive and negative, since its original publication in 1934 and the English translation of Bauer's volume in 1971. This will set the stage for our closer examination of the particulars of Bauer's thesis in chapter 2 and an investigation of the relevant New Testament data in chapter 3.

Walter Bauer and *Orthodoxy and Heresy in Earliest Christianity*

Walter Bauer, born in Königsberg, East Prussia, in 1877, was a German theologian, lexicographer, and scholar of early church history. He was raised in Marburg, where his father served as professor, and studied theology at the universities of Marburg, Strasburg, and Berlin. After a lengthy and impressive career at Breslau and Göttingen, he died in 1960. Although Bauer is best known for his magisterial *Greek-English Lexicon of the New Testament and Other Early Christian Literature*, perhaps his most significant scholarly contribution came with his work *Orthodoxy and Heresy in Earliest Christianity*.[1]

Prior to the publication of this volume, it was widely held that Christianity was rooted in the unified preaching of Jesus' apostles and that it was only later that this orthodoxy (right belief) was corrupted by various forms of heresy (or heterodoxy, "other" teaching that deviated from the orthodox standard or norm). Simply put, orthodoxy preceded heresy. In his seminal work, however, Bauer reversed this notion by proposing that heresy—that is, a variety of beliefs each of which could legitimately claim to be authentically "Christian"—preceded the notion of orthodoxy as a standard set of Christian doctrinal beliefs.

According to Bauer, the orthodoxy that eventually coalesced merely represented the consensus view of the ecclesiastical hierarchy that had the power to impose its view onto the rest of Christendom. Subsequently,

---

[1]Walter Bauer, *Orthodoxy and Heresy in Earliest Christianity*, ed. Robert A. Kraft and Gerhard Krodel, trans. Paul J. Achtemeier (Philadelphia: Fortress, 1971); the original German edition was *Rechtgläubigkeit und Ketzerei im Ältesten Christentum* (Tübingen: Mohr, 1934; 2d ed. Georg Strecker [Tübingen: Mohr Siebeck, 1964]). Other volumes on early Christianity by Bauer include a work on the canon of the epistles, *Der Apostolos der Syrer in der Zeit von der Mitte des vierten Jahrhunderts bis zur Spaltung der Syrischen Kirche* (Giessen: J. Ricker [Alfred Töpelmann], 1903); and a book on Jesus in the age of the New Testament Apocrypha, *Das Leben Jesu: Im Zeitalter der neutestamentlichen Apokryphen* (Darmstadt: Wissenschaftliche Buchgesellschaft, 1967). For a brief overview of other relevant books and articles by Bauer see Hans Dieter Betz, "Orthodoxy and Heresy in Primitive Christianity," *Int* 19 (1965): 299–311. On Bauer's work as a lexicographer, see William J. Baird, *History of New Testament Research*, vol. 2: *From Jonathan Edwards to Rudolf Bultmann* (Minneapolis: Fortress, 2003), 415–17 (with further bibliographic references); on Bauer as a historian and exegete, see ibid., 451–55, esp. 452–54 on *Orthodoxy and Heresy*.

this hierarchy, in particular the Roman church, rewrote the history of the church in keeping with its views, eradicating traces of earlier diversity. Thus what later became known as orthodoxy does not organically flow from the teaching of Jesus and the apostles but reflects the predominant viewpoint of the Roman church as it came into full bloom between the fourth and sixth centuries AD.[2]

Although Bauer provided a historical reconstruction of early Christianity that differed radically from his scholarly predecessors, others had put the necessary historical and philosophical building blocks into place from which Bauer could construct his thesis. Not only had the Enlightenment weakened the notion of the supernatural origins of the Christian message, but the history-of-religions school had propagated a comparative religions approach to the study of early Christianity, and the eminent church historian Adolf von Harnack had engaged in a pioneering study of heresy in general and of the Gnostic movement in particular.[3] Perhaps most importantly, F. C. Baur of the Tübingen School had postulated an initial conflict between Pauline and Petrine Christianity that subsequently merged into orthodoxy.[4]

The "Bauer Thesis"

How, then, did Bauer form his provocative thesis that heresy preceded orthodoxy? In essence, Bauer's method was historical in nature, involving an examination of the beliefs attested at four major geographical centers of early Christianity: Asia Minor, Egypt, Edessa, and Rome. With regard to

---

[2]For a humorous but informative parody of the Bauer thesis see Rodney J. Decker, "The Rehabilitation of Heresy: 'Misquoting' Earliest Christianity" (paper presented at the Bible Faculty Summit, Central Baptist Seminary, Minneapolis, July 2007), 1–2. For a summary of theories of development in early Christianity, see Jeffrey Bingham, "Development and Diversity in Early Christianity," *JETS* 49 (2006): 45–66.

[3]Concerning the history-of-religions school, see Carsten Colpe, "History of Religions School," *Encyclopedia of Christianity* 2:563–65. Concerning Harnack's views on the Gnostics, see Michel Desjardins, "Bauer and Beyond: On Recent Scholarly Discussions of Airesis the Early Christina Era," *SecCent* 8 (1991): 65–82; and Karen L. King, *What Is Gnosticism?* (Cambridge: Harvard University Press, 2003), 55–70. See also Adolf von Harnack, *The Rise of Christian Theology and of Church Dogma*, trans. Neill Buchanan (New York: Russell & Russell, 1958); idem, *What Is Christianity?* (New York: Harper Torchbooks, 1957).

[4]Jerry Rees Flora, "A Critical Analysis of Walter Bauer's Theory of Early Christian Orthodoxy and Heresy" (PhD diss., Southern Baptist Theological Seminary, 1972), 212, suggests that F. C. Baur's construction of early Christianity "proposed the angle of vision adopted" by Walter Bauer. A treatment of scholarly contributions prior to Bauer exceeds the scope of this chapter. For a discussion of Bauer's theory in the context of the history of scholarship see Flora, "Critical Analysis," 37–88. See also William Wrede's proposal of an antithesis between Jesus and Paul in *Paul*, trans. Edward Lummis (Lexington, KY: American Theological Library Association, 1908).

Asia Minor, Bauer pointed to the conflict in Antioch between Peter and Paul (shades of F. C. Baur) and the references to heresy in the Pastoral Epistles and the letters to the seven churches in the book of Revelation.

Bauer observed in Egypt the early presence of Gnostic Christians, contending that there was no representative of truly orthodox Christianity in this locale until Demetrius of Alexandria (AD 189–231). With regard to Edessa, a city located just north of modern Turkey and Syria, Bauer argued that the teaching of Marcion constituted the earliest form of Christianity and that orthodoxy did not prevail until the fourth or fifth century.[5]

Rome, for its part, according to Bauer, sought to assert its authority as early as AD 95 when Clement, bishop of Rome, sought to compel Corinth to obey Roman doctrinal supremacy. In due course, Bauer contended, the Roman church imposed its version of orthodox Christian teaching onto the rest of Christendom. What is more, the Roman church rewrote history, expunging the record of deviant forms of belief, in order to further consolidate its ecclesiastical authority.

By the fourth century, the orthodox victory was assured. However, according to Bauer, true, open-minded historical investigation shows that in each of the four major urban centers of early Christianity, heresy preceded orthodoxy. Diverse beliefs were both geographically widespread and earlier than orthodox Christian teaching. Thus the notion that orthodoxy continued the unified teaching of Jesus and of the apostles was a myth not borne out by serious, responsible historical research.

The Reception of Bauer's Work

Although Bauer's thesis was initially slow to impact scholarship, in part because of the cultural isolation of Germany during the rise of Nazi Germany and World War II, in due course it produced a considerable number of reactions.[6] Two major types of response emerged. One group of scholars

---

[5]Marcionism originated with Marcion of Sinope around AD 144. Marcion taught that Jesus was the Savior sent by God and that Paul was his chief apostle. However, Marcion rejected the Old Testament because he viewed the vindictive God of the Old Testament and the loving God of the New Testament as irreconcilable. On Marcion, see *Marcion und seine kirchengeschichtliche Wirkung*, Texte und Untersuchungen zur Geschichte der altchristlichen Literatur, ed. Gerhard May and Katharina Greschat (Berlin: W. de Gruyter, 2002); and the classic work by Adolf von Harnack, *Marcion: Das Evangelium vom fremden Gott* (Darmstadt: Wissenschaftliche Buchgesellschaft, 1960); *Marcion: The Gospel of the Alien God*, trans. John E. Steely and Lyle D. Bierma, 2d ed. (Durham, NC: Labyrinth, 1990).

[6]Scholars in England and on the Continent widely interacted with Bauer's work following its original publication. However, Bauer's work was rarely discussed in America until after its English translation appeared almost forty years later. Since then, it has become virtually

appropriated Bauer's thesis and used it as a basis for reexamining the origins of Christianity in light of his theory.[7] Another group lodged a series of powerful critiques against the Bauer thesis.[8] In the remainder of this chapter, we will trace these varying responses to Bauer in an effort to gauge the scholarly reception of the Bauer thesis and to lay the foundation for an appraisal of the merits of his work for contemporary investigations of the origins of early Christianity.

Scholarly Appropriations of Bauer

One of the foremost proponents of the Bauer thesis in the twentieth century was Rudolf Bultmann (1884–1976), longtime professor of New Testament studies at the University of Marburg (1921–1951).[9] Bultmann made Bauer's thesis the substructure of his New Testament theology that had a large impact on generations of scholars. Divorcing faith from history in keep-

---

obligatory to discuss the origins of Christianity with reference to Bauer's name. For reactions to Bauer's work between the original German edition and its English translation, see Georg Strecker, "Appendix 2: The Reception of the Book," in Bauer, *Orthodoxy and Heresy*, 286–316.

[7]Arnold Ehrhardt, "Christianity before the Apostles' Creed," *HTR* 55 (1962): 73–119; James M. Robinson and Helmut Koester, *Trajectories through Early Christianity* (Philadelphia: Fortress, 1971); Helmut Koester, "*Gnomai Diaphoroi*: The Origin and Nature of Diversification in the History of Early Christianity," *HTR* 58 (1965): 279–318 (repr. in Robinson and Koester, *Trajectories through Early Christianity*, chap. 4); idem, "Apocryphal and Canonical Gospels," *HTR* 73 (1980): 105–30; James D. G. Dunn, *Unity and Diversity in the New Testament: An Inquiry into the Character of Earliest Christianity*, 2d ed. (Philadelphia: Trinity Press International, 1990); Elaine Pagels, *Beyond Belief: The Secret Gospel of Thomas* (New York: Random House, 2003); and Einar Thomassen, "Orthodoxy and Heresy in Second-Century Rome," *HTR* 97 (2004): 241–56.

[8]Henry E. W. Turner, *The Pattern of Christian Truth: A Study in the Relations Between Orthodoxy and Heresy in the Early Church* (London: A. R. Mowbray, 1954); Flora, "Critical Analysis"; I. Howard Marshall, "Orthodoxy and Heresy in Earlier Christianity," *Them* 2 (1976): 5–14; Brice L. Martin, "Some Reflections on the Unity of the New Testament," *Studies in Religion/Sciences Religieuses* 8 (1979): 143–52; James McCue, "Orthodoxy and Heresy: Walter Bauer and the Valentinians," *VC* 33 (1979): 118–30; Thomas A. Robinson, *The Bauer Thesis Examined: The Geography of Heresy in the Early Christian Church* (Lewiston, NY: Edwin Mellen, 1988); Arland J. Hultgren, *The Rise of Normative Christianity* (Minneapolis: Augsburg Fortress, 1994); Andreas J. Köstenberger, "Diversity and Unity in the New Testament," in *Biblical Theology: Retrospect and Prospect*, ed. Scott J. Hafemann (Downers Grove, IL: InterVarsity, 2002), 144–58; Ivor J. Davidson, *The Birth of the Church: From Jesus to Constantine, A.D. 30–312*, Baker History of the Church 1 (Grand Rapids: Baker, 2004); and Birger A. Pearson, *Gnosticism and Christianity in Roman and Coptic Egypt* (New York: T&T Clark, 2004).

[9]For the following survey see especially Strecker, "Reception of the Book," 286–316; and Daniel J. Harrington, "The Reception of Walter Bauer's *Orthodoxy and Heresy in Earliest Christianity* during the Last Decade," *HTR* 73 (1980): 289–98.

ing with his anti-supernatural, historical-critical methodology, Bultmann believed historical events such as the resurrection were inferior in importance to one's existential faith in Jesus.[10] It followed that, for Bultmann, historical orthodoxy was largely irrelevant. Marshaling Bauer's thesis to support this claim, he stated baldly:

> The diversity of theological interests and ideas is at first great. A norm or an authoritative court of appeal for doctrine is still lacking, and the proponents of directions of thought which were later rejected as heretical consider themselves completely Christian—such as Christian Gnosticism. In the beginning, *faith* is the term which distinguishes the Christian Congregation from the Jews and the heathen, not *orthodoxy* (right doctrine).[11]

Later on in the same volume, Bultmann offered an entire excursus on Bauer's thesis, a testament to its influence on Bultmann.[12] The following quote shows that Bultmann followed Bauer completely in his assessment of the origins of early Christianity:

> W. Bauer has shown that that doctrine which in the end won out in the ancient Church as the "right" or "orthodox" doctrine stands at the end of a development or, rather, is the result of a conflict among various shades of doctrine, and that heresy was not, as the ecclesiastical tradition holds, an apostasy, a degeneration, but was already present at the beginning—or, rather, that by the triumph of a certain teaching as the "right doctrine" divergent teachings were condemned as heresy. Bauer also showed it to be probably that in this conflict the Roman congregation played a decisive role.[13]

Bauer's thesis also provided the matrix for Arnold Ehrhardt (1903–1963), lecturer in ecclesiastical history at the University of Manchester, to examine the Apostles' Creed in relation to the creedal formulas of the early church (e.g., 1 Cor. 15:3–4).[14] Ehrhardt applied Bauer's understanding of diversity in the early church to a study of the formation of the Apostles' Creed. He concluded that the contents of the Apostles' Creed and the New Testament's

---

[10]F. L. Cross, ed., "Bultmann, Rudolf," *ODCC* 1:250.
[11]Rudolf Bultmann, *Theology of the New Testament*, trans. Kendrick Grobel (New York: Charles Scribner's Sons, 1955), 2:135 (emphasis original).
[12]Ibid., 2:137–38.
[13]Ibid., 2:137.
[14]Ehrhardt, "Christianity before the Apostles' Creed."

creedal formulas differed, arguing that the diversity of early Christianity supported this contention. Ehrhardt acknowledged that Bauer made his exploration of this topic possible.[15]

In 1965, Helmut Koester, professor of ecclesiastical history at Harvard University and one of Bultmann's students, applied Bauer's thesis to the apostolic period.[16] In 1971, Koester, joined by James M. Robinson, professor of religion at Claremont University and another of Bultmann's students, expanded his article into a book, *Trajectories through Early Christianity*. In this influential appropriation of Bauer's thesis, Koester and Robinson argued that "obsolete" categories within New Testament scholarship, such as "canonical" or "non-canonical," "orthodox" or "heretical," were inadequate.[17] According to these authors, such categories were too rigid to accommodate the early church's prevailing diversity.

As an alternative, Koester and Robinson proposed the term "trajectory."[18] Rather than conceiving of early church history in terms of heresy and orthodoxy, these scholars preferred to speak of early trajectories that eventually led to the formation of the notions of orthodoxy and heresy, notions that were not yet present during the early stages of the history of the church.[19] Koester's and Robinson's argument, of course, assumed that earliest Christianity did not espouse orthodox beliefs from which later heresies diverged. In this belief these authors concurred entirely with Bauer, who had likewise argued that earliest Christianity was characterized by diversity and that the phenomenon of orthodoxy emerged only later.

James D. G. Dunn, professor of divinity at the University of Durham, embarked on a highly influential appropriation of the Bauer thesis in his

---

[15]Ibid., 93.

[16]Koester, "*Gnomai Diaphoroi*."

[17]Robinson and Koester, *Trajectories*, 270.

[18]Concerning Robinson's and Koester's "newly" coined term, I. Howard Marshall rightly states, "[Their use of the label] 'trajectories' to give expression of this kind of approach . . . is simply a new invention to describe a concept of which scholars have long been conscious" ("Orthodoxy and Heresy," 6–7).

[19]Koester made a similar argument ten years later in "Apocryphal and Canonical Gospels" (*HTR* 73 [1980]: 105–30). He suggested that four apocryphal gospels (*The Synoptic Sayings Source*, *The Gospel of Thomas*, the *Unknown Gospel* of *Papyrus Egerton 2*, and *The Gospel of Peter*) are "at least as old and as valuable as the canonical gospels as sources for the earliest developments of the traditions about Jesus" (p. 130). As a result, Koester suggested, the terms "apocryphal" and "canonical" should be dropped since they reflected "deep-seated prejudices" (p. 105). Koester reached these conclusions by applying Bauer's thesis to the Gospel traditions.

1977 work *Unity and Diversity in the New Testament*.[20] Whereas Bauer (despite the title of his work!) primarily focused on the second-century situation; while Ehrhardt compared the Apostles' Creed to selected New Testament passages; and while Koester and Robinson explored extrabiblical trajectories, Dunn applied Bauer's thesis squarely to the New Testament itself. Dunn's conclusion was that, in line with Bauer's findings, diversity in the New Testament trumped unity. At the same time, Dunn suggested that the New Testament contained a general unifying theme, a belief in Jesus as the exalted Lord. According to Dunn:

> ↳ Paul ↳ -

> That unifying element was the unity between the historical Jesus and the exalted Christ, that is to say, the conviction that the wandering charismatic preacher from Nazareth had ministered, died and been raised from the dead to bring God and man finally together, the recognition that the divine power through which they now worshipped and were encountered and accepted by God was one and the same person, Jesus, the man, the Christ, the Son of God, the Lord, the life-giving Spirit.[21]

At first glance, Dunn's proposed unifying theme runs counter to Bauer's thesis that there was no underlying doctrinal unity in earliest Christianity. However, as Daniel Harrington stated, "the expression of this unifying strand is radically diverse—so diverse that one must admit that there was no single normative form of Christianity in the first century."[22] What is more, Dunn believed that this unifying theme resulted from a struggle between differing viewpoints, with the winners claiming their version of this belief as orthodox. Dunn, then, was the first to provide a thorough assessment of the New Testament data against the backdrop of Bauer's thesis and to affirm the thesis's accuracy when held up to the New Testament evidence.

The Bauer Thesis Goes Mainstream

While Bauer, Ehrhardt, Koester, Robinson, and Dunn wrote primarily for their academic peers, Elaine Pagels, professor of religion at Princeton University, and Bart Ehrman, professor of religious studies at the University

---

[20]Dunn, *Unity and Diversity*; 2d ed. 1990. Dunn wrote a briefer version of *Unity and Diversity* and discussed how his arguments relate to the question of the continuing efficacy of the canon in "Has the Canon a Continuing Function?" in *The Canon Debate*, ed. Lee Martin McDonald and James A. Sanders (Peabody, MA: Hendrickson, 2002), 558–79. This essay includes Dunn's updated reflections on this topic.

[21]Dunn, *Unity and Diversity*, 369.

[22]Harrington, "Reception of Walter Bauer's *Orthodoxy and Heresy*," 297.

of North Carolina at Chapel Hill, chose to extend the discussion to a popular audience.[23] In her 1979 work *The Gnostic Gospels*, Pagels popularized Bauer's thesis by applying it to the Nag Hammadi documents, which were not discovered until 1945 and thus had not been available to Bauer. Pagels contended that these Gnostic writings further supported the notion of an early, variegated Christianity that was homogenized only at a later point.[24]

In 2003, Pagels reengaged the Bauer thesis in *Beyond Belief: The Secret Gospel of Thomas*, another work directed toward a popular readership. In this latter work, Pagels examined the *Gospel of Thomas*, a Nag Hammadi document, and claimed that modern Christians should move beyond belief in rigid dogmas to a healthy plurality of religious views since the early Christians were likewise not dogmatic but extremely diverse. As the first century gave way to the second, Pagels argued, Christians became increasingly narrow in their doctrinal views. This narrowing, so Pagels, caused divisions between groups that had previously been theologically diverse. The group espousing "orthodoxy" arose in the context of this theological narrowing and subsequently came to outnumber and conquer the Gnostics and other "heretics."

Bart Ehrman, even more than Pagels, popularized the Bauer thesis in numerous publications and public appearances, calling it "the most important book on the history of early Christianity to appear in the twentieth century."[25] Besides being a prolific scholar, having published more than twenty books (some making it onto bestseller lists) and contributing frequently to scholarly journals, Ehrman promotes the Bauer thesis in the mainstream media in an unprecedented way. Ehrman's work has been featured

---

[23]Others who have popularized Bauer's thesis in various ways include the following: Gregory J. Riley, *One Jesus, Many Christs: How Jesus Inspired Not One True Christianity, But Many* (San Francisco: Harper, 1997); Gerd Lüdemann, *Heretics: The Other Side of Early Christianity* (Louisville, KY: Westminster, 1996); Keith Hopkins, *A World Full of Gods: Pagans, Jews and Christians in the Roman Empire* (New York: Free Press, 2000); John Dart, *The Jesus of Heresy and History* (San Francisco: Harper & Row, 1988); Robert W. Funk, *Honest to Jesus: Jesus for a New Millennium* (San Francisco: Harper, 1996); and Rosemary Radford Ruether, *Women and Redemption: A Theological History* (Minneapolis: Fortress, 1998). See Decker, "Rehabilitation of Heresy," 3.

[24]The arguments of Bauer and Pagels are not new. Prior to the Nag Hammadi discoveries and subsequent to the Enlightenment, scholars have often depicted a Jesus who differs from the orthodox presentation of him. See Philip Jenkins, *Hidden Gospels: How the Search for Jesus Lost Its Way* (New York: Oxford University Press, 2001), 13–15.

[25]Bart D. Ehrman, *Lost Christianities: The Battles for Scripture and the Faiths We Never Knew* (Oxford: Oxford University Press, 2003), 173.

in publications such as *Time*, *The New Yorker*, and the *Washington Post*, and he has appeared on *Dateline NBC*, *The Daily Show with Jon Stewart*, CNN, The History Channel, National Geographic, the Discovery Channel, the BBC, NPR, and other major media outlets.[26]

Part Two of Ehrman's book *Lost Christianities*, "Winners and Losers," demonstrates his commitment to, and popularization of, the Bauer thesis.[27] Ehrman argues that the earliest proponents of what later became orthodox Christians (called "proto-orthodox" by Ehrman) triumphed over all other legitimate representations of Christianity (chap. 8). This victory came about through conflicts that are attested in polemical treatises, personal slurs, forgeries, and falsifications (chaps. 9–10). The final victors were the proto-orthodox who got the "last laugh" by sealing the victory, finalizing the New Testament, and choosing the documents that best suited their purposes and theology (chap. 11).[28] In essence, Ehrman claims that the "winners" (i.e., orthodox Christians) forced their beliefs onto others by deciding which books to include in or exclude from Christian Scripture. Posterity is aware of these "losers" (i.e., "heretics") only by their sparsely available written remains that the "winners" excluded from the Bible, such as *The Gospel of Peter* or *The Gospel of Mary* and other exemplars of "the faiths we never knew."

Summary

Scholars favorable to the Bauer thesis have appropriated his theory in a variety of ways. They have made it the central plank in their overall conception of New Testament Christianity (Bultmann); have used it to revision early church history (Ehrhardt); have taken it as the point of departure to suggest alternate terminology for discussions of the nature of early Christianity (Koester and Robinson); and employed it in order to reassess the unity and diversity of New Testament theology (Dunn).

More recently, scholars such as Pagels and Ehrman have promoted the Bauer thesis in the popular arena, making the case that contemporary Christians should move beyond the anachronistic and dogmatic notion of

---

[26]http://www.bartdehrman.com. Accessed December 15, 2008.

[27]Ehrman, *Lost Christianities*, 159–257. Ehrman's other major publications on early Christianity include *Lost Scriptures: Books That Did Not Make It into the New Testament* (New York: Oxford University Press, 2003); *The Orthodox Corruption of Scripture: The Effect of Early Christological Controversies on the Text of the New Testament* (New York: Oxford University Press, 1993); and *Misquoting Jesus: The Story Behind Who Changed the Bible and Why* (New York: Harper, 2005).

[28]Ehrman, *Lost Christianities*, 188.

orthodoxy and instead embrace a diversity of equally legitimate beliefs. In this they appealed to the Bauer thesis, according to which it was diversity that prevailed also during the days of the early church before the institutional hierarchy imposed its orthodox standards onto the rest of Christendom.

Critiques of Bauer[29]
Initial Reviews

While, as we have seen, many viewed Bauer's thesis favorably and appropriated it for their own purposes, there were others who took a more critical stance. Georg Strecker observes that in the years following the 1934 publication of Bauer's work, more than twenty-four book reviews appeared in six different languages. Although most reviews were appreciative, the following four points are representative of the tenor of the critical reviews that appeared.[30]

First, Bauer's conclusions were unduly conjectural in light of the limited nature of the available evidence and in some cases arguments from silence altogether.

Second, Bauer unduly neglected the New Testament evidence and anachronistically used second-century data to describe the nature of "earliest" (first-century) Christianity. Bauer's neglect of the earliest available evidence is especially ironic since the title of his book suggested that the subject of his investigation was the *earliest* form of Christianity.

Third, Bauer grossly oversimplified the first-century picture, which was considerably more complex than Bauer's portrayal suggested. For example, orthodoxy could have been present early in more locations than Bauer acknowledged.

Fourth, Bauer neglected existing theological standards in the early church. The remainder of this chapter will explore how later critics built upon these early reviews in a variety of ways.

Later Critiques

Henry E. W. Turner, Lightfoot Chair of Divinity at Durham, offered the first substantial critique of Bauer's thesis in 1954 when delivering the prestigious Bampton Lectures at Oxford University.[31] Turner conceded that

---

[29]See especially the detailed discussion in Strecker, "Reception of the Book," 286–316.
[30]For a more thorough treatment of these reviews and critiques see ibid., 286–97.
[31]These lectures were published the same year in Henry E. W. Turner, *The Pattern of Christian Truth: A Study in the Relations between Orthodoxy and Heresy in the Early Church* (London: A. R. Mowbray, 1954).

theologians prior to Bauer "overestimated the extent of doctrinal fixity in the early church."[32] However, he argued that Bauer caused the pendulum to swing too far in the opposite direction, charging that followers of Bauer "imply too high a degree of openness or flexibility."[33] Over against Bauer's diagnosed prevailing diversity in early Christianity, Turner argued for the following three kinds of "fixed elements."[34]

First, the core of early Christianity included what Turner called "religious facts": a "realistic experience of the Eucharist"; belief in God as Father-Creator; belief in Jesus as the historical Redeemer; and belief in the divinity of Christ. Second, Turner maintained that the early Christians recognized the centrality of biblical revelation. However one delineates the New Testament canon and views its closure, the early church viewed it (at least in part) as revelatory. Third, the early believers possessed a creed and a rule of faith.[35] Turner here refers to the "stylized summaries of *credenda* which are of frequent occurrence in the first two Christian centuries to the earliest creedal forms themselves."[36] Such creeds include the earliest affirmations that "Jesus is Messiah" (Mark 8:29; John 11:27); "Jesus is Lord" (Rom. 10:9; Phil. 2:11; Col. 2:6); and "Jesus is the Son of God" (Matt. 14:33; Acts 8:37).

These fixed elements did not result in a rigid first-century theology. Instead, early Christianity, according to Turner, had the following three "flexible elements." First, there were "differences in Christian idiom."[37] For example, within early Christianity, an eschatological and a metaphysical interpretation existed side by side. However, Turner suggested that "it could be maintained that the Christian deposit of faith is not wedded irrevocably to either idiom."[38] Second, there were differences in backgrounds of thought. In other words, there existed varying philosophical viewpoints among the earliest Christians that resulted in different ways of explaining the same phenomena.[39] A final element of flexibility in early Christianity "arises from the individual characteristics of the theologians themselves."[40] The biblical writers were not monolithic but had diverse intellects and personalities.

---

[32]Ibid., 26.
[33]Ibid.
[34]Ibid., 26–35.
[35]Ibid., 28–31.
[36]Ibid., 30.
[37]Ibid., 31.
[38]Ibid.
[39]Ibid., 31–34.
[40]Ibid., 34.

Turner also more methodically confirmed the diagnosis of earlier reviewers that Bauer's thesis was drawn from an insufficient evidentiary base and did not demonstrably follow from the evidence he adduced. He also observed that Bauer's conception of "orthodoxy" was unduly narrow, while orthodoxy was "richer and more varied than Bauer himself allows."[41]

While Turner critiqued Bauer by noting both fixed and flexible elements in early Christianity, Jerry Flora sought to establish a historical continuity between early and later orthodoxy. In his doctoral dissertation, submitted in 1972, Flora set out to delineate, analyze, and evaluate Bauer's hypothesis.[42] He argued that the notion of orthodoxy that came to prevail in Rome had already been "growing in the soil of the church's first two generations."[43] Thus Flora maintained that there was essential historical continuity between earlier and later orthodoxy, contending that later orthodoxy was grounded in earlier doctrinal convictions that through the early apostles extended all the way back to Jesus himself: "What became the dogma of the church ca. AD 200 was a religious life which [was] determined throughout by Jesus Christ."[44] According to Flora, later orthodoxy "demonstrated historical continuity, theological balance, and providential guidance."[45]

I. Howard Marshall, professor of New Testament exegesis at the University of Aberdeen, Scotland, critiqued Bauer from a New Testament vantage point by establishing the presence of early orthodoxy. In an influential 1976 article, Marshall suggested that by the end of the first century a clear distinction already existed between orthodoxy and heresy. Marshall argued that orthodoxy was not a later development and that Bauer's argument does not fit the New Testament data. The New Testament writers, Marshall maintained, "often see quite clearly where the lines of what is compatible with the gospel and what is not compatible are to be drawn."[46] In some places, heresy may have preceded orthodoxy, but Bauer was wrong to suggest that orthodoxy developed later. The only point that Bauer's thesis proves is that "there was variety of belief in the first century."[47] *That is enough!*

In an article published in 1979, Brice Martin, lecturer in New Testament at Ontario Bible College, explored the unity of the New Testament

---

[41]Ibid., 80.
[42]Flora, "Critical Analysis," 4.
[43]Ibid., 214–15.
[44]Ibid., 219.
[45]For a more thorough explanation, see ibid., 220.
[46]Marshall, "Orthodoxy and Heresy," 13.
[47]Ibid.

using the historical-critical method.[48] As a foil, Martin took Werner Georg Kümmel who stated, "The unity of the New Testament message . . . cannot be presupposed as obvious on the basis of strictly historical research."[49] Martin argued just the opposite. His concern was not to study particular places where supposed New Testament contradictions occur but to offer a methodology that allows for a unified New Testament. He suggested that "significant differences are not significant contradictions (e.g., Paul versus James)."[50]

James McCue leveled a critique against Bauer through a narrower historical angle in a 1979 article, "Orthodoxy and Heresy: Walter Bauer and the Valentinians." McCue did not set out to correct Bauer's entire thesis but only to provide a refutation of Bauer's perception of the relationship between orthodoxy and heresy among the Valentinians.[51] The Valentinians were early second-century followers of Valentinus (c. AD 100–160), a Gnostic who founded a school in Rome.[52] McCue argued that the Valentinians originated and evolved from orthodoxy rather than, as Bauer had suggested, from an early heresy. In other words, Bauer was incorrect to suggest that the Valentinians were an example of heresy that preceded orthodoxy.

In 1989 Thomas Robinson, in a revised version of his McMaster PhD dissertation, took the Bauer thesis head on in *The Bauer Thesis Examined: The Geography of Heresy in the Early Christian Church*. He approached the issue of orthodoxy and heresy in the first century from the same perspective as Bauer, namely by reviewing the evidence region by region. In addition, Robinson rebutted the arguments of later scholars who built upon Bauer. Robinson consistently argued that the evidence in these geographical regions was inadequate for Bauer to lodge his claims. He concluded that

---

[48]Although Martin does not explicitly refute Bauer, his article does so by default. Martin's omission of Bauer's name while addressing his thesis attests to the pervasive impact Bauer's thesis had on scholarship.

[49]Werner Georg Kümmel, *The New Testament: The History of the Investigation of Its Problems*, trans. S. McLean Gilmour and Howard C. Kee (Nashville/New York: Abingdon, 1972), 403.

[50]Martin, "Some Reflections on the Unity of the New Testament," 152.

[51]McCue, "Orthodoxy and Heresy," 151–52. Others have critiqued Bauer similarly: A. I. C. Heron, "The Interpretation of 1 Clement in Walter Bauer's *Rechtgläubigkeit und Ketzerei im Ältesten Christentum: A Review Article*," *Ekklesiastikos Pharos* 55 (1973): 517–45. Fredrick W. Norris, "Ignatius, Polycarp, and 1 Clement: Walter Bauer Reconsidered," in *Orthodoxy, Heresy, and Schism in Early Christianity*, Studies in Early Christianity 4, ed. Everett Ferguson (New York: Garland, 1993), 237–58.

[52]See Ismo Dunderberg, "The School of Valentinus," in *A Companion to Second-Century Christian 'Heretics,'* ed. Antti Marjanen and Petri Luomanen (Leiden: Brill, 2005), 64–99.

That is enough [handwritten]

Bauer's work provided "an adequate basis for no conclusion other than that early Christianity was diverse."[53] In direct opposition to Bauer, Robinson argued that heresy in Ephesus and western Asia Minor, where evidence is more readily available, was neither early nor strong; rather, orthodoxy preceded heresy and was numerically larger. This conclusion, especially in light of the limited evidence, showed that the "failure of [Bauer's] thesis in the only area where it can be adequately tested casts suspicion on the other areas of Bauer's investigation."[54]

So what, that is what Ehrman contends [handwritten marginal note]

In 1994, Arland J. Hultgren, professor of New Testament at Luther Seminary, argued similarly to Flora that in the first century "there was a stream of Christianity—which indeed was a *broad* stream—that claimed that there were limits to diversity, and that persisted from the beginning on into the second century, providing the foundations for orthodoxy."[55] Although the orthodoxy of the fourth century did not exist in the first, its essential identity had been established and could not be divorced from its later, fuller manifestation. This identity had been forged from a struggle "for the truth of the gospel (right confession of faith)," which shaped "a normative tradition that provided the basis for the emergence of orthodoxy."[56] This orthodoxy was characterized by the following beliefs: (1) apostolic teaching is orthodox; (2) Jesus is Messiah, Lord, and God's Son; (3) Christ died for humanity's sins, was buried, and was raised from the dead; (4) the Lord is the God of Israel as the Creator, the Father of Jesus, the Father of humanity, and as the gift of the Spirit to the faithful. Early Christianity and later orthodoxy, then, stood in continuity with one another. Going back even farther than the early church, Hultgren argued that "there are clear lines of continuity between the word and deeds of the earthly Jesus and core affirmations of normative Christianity."[57] Thus, Hultgren agreed with Bauer that diversity existed in the earliest stages of the church, but suggested the following six unifying elements: theology, Christology, soteriology, ethos, the church as community, and the church as extended fellowship.[58]

I (Andreas Köstenberger) wrote an essay in 2002 that discussed the New Testament's diversity and unity. I argued that legitimate, or acceptable, diversity existed in the New Testament. It did not follow, however, that

---

[53]Robinson, *Bauer Thesis Examined*, 28.
[54]Ibid., 204.
[55]Hultgren, *Normative Christianity*, 22.
[56]Ibid., 104.
[57]Ibid., 106.
[58]Ibid., 87–103.

that is horse manure !

this diversity rose to the level of mutually contradictory perspectives.[59] I demonstrated my thesis by examining the unity in the midst of diversity between Jesus and Paul, the Synoptics and John, the Paul of Acts and the Paul of the Epistles, and between Paul and Peter, John, and James. After describing genuine elements of diversity (in the sense of mutually complementing perspectives) in the New Testament, I turned to a discussion of its unity. I proposed three integrating motifs: (1) monotheism, that is, belief in the one God, Yahweh, as revealed in the Old Testament; (2) Jesus as the Christ and the exalted Lord; and (3) the saving message of the gospel.[60] My conclusion was diametrically opposed to the Bauer thesis: "While Walter Bauer believed he could detect a movement from diversity to unity within the early church, the first Christians rather developed from unity to diversity."[61]

Conclusion

Nearly seventy-five years after Bauer proposed his thesis that heresy preceded orthodoxy, scholars are still wrestling with the implications of his theory. McCue states that "[Bauer's work] . . . remains . . . one of the great undigested pieces of twentieth-century scholarship."[62] What is beyond dispute is Bauer's influence, which extends to virtually every discipline related to Christian studies. In fact, one of the ramifications of Bauer's work is that many scholars no longer use the terms *orthodoxy* and *heresy* without accompanying quotation marks. As Robert Wild observed, Bauer's work "has forced a generation of scholars to reflect upon early Christianity in a new way."[63]

As we have seen, while many appropriated Bauer's thesis in support of their own scholarly paradigms, others lodged weighty criticisms against the theory. They persuasively argued that legitimate elements of diversity in the New Testament did not negate its underlying doctrinal unity (Turner, Martin, Hultgren, and Köstenberger) and that historical con-

---

[59]On the issue of legitimate vs. illegitimate diversity, see further the discussion in chap. 3 below. It should be noted here that when we speak of "legitimate" or "illegitimate" diversity, we mean, in historical terms, diversity that was doctrinally acceptable or unacceptable from the vantage point of the New Testament writers, judging from their writings included in the New Testament canon. As will be argued more fully in chap. 3, at the root of the early church's doctrinal core was the teaching of Jesus as transmitted by the apostles and as rooted in Old Testament theology.
[60]Köstenberger, "Diversity and Unity," 154–57.
[61]Ibid., 158.
[62]McCue, "Orthodoxy and Heresy: Walter Bauer and the Valentinians," 118.
[63]Robert A. Wild, review of Thomas A. Robinson, *The Bauer Thesis Examined: The Geography of Heresy in the Early Christian Church*, CBQ 52 (1990): 568–69.

tinuity existed between the theologies of first-century Christians and the church of subsequent centuries (Flora). They also demonstrated the weaknesses of Bauer's thesis by challenging his methodology and by subjecting his views to concrete—and damaging—examination in individual cases (McCue and Robinson) and by investigating his thesis in light of the New Testament data and finding it wanting (Marshall).

In more recent days, Bauer's thesis has received a new lease on life through the emergence of postmodernism, the belief that truth is inherently subjective and a function of power.[64] With the rise of postmodernism came the notion that the only heresy that remains is the belief in absolute truth—orthodoxy. Postmodernism, for its part, contends that the only absolute is diversity, that is, the notion that there are many truths, depending on a given individual's perspective, background, experience, and personal preference. In such an intellectual climate, anyone holding to particular doctrinal beliefs while claiming that competing truth claims are wrong is held to be intolerant, dogmatic, or worse.[65] It is no surprise that in this culture Bauer's views are welcomed with open arms. The Bauer thesis, as propagated by spokespersons such as Bart Ehrman, Elaine Pagels, and the fellows of the Jesus Seminar, validates the prevailing affirmation of diversity by showing that diversity reaches back as far as early Christianity.

On a methodological level, Bauer bequeathed on scholarship a twofold legacy: (1) the historical method of examining the available evidence in the

---

[64]See esp. J. P. Moreland, "Truth, Contemporary Philosophy, and the Postmodern Turn," in *Whatever Happened to Truth?* Andreas J. Köstenberger, ed. (Wheaton, IL: Crossway, 2005), 75–92, and the other essays in this volume; D. A. Carson, *The Gagging of God: Christianity Confronts Pluralism* (Grand Rapids: Zondervan, 1996); Douglas R. Groothuis, *Truth Decay: Defending Christianity against the Challenges of Postmodernism* (Downers Grove, IL: InterVarsity, 2000); Millard J. Erickson, *Truth or Consequences: The Promise and Perils of Postmodernism* (Downers Grove, IL: InterVarsity, 2002); and David F. Wells, *Above All Earthly Pow'rs: Christ in a Postmodern World* (Grand Rapids: Eerdmans, 2005).

[65]For a trenchant critique of Ehrman in this regard, see Craig A. Blaising, "Faithfulness: A Prescription for Theology," *JETS* 49 (2006): 6–9, who writes: "Ehrman presents these proto-orthodox as especially vitriolic, slanderous, as fabricators of lies. All of the groups, he says, forged religious texts, but the proto-orthodox were especially clever at it. They also took over some earlier Christian writings and subtly inserted textual changes to make them appear to proscribe the views of their opponents. And then, in the height of arrogance, they came up with the concept of canon, which no one had thought of before, and by declaring officially the list of acceptable books they banished into obscurity the rich textual diversity of those early years of Christian history. All that was necessary after that was to rewrite history in favor of the proto-orthodox party. But, says Ehrman, that is not quite the end of the story, because the exclusivism and intolerance of the proto-orthodox spirit finally turned against itself, disenfranchising many of its own party as proto-orthodoxy itself was eliminated to make way for—Christian orthodoxy."

different geographical locales where Christianity emerged as the dominant religion; and (2) the contention that the Church Fathers overstated their case that Christianity emerged from a single, doctrinally unified movement.[66] These two planks in Bauer's scholarly procedure form the subject of the following chapter, where we will ask the question: Taken on its own terms, is Bauer's historical reconstruction of second-century Christianity accurate? In order to adjudicate the question, we will examine Bauer's geographical data cited in support of the pervasive and early presence of heresy. We will also look at the early patristic evidence to see whether orthodoxy was as sporadic and late as Bauer alleged.

---

[66]Darrell L. Bock, *The Missing Gospels: Unearthing the Truth behind Alternative Christianities* (Nashville: Nelson, 2006), 48–49.

2

Unity and Plurality

How Diverse Was Early Christianity?

Just how diverse was early Christianity? While, as mentioned, Bauer's claim to have investigated "earliest" Christianity while neglecting the New Testament evidence is dubious, before turning to the New Testament in chapter 3 we will first examine the Bauer thesis on its own terms. The present chapter is therefore devoted to an examination of the geographical evidence adduced by Bauer in support of his thesis that heresy regularly preceded orthodoxy in the major urban centers where Christianity was found. We will also examine the evidence from the early Church Fathers regarding the question of heresy and orthodoxy in the early stages of Christianity. As will be seen, Bauer's arguments regularly fall short of demonstrating the validity of his thesis that heresy preceded orthodoxy. First, then, let us examine the existence of heresy and orthodoxy in some of the major geographical locales where Christianity became the dominant religion.

Orthodoxy and Heresy in Major Urban Centers

As mentioned, Bauer examined four major second-century urban centers: Asia Minor (in modern Turkey), Egypt, Edessa (located east of modern Turkey about 500 miles northeast of Jerusalem near the Tigris and Euphrates rivers), and Rome. He concluded that in each of these regions heresy preceded orthodoxy. As we have seen in the previous chapter, Bauer's arguments have not gone unchallenged. In the following discussion, we revisit these ancient urban centers in order to examine Bauer's contentions firsthand.

As we do so, three preliminary remarks may be helpful. First, it will be important to determine whether a large degree of theological uniformity existed in a given major urban center, a uniformity that did not extend to orthodox groups.[1] Second, there was considerable geographical movement among early adherents to Christianity so that claims assuming geographical isolation are precarious.[2] Third, dogmatism should be avoided in light of the limitations posed by the available evidence.

Asia Minor

Paul Trebilco recently subjected Bauer's claims regarding Asia Minor to meticulous examination.[3] The two most important ancient witnesses to heresy and orthodoxy in Asia Minor are the New Testament book of Revelation and the early church father Ignatius. The book of Revelation was written to seven churches in Asia Minor: Ephesus, Smyrna, Pergamum, Thyatira, Sardis, Philadelphia, and Laodicea.

Ignatius, the third bishop of Antioch, wrote a series of letters to several churches in Asia Minor enroute to his martyrdom in Rome. The cities to which he wrote were Ephesus, Magnesia, Tralles, Rome, Philadelphia, and Smyrna. The Apocalypse and Ignatius's letters preserve glimpses of these churches at the close of the New Testament era.

Bauer offered three reasons why John's and Ignatius's writings supported the notion that heresy preceded orthodoxy in Asia Minor. First, he contended that these two writers wrote letters only to church leaders in locations where a form of Christianity prevailed that resembled their own views. If the cities not addressed by John and Ignatius had contained like-minded churches, they would have sent letters to them as well. Bauer surmised that the groups not addressed by John and Ignatius were Gnostics, who would have rejected written correspondences from them.

Trebilco rightly points out the following problems with this argument. First, most scholars now believe that full-fledged Gnosticism had not yet

---

[1]Thomas A. Robinson, *The Bauer Thesis Examined: The Geography of Heresy in the Early Christian Church* (Lewiston, NY: Mellen, 1988), 37–38.
[2]Ibid., 38–39.
[3]Paul Trebilco, "Christian Communities in Western Asia Minor into the Early Second Century: Ignatius and Others as Witnesses against Bauer," *JETS* 49 (2006): 17–44.

come into existence during John's and Ignatius's time.[4] Instead, it is more likely that John wrote with a variety of other heretical groups in mind, while "Ignatius faced two sets of opponents—Judaizers in Magnesia and Philadelphia, and Docetists in Tralles and Smyrna."[5] As the following discussion reveals, the evidence suggests that neither of these opponents preceded orthodoxy in Asia Minor.

Judaizers taught that Christians should obey the Old Testament law alongside of Jesus' commands. While Ignatius mentions Judaizers in Magnesia and Philadelphia, John does not make reference to them in the letter to the church in Philadelphia (Rev. 3:7–13). The most likely reconstruction of the historical evidence suggests that Judaizers appeared in Philadelphia *after* the writing of Revelation and *before* Ignatius wrote to the same church and that the Judaizing heresy was not the original form of Christianity there.

The second group of opponents Ignatius faced was the Docetists. This particular group believed that Jesus' physical body and his death on the cross were only *apparent* (from the Greek word *dokeō*, "to appear") rather than real. For this reason, "the actual *nature* of Docetism," Trebilco observes, "seems to presuppose an underlying high Christology to start with."[6] It seems more likely, then, that the standard teaching of Jesus' life, death, and bodily resurrection preceded Docetism's spiritualized conception of these events. It is difficult to imagine that communities that had never heard of the major events of Jesus' life would have understood and embraced Docetism.

What is more, Docetism is not attested in the mid-first century but only surfaces in rudimentary form at the end of the New Testament period. This is evident from the letter to the church at Smyrna in the book of Revelation, which contains no reference to Docetism (Rev. 2:8–11). If Docetism had been present in Smyrna at that time, the letter most likely would have addressed it. The lack of reference to Docetism in Revelation suggests that this teaching most likely arose between the time Revelation was written and Ignatius's writings. If so, Docetism was not the original form of Christianity in Smyrna.

A second argument made by Bauer concerning Asia Minor is that the reason why John and Ignatius did not write to two known churches in that area, namely Colossae (Col. 1:7–8; 4:12) and Hierapolis (Col. 4:13), is that they knew that these churches would have rejected their letters because

---

[4]Ibid., 22.
[5]Ibid.
[6]Ibid., 23.

these churches were heretical. However, Trebilco notes that Colossae was overshadowed by Laodicea, the most prominent city in the Lycus Valley and recipient of one of the letters to the churches in Revelation (Rev. 3:14–22). What is more, the Roman historian Tacitus mentions that Laodicea was destroyed by an earthquake in AD 60 (*Ann.* 14.27.1). Since Colossae was only eleven miles away, it was almost certainly damaged severely as well.[7] Most likely, John and Ignatius did not write letters to the church at Colossae because the city was small and less significant than the adjacent Laodicea, especially in the aftermath of the earthquake of AD 60.

Concerning Hierapolis, all that is known from the extant data is that Papias occupied the office of bishop and that Philip, along with some of his daughters (see Acts 21:8–9), settled there around AD 70. It is unwise for Bauer to draw any firm conclusions about Hierapolis based on such scant data.

In addition, there are numerous possible reasons why the particular churches mentioned in the book of Revelation were chosen as recipients of the letters. Most likely, these churches were located along a postal route, which would account for the order in which they are mentioned in Revelation.[8] As Trebilco rightly observes, "we cannot say that there were heretical communities in Colossae, Hierapolis, Pergamum, Thyatira, Sardis, and Laodicea simply on the basis that John and/or Ignatius did not write to these places."[9] Even Bauer admitted that his thesis was based on sparse data and that firm conclusions were unwarranted: "To be sure, this is only a conjecture and nothing more!"[10]

A third argument by Bauer was that theological diversity in Asia Minor took on the form of doctrinal disagreements between church leaders and church members. Trebilco, however, plausibly responds that while there may have been theological tensions between bishops and church members, the primary disagreements were over issues related to church leadership.[11] If so, the church members were not "heretics" but advocated a different type of church structure. Bauer fails to recognize this and, in so doing,

---

[7]No records survive that indicate how long it took Colossae to recover from the devastation following the earthquake.
[8]Colin J. Hemer, *The Letters to the Seven Churches of Asia in Their Local Setting*, JSNT Sup 11 (Sheffield: JSOT, 1989), 15.
[9]Trebilco, "Christian Communities," 27.
[10]Walter Bauer, *Orthodoxy and Heresy in Earliest Christianity*, ed. Robert A. Kraft and Gerhard Krodel, trans. Paul J. Achtemeier (Philadelphia: Fortress, 1971), 75.
[11]Trebilco, "Christian Communities," 28–30.

"*overestimates* the theological diversity among his addressees in Asia Minor."[12]

Fourth, Bauer argued that since Paul founded a church in Ephesus but John mentioned neither Paul's name nor his theology in the letter to the Ephesian church (Rev. 2:1–7), the church at that time had no memory of Paul's influence in that city. The lack of reference to Paul's theology, Bauer believed, was evidence that Paul had lost the struggle with the "enemies" through "internal discord and controversies."[13] Yet John may have been aware of Paul's teaching but chosen not to mention it. In light of Paul's extensive ministry in Asia Minor, it is highly improbable that Paul was forgotten there within one generation.

In light of the available evidence from Asia Minor, there is no reason to suppose that heresy preceded orthodoxy in this region. To the contrary, it is more likely that the original form of Christianity in Asia Minor was orthodox and that only later heretical teaching deviated from the original orthodox teaching.

Egypt

Alexandria was a strategic city on the Mediterranean coastline in northern Egypt that represented a bastion of learning and culture. While the literary evidence concerning early Egyptian Christianity is scant, Bauer claimed that Gnostic-style heresies preceded Christian orthodoxy in Alexandria. He suggested that orthodox Christianity did not arrive in Egypt until the appointment of Bishop Demetrius in the early third century.[14]

Darrell Bock and a host of other scholars offer five major responses to Bauer's assertion.[15] First, Bauer's argument assumes that the *Epistle of Barnabas*, a second-century work, was Gnostic rather than orthodox. He reaches this conclusion by "extrapolating backward from the time of Hadrian, when such Gnostic teachers as Basilides, Valentinus, and Carpocrates were active."[16] However, this is erroneous since "the exegetical and halakhic gnosis of *Barnabas* bears no relationship at all to the gnosis of Gnosticism.

---

[12]Ibid., 33 (italics original).
[13]Bauer, *Orthodoxy and Heresy*, 85.
[14]Ibid., 44–60.
[15]Darrell L. Bock, *The Missing Gospels: Unearthing the Truth behind Alternative Christianities* (Nashville: Nelson, 2006), 52–53. See further the discussion below.
[16]Birger A. Pearson, *Gnosticism and Christianity in Roman and Coptic Egypt*, Studies in Antiquity and Christianity (New York: T&T Clark, 2004), 89.

Rather, it can be seen as a precursor to the 'gnostic' teaching of Clement of Alexandria and as implicitly anti-Gnostic."[17]

This leads to a second response, also related to the *Epistle of Barnabas*. Instead of standing in a Gnostic trajectory, the letter more likely exhibits orthodox Christian beliefs. To begin with, it "reflects an apocalyptic concern with the end of history that is like Judaism." This orientation, which includes a "consciousness of living in the last, evil stages of 'the present age' before the inbreaking of the 'age to come'" (*Barn.* 2.1; 4:1, 3, 9),[18] is more akin to orthodox Christianity than to early Gnosticism. Also, the letter reflects "strands of Christianity with Jewish Christian roots" that reach back to Stephen's speech in Acts 7.[19] Examples include the attitude expressed toward the Jerusalem temple and its ritual (Acts 7:42–43, 48–50; *Barn.* 16.1–2; 2.4–8); the interpretation of the golden calf episode in Israel's history (Acts 7:38–42a; *Barn.* 4.7–8); and Christology, especially the application of the messianic title "the Righteous One" to Jesus (Acts 7:52; *Barn.* 6.7).[20]

A third response concerns another late second-century Egyptian document, the *Teachings of Silvanus*. Instead of espousing Gnostic principles, this letter, too, stands in the conceptual trajectory that led to the later orthodoxy of Egyptian writers such as Clement, Origen, and Athanasius.[21]

Fourth, Bauer ignores the fact that Clement of Alexandria, one of Egypt's most famous second-century orthodox Christian teachers, and Irenaeus, a second-century bishop in Gaul, independently of one another claimed that orthodoxy preceded the rise of the Valentinians, an influential Gnostic movement founded by Valentinus. James McCue offers three points about Valentinian thought that Bauer overlooks: (1) The orthodox play a role in Valentinian thought such that they seem to be part of the Valentinian self-understanding. (2) This suggests that the orthodox are the main body, and at several points explicitly and clearly identifies the orthodoxy as the many over against the small number of Valentinians. (3) The Valentinians of the decades prior to Irenaeus and Clement of Alexandria use the books of the orthodox New Testament in a manner that is best accounted for by supposing that Valentinianism developed within a mid-second-century orthodox matrix.[22]

---

[17]Ibid., 90. For the complete argument see pp. 90–95.

[18]Ibid., 93.

[19]Ibid., 92–93; cf. Bock, *Missing Gospels*, 53.

[20]Pearson, *Gnosticism and Christianity*, 92.

[21]Ibid., 95–99; Bock, *Missing Gospels*, 53.

[22]James F. McCue, "Orthodoxy and Heresy: Walter Bauer and the Valentinians," *VC* 33 (1979): 120.

Fifth, Birger Pearson, citing Colin Roberts, points out that there are only fourteen extant second- or third-century papyri from Egypt.[23] Of these, only one, the *Gospel of Thomas*, may possibly reflect a Gnostic context, which calls into question Bauer's argument for a prevailing Gnostic presence in Alexandria prior to the arrival of orthodoxy.[24] What is more, as Pearson rightly notes, it is far from certain that even the *Gospel of Thomas* had Gnostic origins.[25] In addition, Arland Hultgren observes that "the presence of Old Testament texts speaks loudly in favor of the nongnostic character of that community."[26] Bauer's argument that Gnosticism was preeminent in Alexandria, then, is supported by one out of fourteen papyri that may be Gnostic.[27] This hardly supports Bauer's thesis that Gnosticism preceded orthodoxy in Alexandria.[28]

The five responses detailed above combine to suggest that Bauer's argument fails to obtain also with regard to Egypt. Rather than support the

---

[23]Birger A. Pearson, "Earliest Christianity in Egypt: Some Observations," in *The Roots of Egyptian Christianity*, Studies in Antiquity and Christianity, ed. Birger A. Pearson and James E. Goehring (Philadelphia: Fortress, 1986), 132–33; Colin H. Roberts, *Manuscript, Society and Belief in Early Christian Egypt*, The Schweich Lectures of the British Academy 1977 (London: Oxford University Press, 1979), see esp. 12–14. According to Roberts's analysis of the earliest Christian papyri from Egypt (NT, OT, and patristic works), there is little indication that Gnosticism had a foothold in the second century.

[24]Most relevant ancient manuscripts have been discovered in the Egyptian city of Oxyrhynchus, which has provided us with over 40 percent of our New Testament papyri—more than any other single location—covering at least fifteen of our twenty-seven New Testament books, and many of these papyri date to the second or third centuries (e.g., P.Oxy. 4403 and 4404). When one considers the fact that many of our New Testament papyri have unknown provenances (e.g., $\mathfrak{P}52$), and may have actually come from Oxyrhynchus, then this percentage could be even higher. For more information see Eldon Jay Epp, "The New Testament Papyri at Oxyrhynchus in their Social and Intellectual Context," in *Sayings of Jesus: Canonical and Non-Canonical*, ed. William L. Petersen (Leiden: Brill, 1997), 47–68; idem, "The Oxyrhynchus New Testament Papyri: 'Not Without Honor Except in Their Hometown'?" *JBL* 123 (2004): 5–55; and Peter M. Head, "Some Recently Published NT Papyri From Oxyrhynchus: An Overview and Preliminary Assessment," *TynBul* 51 (2000): 1–16. For more on the site of Oxyrhynchus as a whole see AnneMarie Luijendijk, *Greetings in the Lord: Early Christians in the Oxyrhynchus Papyri* (Cambridge, MA: Harvard University Press, 2008); P. J. Parsons et al., ed., *Oxyrhynchus: A City and Its Texts* (London: Egypt Exploration Society, 2007); and E. G. Turner, "Roman Oxyrhynchus," *JEA* 38 (1952): 78–93.

[25]Pearson, "Earliest Christianity in Egypt," 133.

[26]Arland J. Hultgren, *The Rise of Normative Christianity* (Minneapolis: Fortress, 1994), 11–12.

[27]In fairness to Bauer, these manuscripts were not discovered until after he published his work.

[28]Winrich A. Löhr, *Basilides und seine Schule: Eine Studie zur Theologie und Kirchengeschichte des zweiten Jahrhunderts*, WUNT 83 (Tübingen: Mohr Siebeck, 1996), 33–34 (cited in Bock, *Missing Gospels*, 53).

notion that Gnosticism preceded orthodoxy, the available evidence from Alexandria instead suggests that orthodox Christianity preceded Gnosticism also in that locale.

Edessa

Edessa was the primary focus of Bauer's research because he believed that there Marcionism preceded orthodoxy.[29] It is curious that Bauer focused so much attention on Edessa since literary data from that region is extremely limited, requiring the historian to fill many historical gaps with conjecture. Also, Edessa was not nearly as major a center of early Christianity as Ephesus or Rome. In any case, as Thomas Robinson has cogently argued, while Edessa is the one urban center where Bauer's argument might hold, even there his thesis is fraught with error.[30]

The primary problem with Bauer's thesis concerning Marcionism in Edessa, according to Robinson, is that "if we say that the earliest form of Christianity in Edessa was Marcionism we are forced to account for at least a century during which Edessa had no Christian witness."[31] This is the case because Marcionism did not arise until Marcion was excommunicated in Rome in c. AD 144. This means that Marcionism would not have arrived in Edessa until approximately AD 150. Is it likely, Robinson asked, that Edessa was without Christian influence from c. AD 50 until about 150?

In theory, it is conceivable that Edessa remained impervious to Christianity during this one-hundred-year period since Edessa did not become part of the Roman Empire until AD 216. Prior to this date, convenient travel for early Christian missionaries to Edessa could have been limited or prohibited.[32] Robinson, however, challenges this contention of an Edessa isolated from Christianity: "Although Edessa was not part of the Roman [E]mpire at the beginning of the Christian church, it was, as a city on a major trade route in a bordering state, not isolated from the Roman [E]mpire."[33]

---

[29]Bauer, *Orthodoxy and Heresy*, 22.

[30]Helmut Koester, an adherent to Bauer's thesis (see chap. 1), concurred that orthodoxy did not precede heresy in Edessa. He believed, however, that a non-orthodox "Thomas tradition" arrived first in Edessa ("Gnomai Diaphoroi"; for a rebuttal of this view see Robinson, *Bauer Thesis Examined*, 52–59). Koester's argument is interesting because it exemplifies the lack of consensus concerning what type of Christianity first appeared in Edessa even among those who are committed to the thesis that heresy preceded orthodoxy in that location.

[31]Robinson, *Bauer Thesis Examined*, 47.

[32]Ibid., 47–48.

[33]Ibid., 48.

Moreover, since a prominent Jewish community existed in Edessa, it seems unlikely that there would have been no contact with Antioch, the largest Jewish center in the area. Although Antioch was a considerable distance from Edessa (c. 250 miles), the Jewish capital Jerusalem was a distant 750 miles away. Thus Jews in Edessa would have communicated more readily with their closer compatriots in Antioch. What is more, during the earliest years of Christianity Jews and Christians were in close contact. In light of this, it is unlikely that the Jews of Edessa were unaware of Christianity.[34] This is further unlikely in view of the contact "between Jews and Christians in most of the major cities of the Roman world."[35]

In fact, the very attestation of Marcionism may indicate a form of Christianity that preceded Marcionism. This is indicated by the very nature of Marcionism:[36] "All our evidence indicates that Marcion's activities were directed not at the conversion of pagans but at a reformation of the catholic church in terms of a radical Paulinism."[37] By virtue of denying the validity of the Old Testament Scriptures and by critically editing the Pauline literature, Marcionism was a message most apt for people steeped in the Jewish Scriptures and in the writings of Paul. For this reason Marcionism was most likely a corrective rather than a converting movement, seeking to change how people viewed Christianity rather than teaching it for the first time.

If so, it may be surmised that an element of Pauline or Jewish Christianity was present in Edessa that Marcionism subsequently sought to correct. As Robinson aptly notes:

> Quite simply, the Marcionite message had too many Christian assumptions at its core for its primary audience not to have been the larger Christian community. If, then, early Marcionism neither looked for nor found an audience other than an already Christian one, the success of Marcionism in Edessa would seem to serve (against Bauer) as evidence *for*, rather than against, an early catholic-like Christianity there.[38]

It is possible that a substantially altered form of Marcionism, one more intelligible for an audience not steeped in a form of Christianity, arrived in Edessa at a later time. If so, Marcionism made its way to Edessa no earlier than c. AD 145–150. Since, as mentioned, the earliest form of Marcionism

---

[34]Ibid.
[35]Ibid.
[36]This argument is similar to the one regarding Docetism above.
[37]Robinson, *Bauer Thesis Examined*, 49.
[38]Ibid., 51 (italics original).

addressed an already existing version of Christianity, more time would have had to elapse to allow Marcionism to change its primary emphasis. Yet such a late date for the arrival of Marcionism in Edessa seems unlikely in a predominantly Jewish city in relatively close proximity to Antioch, Christianity's early hub of activity (Acts 11:26).[39]

Evidence is lacking, therefore, that heresy preceded orthodoxy in Edessa. As far as we can tell, when Marcionite teaching arrived, it most likely set itself against an earlier form of Christianity that may well be characterized as orthodox.

Rome

As mentioned in chapter 1, Rome played an especially crucial role in Bauer's argument. Primarily from *1 Clement* (c. AD 95), Bauer claimed that orthodoxy had a firm stronghold in Rome and that Roman leaders, by virtue of their power over other churches in different locations, imposed their orthodoxy throughout the Empire. This form of orthodoxy, Bauer maintained, had nothing to do with an original form of Christianity that can be traced back to the New Testament or to Jesus. Instead, it was simply the belief of the Roman church. The heretics of other cities and their theologies were relegated to the sidelines largely because they lost the battle with Rome.[40]

As Darrell Bock contends, if Rome was the impetus for orthodoxy, Bauer must demonstrate two facts.[41] First, he must show that orthodoxy did not exist elsewhere, since, if it did, orthodoxy was not a characteristic solely of the Roman church, nor was it necessarily original with Rome. Second, Bauer must show that "Roman communication in *1 Clement* . . . to Corinth was not merely an attempt to persuade but was a ruling imposed on Corinth."[42]

However, the data does not support Bauer's thesis in these respects. First, as noted above, orthodoxy was present in Asia Minor and most likely also prevailed in Egypt and Edessa. Orthodox teaching, then, was not a characteristic solely of the Roman church but a feature attested also in other regions. Second, when one compares the tone of *1 Clement* to that of other letters from the same time period, it is evident that the letter did not aim to impose a theological position onto the Corinthian church but to persuade

---

[39]Ibid., 51–52.
[40]See Bauer, *Orthodoxy and Heresy*, 229.
[41]Bock, *Missing Gospels*, 50.
[42]Ibid. For a full critique of Bauer's reconstruction of early Christianity in Corinth, see Robinson, *Bauer Thesis Examined*, 69–77.

the Christians there to accept it.[43] If the Roman church had carried the authority Bauer ascribed to it, one would expect *1 Clement* to convey an authoritative tone that would tolerate no dissent. Since *1 Clement* does not exhibit such a tone, Rome, though wielding wide and increasing influence during the patristic era, had not yet become the sole locus of authority.

Bock registers six additional arguments against the Roman control thesis.[44] First, the idea of each city appointing only one bishop probably did not originate with Rome but most likely began in Jerusalem and Syria. There is evidence that James was the leader of the Jerusalem church (Acts 15; Gal. 2:9). In addition, Frederick Norris presents a strong argument that while the case Ignatius made for the theological and organizational significance of the bishop may have been new, "prior to his writing, the offices existed and were distinguished from each other in Asia Minor, and probably Western Syria."[45] This is important because Bauer believed that the centralization of the episcopal office in Rome was central to Rome's power. If this practice originated outside of Rome, however, Rome's power may not have given birth to orthodoxy but simply replicated what Rome had already inherited.

Second, Ignatius, who was not from Rome, spoke of theological schisms between opposing groups. Since Ignatius is considered by most to be part of the orthodox, this intimates a competition between heresy and orthodoxy. This competition suggests the presence of orthodoxy outside of Roman control, an orthodoxy that did not originate with Rome and was not imposed by her.

Third, Asia Minor, a location far away from the city of Rome, is the likely provenance of many extant "orthodox" materials such as John's Gospel, his three letters, Revelation, and several of Paul's letters. To argue that Rome imposed orthodoxy on other geographical regions later on gives insufficient consideration to orthodox activity already attested in locations such as Asia Minor.

Fourth, Marcion of Sinope, who was branded as a heretic by many early Christians, assumed the authority of some works that were later recognized as orthodox. In the mid-second century, Marcion developed a canon that

---

[43]On this point, see Fredrick W. Norris, "Ignatius, Polycarp, and 1 Clement: Walter Bauer Reconsidered," in *Orthodoxy, Heresy, and Schism in Early Christianity,* Studies in Early Christianity 4, ed. Everett Ferguson (New York: Garland, 1993), 36–41.

[44]Bock, *Missing Gospels,* 51.

[45]For the complete argument, see Frederick W. Norris, "Ignatius, Polycarp, and I Clement: Walter Bauer Reconsidered," *VC* 30 (1976): 23–44 (esp. 29–36).

included an edited version of Luke and ten of Paul's epistles, rejecting all other gospels and letters. Marcion formed his canon either in reaction to an already established standardized collection in the early church or he pioneered the idea himself. Either way, it is notable that within his system he depended on works that later achieved orthodox status, and this apart from Rome.

Fifth, as Bock observes, the earliest liturgical texts that we possess come from Syria, not Rome.[46]

Sixth, Pliny the Younger wrote to the Roman emperor Trajan with regard to a Christian community in Bythynia that worshiped Jesus, a practice that points to the existence of orthodox belief there (*Ep.* 10.96–97).[47]

For these reasons it is evident that orthodoxy existed in locations other than Rome. Although Roman control certainly solidified in subsequent centuries, it is erroneous to suggest, as Bauer did, that early orthodoxy did not exist elsewhere. In fact, the existence of orthodoxy in other locations may well explain Rome's relatively easy success in acquiring ecclesiastical power and in demanding adherence to orthodoxy. If other cities had been mired in a plethora of diverse forms of Christianity, doctrinal uniformity would have been much more difficult to enforce. On the other hand, if Rome were not the driving force behind the consolidation of orthodoxy in earliest Christianity, orthodoxy must have been less isolated and more widespread than Bauer was willing to concede.

Summary
The above examination of the extant evidence has shown that in all the major urban centers investigated by Bauer, orthodoxy most likely preceded heresy or the second-century data by itself is inconclusive.

Indications of Early Orthodoxy in Patristic Literature
Apart from what we know about the presence of orthodoxy and/or heresy in the major urban centers of early Christianity, what can we know about these phenomena more broadly? Bart Ehrman opens his book *Lost Christianities* with a dramatic statement about how diverse the early church was, suggesting that early Christianity was so fragmented that, essentially, there were possibly as many forms of Christianity as there were people.[48] Does Ehrman's statement about this period square with the evidence?

---

[46]Bock, *Missing Gospels*, 51.
[47]Ibid.
[48]Bart D. Ehrman, *Lost Christianities: The Battles for Scripture and the Faiths We Never Knew* (Oxford: Oxford University Press, 2003), 2–3.

In this section, we examine both orthodoxy and heresy in the patristic era in order to show that Ehrman's assessment of the data is inadequate. First, we will investigate orthodoxy in the early centuries of the Christian era. As will be seen, the church fathers, far from being innovators, were committed to the New Testament orthodoxy that preceded them. Second, we will examine heresy in the same period, showing that orthodoxy served as the theological standard from which various forms of heresy deviated.

Before embarking on this examination, a brief look at four principal views concerning the progression of early Christianity will help frame the discussion.[49] The first position was espoused by Adolf von Harnack (1851–1930), who suggested that Hellenism influenced the post–New Testament church to the point of eradicating the original sense of the gospel message.[50] The later church accommodated the surrounding culture, adding layers to the gospel that resulted in a message that significantly differed from the original.

John Henry Newman (1801–1890), a Roman Catholic priest, proposed a second view: the Christianity that originated with Jesus and his apostles was merely the starting point of a series of theological developments that continued to evolve over the centuries. As a result, fourth-century orthodoxy was but vaguely connected to the original.[51] A third view is that of Walter Bauer, Bart Ehrman, and others—the Bauer-Ehrman thesis—which, since it was already dealt with in chapter 1, needs no further discussion here.

Finally, John Behr, dean and professor of patristics at St. Vladimir's Theological Seminary, argues that the theology that emanated from the New Testament, continued through the church fathers, was guarded by the Apologists,[52] and solidified in the ecumenical church councils[53] represents a continuous uninterrupted stream.[54] The theology espoused by the orthodox

---

[49]For a fuller exploration and description of the progression of early Christianity, see Jeffrey Bingham, "Development and Diversity in Early Christianity," *JETS* 49 (2006): 45–66.

[50]Adolf von Harnack, *The History of Dogma*, trans. Neil Buchanan (London: Williams & Northgate, 1894).

[51]John Henry Newman, *Essay on the Development of Christian Doctrine* (London: Longmans Green, 1888; repr., London: Sheed & Ward, 1960).

[52]The Apologists were early Christian writers (c. AD 120–220) who defended the Christian faith and commended it to outsiders.

[53]The so-called First Ecumenical Council of Nicaea (AD 325) produced the Nicene Creed. Six subsequent councils convened in AD 381, 431, 451, 553, 680–681, and 787, respectively.

[54]John Behr, *The Way to Nicaea*, The Formation of Christian Theology, vol. 1 (Crestwood, NY: St. Vladimir's Seminary Press, 2001).

clarified, elucidated, and expounded the theology of the New Testament without deviating from it, and the creeds accurately represent the essence of the apostolic faith.

As the following discussion will show, Behr's position does the most justice to the available evidence from the first two centuries of the church.

Orthodoxy in the Patristic Era

As we will see, the essential theological convictions of Jesus and the New Testament writers continued into the second-century writings of the church fathers. The place to begin this exploration is with the pervasive and decisive role that the "Rule of Faith"[55] (Latin *regula fidei*) played in the post–New Testament church. The Rule appeared as early as *1 Clement* 7.2 in an undeveloped form and is found in virtually all the orthodox writings of the patristic era from varied geographical locales including Irenaeus (c. 130–200), Tertullian (c. 160–225), Clement of Alexandria (c. 150–215), Origen (c. 185–254), Hippolytus (c. 170–236), Novatian (c. 200–258), Dionysius of Alexandria (c. 200–265), Athanasius (c. 296–373), and Augustine (c. 354–430). Irenaeus and Tertullian were the first writers to discuss the Rule at length. Irenaeus identified it with the central governing sense or overarching argument of Scripture (*Haer.* I. 9–10).[56] Similarly, Tertullian called it the "reason" or "order" of Scripture (*Praescr.* 9).

Although the church fathers never explicitly spelled out for posterity the Rule's specific theological content,[57] there is relative consensus among scholars that it served as a minimal statement concerning the church's common faith. It has variously been called "the sure doctrine of the Christian faith";[58] a "concise statement of early Christian public preaching and communal belief, a normative compendium of the *kerygma*";[59] a "sum-

---

[55]Also variously referred to by the post–New Testament writers as Rule of Piety, Ecclesiastical Rule, Rule of the Church, Evangelical Rule, Rule of the Gospel, Rule of Tradition, Sound Rule, Full Faith, Analogy of Faith, Law of Faith, Canon of the Truth, Canon of the Church, and Preaching of the Church.

[56]See Paul Hartog, "The 'Rule of Faith' and Patristic Biblical Exegesis," *TJ* NS 28 (2007): 67.

[57]For a brief look at how scholars have delineated the Rule, see Paul M. Blowers, "The Regula Fidei and the Narrative Character of Early Christian Faith," *ProEccl* 6 (1997): 199–228.

[58]M. Eugene Osterhaven, "Rule of Faith" in *Evangelical Dictionary of Theology* (2d ed.; Grand Rapids: Baker, 2001), 1043.

[59]Hartog, "The 'Rule of Faith,'" 66, summarizing Eric F. Osborn, "Reason and Rule of Faith in the Second Century AD," in *Making of Orthodoxy* (Cambridge: Cambridge University Press, 1989), 48.

mary of the main points of Christian teaching . . . the form of preaching that served as the norm of Christian faith . . . the essential message . . . fixed by the gospel and the structure of Christian belief in one God, reception of salvation in Christ, and experience of the Holy Spirit";[60] and "the substance of [the] Christian faith, or truth as a standard and normative authority."[61]

Bart Ehrman concurs with these descriptions of the Rule: "The [Rule] included the basic and fundamental beliefs that, according to the proto-orthodox, all Christians were to subscribe to, as these had been taught by the apostles themselves."[62] As will be discussed in chapter 3, the apostles and New Testament writers adhered to an orthodoxy that centered on Jesus' death, burial, and resurrection for the forgiveness of sins. The Rule of Faith contained and proclaimed this core New Testament message as the central tenet of Christianity. Nearly from the beginning of the post–New Testament era, then, a geographically pervasive group of Christian writers espoused a theological standard that unified them.

The church fathers saw their role as propagators, or conduits, of this unified and unifying theological standard. They used the nomenclature of "handing down" to describe their role (e.g., Irenaeus, *Haer.* 3.3.3). Their self-perceived calling was to take what they had received from the apostles and hand it down to their generation and to posterity. This idea of propagating what was received appears as early as Clement of Rome (*1 Clem.* 42.1–3; c. AD 96) and Ignatius (*Magn.* 13.1; 6.1; *Phld.* 6.3; c. AD 110) who encouraged their readers to remain in the teachings of Christ and the apostles (cf. Pol. *Phil* 6.3). Irenaeus continues to speak in these terms: "Such is the preaching of the truth: the prophets have announced it, Christ has established it, the apostles have transmitted it, and everywhere the church presents it to her children" (*Epid.* 98; cf. *Haer.* 3.1.1; 3.3.1). Not only did the early Fathers see themselves as proclaiming the gospel, but they also viewed themselves as the guardians of the message (e.g., *1 Clem.* 42).

The origin of this theological standard that the Fathers passed on was perceived to be the Old Testament (e.g., Justin, *Dial.* 29; Justin, *Apol.* 1.53; *Barn.* 14.4). The Fathers taught that the gospel originated with the Old Testament prophets, whose message was taken up by the apostles who,

---

[60]Everett Ferguson, "Rule of Faith," in *Encyclopedia of Early Christianity*, ed. Everett Ferguson (New York: Garland, 1990), 804–5.

[61]Geoffrey W. Bromiley, "Rule of Faith," in *The Encyclopedia of Christianity*, vol. 4 (Grand Rapids: Eerdmans, 1997), 758.

[62]Ehrman, *Lost Christianities*, 194.

like the prophets, were sent by God.[63] This self-understanding stands in marked contrast to second-century sects that sought to strip the gospel of its Old Testament roots. Rather than being devoted to and dependent on the teaching of the apostles, these groups held that secretly revealed knowledge about Jesus trumped historical and theological continuity. The Fathers, on the other hand, taught that the Rule of Faith originated with the Old Testament prophetic message, which was fulfilled in Jesus and proclaimed by the apostles. The Fathers, in turn, guarded this message and passed it on to others, handing the baton to subsequent generations of believers.

What happened to the Rule of Faith after the Fathers passed it along? Its contents, that is, the core gospel message, made its way into the third- and fourth-century creeds. In two recently published works, Gerald Bray argues this point by investigating the Nicene Creed and concluding that its authors did not anachronistically read orthodoxy back into previous centuries. Examining the Nicene Creed step by step, Bray traces every detail of its theological contents from the New Testament through the Fathers to its codification in the creed. For example, concerning the first article of the Nicene Creed, Bray remarks, "The bedrock of the church's beliefs remained unaltered, and in the first article of the creed we can be confident that we are being transported back to the earliest days of the apostolic preaching."[64] D. A. Carson agrees: "[While it may be erroneous] to read . . . fourth-century orthodoxy back into the New Testament . . . it is equally wrong to suggest that there are few ties between fourth-century orthodoxy and the New Testament."[65]

That the Fathers preserved the orthodoxy of the New Testament and delivered it to those who formulated the creeds does not necessarily mean that the New Testament writers would have conceived of their theology in the same exact constructs as those of the creeds. For example, although the term "Trinity" does not appear in the New Testament, the concept is clearly present (e.g., Matt. 28:19; 1 Pet. 1:2). Creedal third- and fourth-century orthodoxy, then, is not in opposition to the orthodoxy purported in the New Testament and propagated by the Fathers. It is, as Behr suggests, an organic continuation of what the New Testament writers began without

---

[63] Joseph F. Mitros, "The Norm of Faith in the Patristic Age," *TS* 29 (1968): 448.

[64] Gerald L. Bray and Thomas C. Oden, eds., *Ancient Christian Doctrine I* (Downers Grove, IL: InterVarsity, 2009), xxxvi.

[65] D. A. Carson, *The Gagging of God: Christianity Confronts Pluralism* (Grand Rapids: Zondervan, 1996), 31.

any transmutation of the DNA of the New Testament gospel message, which, in turn, is rooted in the Old Testament.[66] This is especially evident in the similarities between the following words of Irenaeus and those of the later creeds:

> [The Church believes] in one God, the Father Almighty, Maker of Heaven and earth, and the sea, and all things that are in them; and in one Christ Jesus, the Son of God, who became incarnate for our salvation; and in the Holy Spirit, who proclaimed by the prophets the (divine) dispensations and the coming of Christ, his birth from a virgin, his passion, his rising from the dead, and the bodily ascension into heaven of our beloved Lord Jesus Christ, and his manifestation from heaven in the glory of the Father to sum up all things in one and to raise up again all flesh of the whole human race. (*Haer.* 1.10.1)

Therefore, as Larry Hurtado contends:

> Well before the influence of Constantine and councils of bishops in the fourth century and thereafter, it was clear that proto-orthodox Christianity was ascendant, and represented the emergent mainstream. Proto-orthodox devotion to Jesus of the second century constitutes the pattern of belief and practice that shaped Christian tradition thereafter.[67]

To sum up, then, the church fathers' Rule of Faith served both as a theological continuation of New Testament orthodoxy and as a conduit to the orthodoxy of the creeds.

However, affirming an essential theological unity among the church fathers, the basic content of whose essential teaching derived from their apostolic forebears, does not by itself address the degree to which their teaching was prevalent among early Christianity at large. The question remains whether the orthodox represented but a (small) part of second-century Christianity as Ehrman contends, with alternate forms of Christianity being equally, if not more, prominent, or whether orthodox Christianity constituted the prevailing form of Christianity not only in the fourth century but already in the second century. To answer this question, we now turn our attention to the heresies attested in this period.

---

[66]Behr, *Way to Nicaea.*
[67]Larry W. Hurtado, *Lord Jesus Christ: Devotion to Jesus in Earliest Christianity* (Grand Rapids: Eerdmans, 2003), 561.

Heresy in the Patristic Era

As mentioned, Bart Ehrman and others argue that the proponents of second-century orthodoxy represented, at best, a minor group in a diverse religious landscape that featured a large variety of alternative forms of Christianity. In the next chapter, we will seek to demonstrate that orthodoxy emerged in the New Testament period and was passed along by the apostolic fathers. In the remainder of this chapter, we will attempt to show that the various forms of heresy in the patristic era were not as widespread as Ehrman contends and that these heretics were not nearly as unified as the orthodox. In fact, the available evidence suggests that heretical groups were regularly parasitic of the proponents of orthodoxy that were already well established and widespread.

The second century produced numerous heretical groups. For example, the Ebionites were a leading group of Jewish Christians who, because of their Jewish roots, denied Jesus' divinity. Another example is furnished by the Docetists who held that Jesus only appeared to be, but was not in fact, human. The only second-century group, however, that remotely rivaled and presented a serious challenge to orthodoxy was Gnosticism.[68] The Gnostic movement was more widespread than any other second-century heresy and was the only one that offered an alternative to orthodoxy that had "potential staying power."[69] For this reason, we use Gnosticism as a test case in order to examine the nature of second-century heresy and how it related to its orthodox counterpart.[70]

---

[68]Some classify various subsets to Gnosticisms (i.e., Syrian gnosis, Marcionism, Valentinism, and the Basilidian movement; later movements include the Cainites, Peratae, Barbelo-Gnostics, the Sethians, and the Borborites, to mention only a few) as individual religio-philosophical systems. In this section, they are presumed to be loosely connected under the broader umbrella of Gnosticism. If, however, these sects do represent independent and unrelated entities, then the argument of this section is considerably strengthened to the extent that discussion becomes nearly moot. For a fuller explanation of the complexities of these movements, see Hurtado, *Lord Jesus Christ*, 519–61. Our information about the Gnostics comes from the Nag Hammadi documents and from the following church fathers who refuted them: Irenaeus, *Against Heresies*; Hippolytus, *Refutations of all Heresies*; Epiphanius, *Panarion*; and Tertullian, *Against Marcion*. For more information on Gnosticism, see Pheme Perkins, "Gnosticism," *NIB* 2:581–84, and David M. Scholer, "Gnosis, Gnosticism," in *DLNT*, 400–412.

[69]Bock, *Missing Gospels*, 25.

[70]Although we limit this section to a study of Gnosticism because of space and because of Gnosticism's influence, comparable information concerning other second-century texts is mentioned in various footnotes. The conclusions reached in this section regarding Gnosticism apply equally to other second-century sects. For a fuller overview of all the known sects of the second century see Antti Marjanen and Petri Luomanen, eds., *A Companion to Second-Century Christian "Heretics,"* Supplements to VC (Boston: Brill, 2005) (note accompanying

Specifically, we will investigate whether second-century orthodoxy was just one among many forms of Christianity that was caught in a struggle against a large number of alternatives. The following three points concerning Gnosticism reveal that orthodoxy was the norm of earliest Christianity and that Gnosticism was subsidiary and comparatively less pervasive.

First, Gnosticism was a diverse syncretistic religious movement that, although loosely sharing a few key thematic elements,[71] never emerged as a singularly connected movement.[72] In light of this diversity, it is debatable whether a singular term such as "Gnostic" adequately encapsulates the movement. Gnosticism, in essence, was demonstrably diverse and only loosely connected by an overall philosophical framework. As a result, or perhaps because, of this diversity, Gnosticism never formed its own church or groups of churches. Instead, the Gnostics were basically "a conglomeration of disconnected schools that disagreed with each other as well as with the traditional Christians."[73]

On the other hand, there is ample evidence that second-century orthodox Christianity was largely unified. To begin with, as mentioned in the previous section, the prevalence of the Rule of Faith in the writings of the second-century Fathers demonstrates the pervasive unity on core Christian doctrines. Also, orthodox Christians founded thriving churches as early as the AD 50s, which is attested by Paul's many letters. Paul wrote to established churches in Galatia, Thessalonica, Corinth, Rome, Philippi, Ephesus, and other locations.[74] Moreover, there is ample evidence that these congregations exhibited "an almost obsessional mutual interest and interchange" among themselves.[75] In other words, these congregations, although spread throughout the known world, viewed themselves as a

---

bibliographies for further study) and Chas S. Clifton, *Encyclopedia of Heresies and Heretics* (Santa Barbara: ABC-Clio, 1992).

[71] For a brief summation of these key elements see Pheme Perkins, "Gnosticism," *NIB* 2:583–84. Docetism, likewise, was extremely variegated (D. F. Wright, "Docetism," *DLNT* 306). The data concerning the Ebionites is too scant to know the degree of unity which this sect possessed. Wright states, "Making consistent and historically plausible sense of patristic testimonies to the Ebionites is a taxing assignment" (D. F. Wright, "Ebionites," *DLNT* 315).

[72] Bock, *Missing Gospels*, 23.

[73] Ibid., 23–24.

[74] That Paul addresses "overseers and deacons" in Phil. 1:1 indicates that he is writing to an established church.

[75] See Rowan Williams, "Does It Make Sense to Speak of Pre-Nicene Orthodoxy?" in *The Making of Orthodoxy: Essays in Honour of Henry Chadwick*, ed. Rowan Williams (Cambridge: Cambridge University Press, 1989), 11–12.

unified network of churches.[76] Orthodox Christians, then, organized themselves into local assemblies remarkably early, established leadership (e.g., Acts 14:23; 20:28; Phil. 1:1; Titus 1:5; 1 Pet. 5:2), agreed on fundamental beliefs, and interacted regularly and frequently. These characteristics do not support Ehrman's portrait of an underdeveloped first- and second-century orthodoxy.

Second, to the degree that Gnosticism became organized, it did so substantially later than orthodox Christianity.[77] Historians disagree regarding the origin of Gnosticism. Some believe that it originated independently of and prior to orthodox Christianity.[78] Others think that it originated independently and alongside of orthodox Christianity.[79] Still others argue that it arose as a reaction to either Christianity[80] or Judaism.[81] Darrell Bock is probably right that Gnosticism formed in the shadow of Christianity and/or Judaism.[82] There is no literary evidence that confirms a first-century origin of Gnosticism, contrary to Schmithals's argument that Paul's opponents were Gnostics.[83] The first-century data, rather, reveals, at best, a primitive, incipient form of Gnosticism (e.g., 1 Tim. 6:20; 1 John 2:20;

---

[76]See, e.g., M. B. Thompson, "The Holy Internet: Communication between Churches in the First Christian Generation," in *The Gospels for All Christians: Rethinking the Gospel Audiences*, ed. R. Bauckham (Grand Rapids: Eerdmans, 1998), 49–70. This self-perceived unity continues into the era of the church fathers (see Williams, "Does It Make Sense to Speak of Pre-Nicene Orthodoxy?" in *Making of Orthodoxy*, 12–14).

[77]Although primitive Docetism is perhaps detectable at the end of the first century (1 John 4:2–3; 2 John 7), there is no evidence that it arose concurrently with orthodoxy. Likewise, the evidence is too sparse to draw firm conclusions about the origin of the Ebionites (see Wright, "Ebionites," *DLNT* 315–16).

[78]Carsten Colpe, *Die religionsgeschichtliche Schule: Darstellung und Kritik ihres Bildes vom gnostischen Erlösungsmythus* (FRLANT 78; Göttingen: Vandenhoeck & Ruprecht, 1961); Karl Prümm, *Gnosis an der Wurzel des Christentums? Grundlagenkritik an der Entmythologisierung* (Müller: Salzburg, 1972). But see Edwin M. Yamauchi, *Pre-Christian Gnosticism: A Survey of Proposed Evidences* (Grand Rapids: Eerdmans, 1973).

[79]Kurt Rudolph, *Gnosis: The Nature and History of Gnosticism*, trans. R. M. Wilson (Edinburgh: T&T Clark, 1983), 275–94.

[80]Adolf Harnack, *History of Dogma*, vol. 1, trans. Neil Buchanan (Eugene, OR: Wipf & Stock, 1997), 223–66; Simone Petrément, *A Separate God: The Origins and Teachings of Gnosticism*, trans. Carole Harrison (San Francisco: HarperSanFrancisco, 1990).

[81]R. McL. Wilson, *Gnosis and the New Testament* (Oxford: Basil Blackwell, 1968); Alan F. Segal, *Two Powers in Heaven: Early Rabbinic Reports about Christianity and Gnosticism* (Leiden: Brill, 2002); Carl B. Smith II, *No Longer Jews: The Search for Gnostic Origins* (Peabody, MA: Hendrickson, 2004).

[82]Bock, *Missing Gospels*, 30.

[83]Walter Schmithals, *Gnosticism in Corinth: An Investigation of the Letters to the Corinthians*, trans. John E. Steely (Nashville: Abingdon, 1971).

2 John 1:9).[84] When this first-century data is compared with what we know of Gnosticism from the second century, a picture emerges of a movement that begins to surface in the latter half of the first century and begins to take shape in the first half of the second century (evidenced by the growing body of literature and the church fathers' vehement attacks against it) but never coalesces into a unified entity. In light of the available first-century evidence, any assessment that concludes that Gnosticism was organized earlier than the second century is ultimately an argument from silence.

Orthodox Christianity, conversely, was organized early (in the AD 40s and 50s). Not only is this exhibited in the above-mentioned early formation of churches but also in the early solidification of a core belief system that will be examined in the next chapter. Although the complexity of ecclesiastical organization increased in the second century, the church's foundational organizing principles were already well in place in the first century. The apostolic fathers and subsequent church leaders, therefore, did not supply the original impetus for organizing the church; they had already inherited its foundational structure and core beliefs.

Third, prior to Constantine's Edict of Milan (AD 313) that mandated religious toleration throughout the Roman Empire, adherents of orthodoxy had no official means or power to relegate heretics to a marginal role. Nearly concurrent with this Edict was the Arian controversy (AD 318). Interestingly, there is no significant mention of any Gnostic sect during this controversy. It seems that by that time Gnosticism was either forgotten or so insignificant as to hardly warrant any of the orthodox's attention. This means that prior to Constantine's mandated religious toleration, the orthodox were able decisively to refute these heretical movements. If the heretics were as numerous and pervasive as Ehrman contends and if orthodoxy was relatively insignificant prior to the fourth century, then historical probabilities suggest that it would have been unlikely that orthodoxy would have been able to overturn these heretical movements. Without an official governing body in place, the only way that the orthodox could have "won" prior to Constantine was through the force of sheer numbers. It is clear, then, that second- and third-century Gnosticism could not have been as pervasive and influential as second-century orthodoxy.[85]

---

[84]But note in this regard the recent refutation of the Gnostic background for 1 John by Daniel R. Streett, "'They Went Out from Us': The Identity of the Opponents in First John" (PhD diss.; Wake Forest, NC: Southeastern Baptist Theological Seminary, 2008).

[85]Bray, *Ancient Christian Doctrine I*, xxxix. Cf. Hurtado, *Lord Jesus Christ*, 521. The same applies to other second-century heretical movements.

Nevertheless, the following questions might be asked regarding early Christian heresies. First, some may contend that the archaeological discovery of a Gnostic library in Upper Egypt (Nag Hammadi) suggests that Gnosticism was just as prevalent as orthodoxy. If the writings of the orthodox were the primary witnesses to Christianity during this period, it may be asked, how could so many Gnostic documents survive? In response, Gerald Bray rightly notes that the survival of these texts can be explained by a variety of factors, one of them being the remoteness of the location where these Gnostic texts were found.[86] What is more, even if archaeologists were to discover Gnostic writings in other locations, this would still not overturn the above-stated argument for the prevalence of orthodox Christianity over Gnosticism.

Second, if early Christian heresies were not as pervasive as orthodoxy, then what accounts for the pervasive mention of heresy in the writings of the orthodox "at every turn"?[87] But as Rodney Decker rightly responds, "Intensity of rhetoric does not translate to any particular estimate of numerical predominance."[88] In other words, a vocal minority may receive attention out of proportion to its actual size or influence. In fact, the orthodox very likely engaged heretical groups at great length, not because the heterodox were so large in size, but because the orthodox deemed the heretical message so dangerous.

There is yet another way to examine second-century heresy and how it relates to orthodoxy. One may trace a central orthodox doctrine, such as the deity of Christ, back in history in order to establish which group originated first and which one deviated from the other. Larry W. Hurtado, professor of New Testament language, literature, and theology at the University of Edinburgh, masterfully does this in his work *Lord Jesus Christ: Devotion to Jesus in Earliest Christianity*. In essence, Hurtado demonstrates the swiftness with which monotheistic, Jewish Christians revered Jesus as Lord.[89] This early "Christ devotion," which entailed belief in Jesus' divinity, was amazing especially in light of the Jewish monotheistic belief that was

---

[86]Bray, *Ancient Christian Doctrine I*, xxxix.

[87]Ehrman poses this question in *Lost Christianities*, 176.

[88]Rodney J. Decker, "The Rehabilitation of Heresy: 'Misquoting' Earliest Christianity" (paper presented at the Bible Faculty Summit, Central Baptist Seminary, Minneapolis, July 2007), 29.

[89]Hurtado's argument stands as a corrective to Wilhelm Bousset's hypothesis that Hellenism shaped Christianity's high Christology over time resulting in its gradual emergence (*Kyrios Christos: A History of the Belief in Christ from the Beginnings of Christianity to Irenaeus*, trans. John E. Steely [Nashville: Abingdon Press, 1970]). Other works that trace theological

deeply ingrained in Jewish identity, worship, and culture. The revolutionary nature of the confession of Jesus as Lord and God, especially in such chronological proximity to Jesus' life, cannot be overstated.[90] The study of early Christian worship of Jesus thus further confirms that heresy formed later than, and was parasitic to, orthodoxy. In the following brief survey, we will first trace the belief in Jesus' divinity through the orthodox and then through the heretical literature.

Hurtado's study of early Christian belief in the deity of Christ begins with Paul's writings (limited to the "undisputed Pauline Epistles") because they were written prior to the other New Testament documents.[91] Hurtado shows that there is evidence that the early Christians acknowledged Jesus as Lord and God as early as twenty years after his death (1 Cor. 8:4–6). What is more, this pattern of devotion to Jesus likely preceded Paul since it is referenced in two pre-Pauline confessions or hymns (1 Cor. 15:3–6; Phil. 2:6–11). When dealing with various doctrinal and practical issues, Paul nowhere defends Jesus' lordship and divinity but regularly assumes the existence of these beliefs among his readers.

It might be objected that devotion to Jesus as Lord did not extend to the church at large but was limited to the "Pauline circle." The evidence, however, suggests otherwise. In light of the evidence from Acts and Paul's letters regarding broader Judean Christianity, which consisted of "followers of Jesus located in Roman Judea/Palestine in the first few decades" of the church's formation, Hurtado concludes that devotion to Jesus as Lord far exceeded Paul's immediate circle of influence.[92] Such devotion to Jesus is evident in the pervasive reference to Jesus as Lord and the "functional overlap" of Jesus and God.[93] Devotion to Jesus as Lord, then, occurred so early that it could not have originated with Paul. This means that "the most influential and momentous developments in devotion to Jesus took place in

---

themes of early Christianity include J. N. D. Kelly, *Early Christian Doctrines*, 5th ed. (London: Adam and Charles Black, 1977); and John Behr, *Way to Nicaea*.

[90]Cf. Ed J. Komoszewski, M. James Sawyer, and Daniel B. Wallace, *Reinventing Jesus: What The Da Vinci Code and Other Novel Speculations Don't Tell You* (Grand Rapids: Kregel, 2006), 170, 259–60, and Ben Witherington III, *What Have They Done with Jesus?: Beyond Strange Theories and Bad History—Why We Can Trust the Bible* (San Francisco: HarperSanFrancisco, 2006), 285–86.

[91]Hurtado, *Lord Jesus Christ*, 79–153.

[92]Ibid., 214.

[93]Ibid., 155–216.

early circles of Judean believers. To their convictions and the fundamental pattern of their piety all subsequent forms of Christianity are debtors."[94]

Turning his attention to the New Testament literature written subsequently to Paul, including the so-called "Q" source and the Synoptic Gospels, Hurtado finds the same devotion to Jesus as Lord in these writings.[95] "Q," presenting "a clear and sustained emphasis on the importance of Jesus," not only emphasizes the centrality of Jesus, but also uses the same Christological categories to describe Jesus. What is more, the fact that "Q" or other sources used by the Synoptic writers already referenced devotion to Jesus most likely was a major reason why Matthew and Luke, in particular, may have drawn on these sources as significantly as they did.[96] The Synoptic Gospels, similar to Paul, continue to depict radical commitment to Jesus as Lord. This is most clearly evident in their consistent application of the honorific titles to Jesus used by Paul and those who preceded him. Many of these adherents to Christianity were Jews who continued to be committed to monotheism, making their devotion to Jesus as Lord all the more remarkable.

When John wrote his Gospel in the AD 80s or early 90s, therefore, far from developing a high Christology of his own, he rather continued and expounded upon the lordship of Jesus that had begun to be confessed already during Jesus' lifetime and almost immediately subsequent to his resurrection.[97] One of the most remarkable elements in John's portrayal of Jesus are the seven "I am"[98] statements, which represent a direct claim of divinity on the part of Jesus, as well as Jesus' explicit affirmation that he and the Father are one (John 10:30).[99]

When one turns to the Christology found in the Gnostic writings, such a variegated picture emerges that discussing it is nearly impossible.[100] This fact

---

[94]Ibid., 216. Cf. Thomas C. Oden, ed., *Ancient Christian Doctrine* series, 5 vols. (Downers Grove, IL: InterVarsity, 2009, and forthcoming).

[95]Hurtado, *Lord Jesus Christ*, 217–347; cf. Bock, *Missing Gospels*, 39–43. *The Gospel of Thomas* also teaches an exalted Jesus (*Thomas* 77; cf. Bock, *Missing Gospels*, 38), contrary to Elaine Pagels's arguments (*Beyond Belief*, 68).

[96]For Hurtado's specific arguments concerning "Q," see *Lord Jesus Christ*, 244–57.

[97]Hurtado, *Lord Jesus Christ*, 349–426.

[98]The expression "I am" clearly echoes God's self-identifying remarks in Exodus 3:14 as taken up in Isaiah 40–66.

[99]For a full-fledged treatment of John's Gospel in the context of first-century Jewish monotheism see Andreas J. Köstenberger and Scott R. Swain, *Father, Son and Spirit: The Trinity and John's Gospel*, NSBT 24 (Downers Grove, IL: InterVarsity, 2008), chap. 1.

[100]The Ebionites, according to the church fathers, rejected both Jesus' virgin birth and his deity (see *Companion to Second-Century Christian "Heretics,"* 247).

alone reveals the degree to which orthodoxy was unified and the degree to which Gnosticism was not. Nevertheless, several pertinent beliefs regarding Jesus can be discerned. First, and most importantly, Gnostics severed any connection between Jesus and the God of the Old Testament. While the orthodox writers portray Jesus and the God of the Old Testament (Yahweh) as integrally related,[101] Gnostics thought that the Old Testament God was inferior and evil and that Jesus was radically different from him. Thus Jesus was not the Creator as John and other New Testament writers affirmed (see, e.g., John 1:1–3) but a creature distinct from the Creator.

Second, the role of Jesus as Redeemer was not to save people from their sins by virtue of his sacrificial death on the cross, but to bring knowledge (*gnōsis*) to entrapped humanity. This knowledge resulted in salvation. By contrast, the orthodox teaching regarding Jesus was that he died as Savior and Lord for the forgiveness of sins.

On the whole, however, what is more important than *what* Gnostics (and other sects) believed about Jesus is *when* they started believing it. Unlike the orthodox, whose core Christological beliefs coalesced in the early to mid-first century, Gnostics did not solidify their Christology—if such solidification ever occurred—until sometime in the second century. The same is true of all other known first- and second-century sects. Orthodoxy, then, emerged first, followed by a variety of rather amorphous second-century heresies. These heresies, for their part, diverted from an orthodox Christology that was already widely believed and taught.

Thus as the first century gave way to the second, what Hurtado calls a "radical diversity" began to emerge.[102] A notable theological shift occurred. The incipient whispers of Gnosticism in the late first century gradually developed more fully and eventually led to the production of Gnostic writings setting forth a variety of Christological and other beliefs. In these works, the presentation of Jesus significantly diverged from the views that had preceded these Gnostic documents for nearly a hundred years.

Two conclusions emerge, therefore, from our study of early Christian views concerning Jesus' deity. First, this core component of Christian orthodoxy—the belief in the divinity of Jesus and worship of him as Lord and God—was not forged in the second century on the anvil of debate among various Christian sects. Instead, such a belief dates back to the very origins of Christianity during and immediately subsequent to Jesus' earthly ministry.

[101]See on this point especially Christopher H. Wright, *The Mission of God: Unlocking the Bible's Grand Narrative* (Downers Grove, IL: InterVarsity, 2006), chap. 4.
[102]Hurtado, *Lord Jesus Christ*, 519–61.

Second, it was only considerably later that various heretical sects deviated from this existing Christological standard trajectory.

Conclusion

Although the late first and early second century gave birth to a variety of heretical movements, the set of (Christological) core beliefs known as orthodoxy was considerably earlier, more widespread, and more prevalent than Ehrman and other proponents of the Bauer-Ehrman thesis suggest. What is more, the proponents of second-century orthodoxy were not innovators but mere conduits of the orthodox theology espoused already in the New Testament period. The following timeline will help summarize and clarify the relationship between orthodoxy and heresy in the patristic era.

- AD 33: Jesus dies and rises from the dead.
- AD 40s–60s: Paul writes letters to various churches; orthodoxy is pervasive and mainstream; churches are organized around a central message; undeveloped heresies begin to emerge.
- AD 60s–90s: the Gospels and the rest of the New Testament are written and continue to propagate the orthodoxy that preceded them; orthodoxy continues to be pervasive and mainstream; heresies are still undeveloped.
- AD 90s–130s: the New Testament writers pass from the scene; the apostolic fathers emerge and continue to propagate the orthodoxy that preceded them; orthodoxy is still pervasive and mainstream; heresies begin to organize but remain relatively undeveloped.
- AD 130s–200s: the apostolic fathers die out; subsequent Christian writers continue to propagate the orthodoxy that preceded them; orthodoxy is still pervasive and mainstream, but various forms of heresy are found; these heresies, however, remain subsidiary to orthodoxy and remain largely variegated.
- AD 200s–300s: orthodoxy is solidified in the creeds, but various forms of heresy continue to rear their head; orthodoxy, however, remains pervasive and mainstream.

This timeline shows that heresy arose after orthodoxy and did not command the degree of influence in the late first and early second century that Ehrman and others claim. Moreover, the orthodoxy established by the third- and fourth-century creeds stands in direct continuity with the teachings of the orthodox writers of the previous two centuries. In essence, when orthodoxy and heresy are compared in terms of their genesis and chronology, it is evident that orthodoxy did not emerge from a heretical morass; instead, heresy grew parasitically out of an already established orthodoxy. And while the church continued to set forth its doctrinal beliefs in a variety of creedal formulations, the DNA of orthodoxy remained essentially unchanged.

3

Heresy in the New Testament

How Early Was It?

Bauer, in proposing his thesis, focused almost exclusively on later, second-century extrabiblical material, bypassing the New Testament as a potential source of primary evidence. The New Testament, Bauer maintained, "seems to be both too unproductive and too much disputed to be able to serve as a point of departure."[1] Bauer's wholesale dismissal of the primary source for our knowledge of earliest Christianity—the New Testament—is problematic, however, because it unduly eliminates from consideration the central figure in all of Christianity, Jesus, as well as the apostles he appointed.

As will be seen below, however, it is precisely Jesus and the apostles who provided the core of early orthodoxy in conjunction with Old Testament messianic prophecy. This explains, at least in part, why Bauer found early Christianity to be diverse and orthodoxy late—he failed to consult the New Testament message regarding Jesus and his apostles. It is to an investigation of the New Testament data regarding orthodoxy and heresy that we now turn, in an effort to move beyond Bauer's biased account to

---

[1]Walter Bauer, *Orthodoxy and Heresy in Earliest Christianity*, ed. Robert A. Kraft and Gerhard Krodel, trans. Paul J. Achtemeier (Philadelphia: Fortress, 1971), xxv.

a proper understanding of the actual first-century condition of *earliest* Christianity.

The Concept of Orthodoxy

As mentioned, the Bauer-Ehrman thesis contends that "orthodoxy" is not a first-century phenomenon but only a later concept that allowed the Roman church to squelch alternate versions of Christianity. We have seen that Bauer virtually ignores the New Testament evidence while believing to find evidence for early heresy and late orthodoxy in various urban centers of the second century. Ehrman, likewise, makes much of second-century diversity and assigns the notion of orthodoxy to later church councils. The precursors of the orthodox, Ehrman calls "proto-orthodox," even though it must, of course, be remembered that at the time this group was not the only legitimate representative of Christianity according to Ehrman, which renders the expression anachronistic.

What are we to say about this way of presenting things? In essence, the argument is circular. Once "orthodoxy" is defined in fourth-century terms as ecclesiastical doctrine hammered out by the various ecumenical councils, any doctrinal core preceding the fourth century can be considered "proto-orthodox" at best. Thus the validation of the Bauer-Ehrman thesis becomes in effect a self-fulfilling prophecy. Bauer, Ehrman, and others have cleverly recast the terminological landscape of the debate, most importantly by narrowing the term "orthodoxy" to a degree of doctrinal sophistication only reached in subsequent centuries, so that everything else falls short by comparison. Then they put "diversity" in the place of what was conventionally understood as orthodoxy.

As we will see below, however, the New Testament presents instead a rather different picture. What we find there is not widespread diversity with regard to essential doctrinal matters, most importantly Christology and soteriology, but rather a fixed set of early core beliefs that were shared by apostolic mainstream Christianity while allowing for flexibility in nonessential areas. In matters of legitimate diversity, there was tolerance; in matters of illegitimate diversity (i.e., "heresy"), no such tolerance existed, but only denunciation in the strongest terms. What is more, as we have seen in the previous chapter, this early agreement on the fundamentals of the Christian faith in no way precludes subsequent theological formulation.

For this reason Christian orthodoxy for our present purposes can be defined as "correct teaching regarding the person and work of Jesus Christ, including the way of salvation, in contrast to teaching regarding Jesus that

By this you mean Paul's Pharisee views —

deviates from standard norms of Christian doctrine. Defined in this way, the questions then become: Is it meaningful and appropriate to speak of the notion of "correct teaching regarding the person and work of Christ" in the first century? Were there standards in place by which what was "correct" and what was "incorrect" could be measured? As we will see, when framing the issue in this manner, the answers that emerge from a close study of the New Testament present themselves quite differently from those given by the Bauer-Ehrman thesis.

One final point should be made here. As in many places, Ehrman places the conventional view in a virtual no-win situation. If the New Testament is held to be essentially unified, this, according to Ehrman, proves that it was "written by the winners" who chose to suppress and exclude all countervailing viewpoints. If the New Testament were to exhibit a considerable degree of diversity, and an unsettled state of affairs as to which theological position represents the standard of orthodoxy, this would be taken as evidence that the Bauer-Ehrman thesis is correct and diversity prevailed in earliest Christianity. Either way, Ehrman is right, and the conventional understanding of orthodoxy wrong. As a debating tactic, this is clever indeed. But will it work?

The Reliability of the Gospel Witness

The first important issue that is at stake when evaluating the gospel evidence is the reliability of the gospel witness. When engaging in historical study, one's conclusions are normally only as valid as the quality of the sources on the basis of which one arrived at these conclusions. For this reason one's selection of sources is of utmost importance. Applied to the study of earliest Christianity, this means that the most helpful documents will be those that date to the time closest to Jesus' ministry and the days of the early church and that were written by reliable eyewitnesses to these events.

Richard Bauckham, in his seminal work *Jesus and the Eyewitnesses: The Gospels as Eyewitness Testimony*, has recently made a compelling case for the New Testament Gospels as eyewitness testimony.[2] According to Bauck-

---

[2]Richard Bauckham, *Jesus and the Eyewitnesses: The Gospels as Eyewitness Testimony* (Grand Rapids: Eerdmans, 2006). (Note, however, that Bauckham's work has not been universally accepted; see the critical reviews by Stephen J. Patterson and Christopher Tuckett in *RBL*, posted at http://www.bookreviews.org.) Reference to Bauckham's work is conspicuously absent in Bart Ehrman's most recent work, *Jesus, Interrupted: Revealing the Hidden Contradictions in the Bible (and Why We Don't Know About Them)* (San Francisco: HarperOne, 2009). See Ehrman's discussion of the Gospels as eyewitness accounts on pp. 102–4, where he denies that Matthew and John wrote the respective Gospels named after them. For a critique, see

ham, the apostles were not merely the authors or sources of information for the canonical Gospels, but they also provided "quality control" during the period of transmission of the gospel tradition, serving as an "authoritative collegium" throughout the period during which the New Testament writings were produced.

The important implication of Bauckham's work is that there was not a span of several decades between Jesus' days and the time at which the Gospels and other New Testament writings were generated, during which there were no sufficient control mechanisms that guaranteed the reliable transmission of the material included in the canonical Gospels. Rather, the apostles played an active role throughout this entire process, culminating in the composition of the canonical Gospels. In the case of Matthew and John, eyewitnesses also served as authors of their respective Gospels. In the case of Mark, he functioned, according to tradition, as the interpreter of Peter. Luke, for his part, while frankly acknowledging that he was not himself an eyewitness, wrote his account on the basis of those who were eyewitnesses of Jesus' life and ministry (see Luke 1:2).

It is no coincidence that those who come to different conclusions regarding the nature of early Christianity regularly turn to alternative gospels or other writings that significantly postdate the canonical Gospels. As will be seen later on in this book, however, the early church distinguished significantly between documents produced during the apostolic period and writings composed only during the second or later centuries. A case in point are the Gnostic gospels, which, as will be seen, were written no earlier than AD 150 and differ in both form and content from the canonical Gospels.[3] The fact remains that there are no other surviving documents that are as reliable and as historically close to Jesus and the early days of the church as

---

Daniel B. Wallace, *The Chicken Little Syndrome and the Myth of "Liberal" New Testament Scholarship: A Critique of Bart Ehrman's Jesus, Interrupted* (n.p.).

[3]See chap. 3 in Andreas J. Köstenberger, L. Scott Kellum, and Charles L. Quarles, *The Cradle, the Cross, and the Crown: An Introduction to the New Testament* (Nashville: Broadman, 2009). Helmut Koester argues that several apocryphal gospels, including the *Gospel of Thomas* and *Secret Mark*, were written as early as those in the New Testament canon (*Ancient Christian Gospels: Their History and Development* [London: SCM, 1990]). His argument, however, is unduly speculative. No reliable evidence exists that indicates that these apocryphal gospels originated early. As even a scholar otherwise favorable to Bauer's thesis, James D. G. Dunn, remarks, "The arguments . . . of Koester . . . have not commanded anything like the same consent as the older source hypotheses and certainly require further scrutiny" (*Jesus Remembered, Christianity in the Making* [Grand Rapids: Eerdmans, 2003], 140, cf. 161–65).

the writings included in the New Testament.[4] This means that a discussion about the earliest strands of orthodoxy and heresy must properly begin with the New Testament itself.[5]

Can Accurate History Be Written by the "Winners"?

A second critical issue in discussing the data is the question of whether accurate history can be written by those who prevailed in the battles over heresy and orthodoxy.[6] Can, or should, one trust documents written by the "winners"? Bart Ehrman argues that "you can never rely on the enemy's reports for a fair and disinterested presentation."[7] Ehrman's argument, however, puts on the New Testament writers an unreasonable requirement of neutrality. Postmodernity has aptly revealed the irrationality of this view. All writers are biased, including Ehrman!

This does not mean, however, that the New Testament authors could not offer a fair and balanced portrait of early Christianity. As with any historical study, while one should always read with a critical eye, it must be remembered that strong convictions do not *mandate* dishonesty or inaccuracy. To be sure, the New Testament data examined below contain a decided vantage point—most importantly, faith in Jesus Christ as Messiah

---

[4]There is considerable debate regarding the dating of individual New Testament writings. For example, many suggest that someone other than Paul wrote several of the letters attributed to him (Ephesians, Colossians, 2 Thessalonians, 1 and 2 Timothy, and Titus) subsequent to the apostle's death. For a defense of early dates for the various New Testament documents see Köstenberger, Kellum, and Quarles, *The Cradle, the Cross, and the Crown*. While in this chapter we assume early dates for the New Testament documents, our argument remains valid even if any of these writings are dated late, because the fact remains that these writings are credible witnesses to the orthodoxy and unity characteristic of early Christian teaching regarding Jesus. The date and nature of other documents such as the *Didache, 1 Clement*, the letters of Ignatius, and the *Gospel of Thomas* will be addressed later on in this volume.
[5]Craig A. Blaising, "Faithfulness: A Prescription for Theology," *JETS* 49 (2006): 8–9, perceptively states, "If the NT writings were not forgeries, then the early Christian writers were not deceitful in their use of them. If the Gospels give a trustworthy account of Jesus and his teaching, then the early church cannot be faulted for appealing to them to adjudicate conflicting claims about what he said, especially if these claims are found in writings that are most likely forgeries. If, in fact, they are authoritative writings from the days of Jesus and his apostles, it is sound to consult them. It is not the case that all such writings are only projections of the diverse religious experiences of later communities. . . . Impugning their claim of faithfulness to Jesus Christ in accordance with his Word is unfair."
[6]This information is indebted to Robert J. Decker, "The Rehabilitation of Heresy: 'Misquoting' Earliest Christianity" (paper presented at the annual meeting of the Bible Faculty Summit of Central Baptist Seminary, Minneapolis, July 2007), 40–41.
[7]Bart D. Ehrman, *Lost Christianities: The Battles for Scripture and the Faiths We Never Knew* (Oxford: Oxford University Press, 2003), 104.

and exalted Lord—but this does not necessarily impugn the credibility of the New Testament writers. When studying orthodoxy and heresy in earliest Christianity, then, the historians' most pertinent data is the New Testament documents, because they are the earliest available materials and are based on eyewitness testimony by those who were the first followers of Jesus.

The remainder of this chapter examines the New Testament data with regard to the question of orthodoxy and heresy in earliest Christianity. Specifically, we will trace the notion of orthodoxy to Jesus, the person to whom Christianity owes its origin, and to the apostles he appointed. The existence of a doctrinal, orthodox Christological core—the gospel—is then followed through the New Testament literature, as are references to heretical teachings.

Orthodoxy and the New Testament
The Teaching of Jesus and of the Apostles

When Jesus summoned his followers at a critical juncture during his earthly ministry, he asked them, "Who do people say that the Son of Man is?" They replied, "Some say John the Baptist, others say Elijah, and others Jeremiah or one of the prophets." He said to them, "But who do you say that I am?" Simon Peter replied, "You are the Christ, the Son of the living God." And Jesus weightily pronounced that Peter had gained this insight on the basis of divine revelation, which, in turn, would provide the very foundation on which he would build his messianic community, the church (Matt. 16:13–19).

This anecdote from Jesus' life, also recounted in the other canonical Gospels (Mark 8:27–20; Luke 9:18–20; cf. John 6:66–69), is relevant for our present discussion for several reasons. First, the disciples' initial response to Jesus' question suggests that there clearly was considerable diversity of opinion regarding Jesus' identity. At the same time, Peter's confession of Jesus as the Christ, the Son of the living God, commended by Jesus as due to divine revelation, indicates that Jesus accepted only *one* belief as accurate: the confession that Jesus had come in fulfillment of Old Testament messianic prediction.

What is more, Jesus declared that his entire church would be built on the basis of this christological confession. Even if this document were not to accurately reflect Jesus' own beliefs, or even if Matthew's—and Mark's, and Luke's, and John's—testimony were mistaken, the fact remains that their Gospels were almost certainly produced well within the first century. Thus their record of these and other Christological confessions on the part of Jesus' first followers constitute important first-century evidence regarding the widespread Christian conviction that Jesus was the Messiah and exalted Lord.

At another critical juncture in his ministry, Jesus appointed his twelve apostles (Matt. 10:1–4; Mark 3:13–15; 6:7–13; Luke 6:13; 9:1–2). These apostles, in turn, were carefully instructed, trained, and commissioned to pass on Jesus' message to subsequent generations (Matt. 28:18–20; Luke 24:45–48; John 20:21–22; Acts 1:8). This witness, for its part, was consistent with Old Testament messianic prophecy (Luke 24:25–26, 44). Thus the New Testament message is one of continuity between the Old Testament, Jesus, and the apostles.

Accordingly, Luke, when describing the early church, states that "they devoted themselves to the apostles' teaching" (Acts 2:42). Assuming the historical accuracy of Luke's account, this reference is to the church's unity of belief at its very inception. The remainder of the book of Acts presents a consistent picture of the church as a group of believers who were primarily concerned, not with fashioning a variety of Christian teachings, or with conflicting doctrinal perspectives, but with propagating a message that did not originate with them.

It is also clear from the book of Acts that great value was placed on the continuity between the teaching of the early church and the teaching of Jesus. Thus it was stipulated that Judas's replacement be an eyewitness of the events "from the baptism of John until the day when [Jesus] was taken up" to heaven (Acts 1:21–22). In the remainder of the book, the early Christians are shown to preach unanimously Jesus as the one who was crucified and subsequently raised from the dead. While the church faced both internal and external challenges and had to deal with doctrinal questions such as the inclusion of the Gentiles into the nascent movement (a challenge that was met as early as AD 49/50; cf. Galatians; Acts 15), it is shown to be utterly unified with regard to its core belief encapsulated in the gospel of salvation through faith in the crucified and risen Jesus.[8]

---

[8]Some may cite the differing perspectives on the inclusion of Gentiles in the early church which necessitated the Jerusalem Council as evidence for early doctrinal diversity in the church. However, the primary question is not "Was there diversity?" but were there mechanisms in place to deal with different perspectives when they affected the integrity of the apostolic gospel preaching? As Acts 15 makes clear, such a mechanism was in fact in place, and the church dealt definitively and decisively with the issue at hand under the leadership of James, Paul, and Peter.

Paul's Conception of the Nature of His Gospel

The continuity between Jesus and his apostles and their grounding in Old Testament messianic prophecy is further extended through Paul and his gospel preaching. Writing in the AD 50s, he says:

> Now I would remind you, brothers, of the gospel I preached to you, which you received, in which you stand, and by which you are being saved, if you hold fast to the word I preached to you—unless you believed in vain. For I delivered to you as of first importance what I also received: that Christ died for our sins in accordance with the Scriptures, that he was buried, that he was raised on the third day in accordance with the Scriptures, and that he appeared to Cephas, then to the twelve. (1 Cor. 15:1–5).

Paul's message of good news of salvation in Jesus Christ, the gospel, did not originate with him, but was a message he had received and merely passed on to others as of first importance. The apostolic message, in turn, was "in accordance with the Scriptures," that is, the Old Testament prophetic prediction that God would send his Messiah to die for people's sins. Paul elaborates on this in his letter to the Romans, written a few short years after 1 Corinthians. According to Paul, he was "a servant of Christ Jesus, called to be an apostle, set apart for the gospel of God, which he promised beforehand through his prophets in the holy Scriptures, concerning his Son" (Rom. 1:1–3).

The way Paul saw it, the message he preached was not his own; it was *God's* message, "the gospel of God," that is, a message that originated with God. He explains that God promised this message in advance through his prophets in the Holy Scriptures. Later on in the preface to the book of Romans, Paul quoted from the prophet Habakkuk, making clear that his gospel of righteousness by faith stood in direct continuity with Habakkuk's statement, "The righteous shall live by faith" (Rom. 1:16–17; cf. Hab. 2:4).

In Rom. 3:21–22, Paul elaborated still further, writing, "But now the righteousness of God has been manifested apart from the law, although *the Law and the Prophets* bear witness to it—the righteousness of God through faith in Jesus Christ for all who believe." Thus, according to Paul, it was the Scriptures *in their entirety*—the Law and the Prophets—that already taught, in a nutshell, the gospel Paul proclaimed: that a person can be made right with God through believing in his Son, Jesus Christ.

To be sure, the Hebrew Scriptures did so by way of anticipation of the coming of the Messiah and his vicarious death for his people, something that now had transpired, so that Paul and the other apostles could look back on the *finished* work of Christ and proclaim it as an accomplished fact. But the prophets' and Paul's message was essentially the same—at least this is what Paul adamantly affirmed. Paul, for his part, was not the one who had created the gospel message out of nothing; he was only the messenger commissioned "to bring about the obedience of faith for the sake of his name among all the nations" (Rom. 1:5).

Liturgical Materials That Precede the New Testament

Another possible indication of early core doctrinal beliefs among the early Christians is provided by the likely inclusion of hymns and other preexisting materials in the writings of the New Testament.[9] Many believe that Philippians 2:6–11 and Colossians 1:15–20 represent early Christian hymns that Paul incorporated into his letters for various purposes.[10] Regarding the "Christ hymn"[11] of 2:6–11, arguments for its pre-Pauline origin include (1) its unusual vocabulary; (2) its rhythmic style; (3) the absence of key Pauline themes such as redemption or resurrection. However, those who think Paul wrote 2:6–11 respond that (1) other Pauline passages contain as many unusual words within a comparable space; (2) other passages convey a rhythmic style; and (3) Paul need not mention all of his theology in every passage.[12]

The debate proceeds along similar lines concerning Colossians 1:15–20, another high point in New Testament Christology where Paul highlights the supremacy of Christ.[13] Features such as the elevated diction and extensive

---

[9]See Darrell L. Bock, "Why Apocryphal Literature Matters for NT Study: Relevance, Models, and Prospects—A Look at the Influence of the New School of Koester-Robinson" (paper presented at the annual meeting of the Evangelical Theological Society, Providence, RI, November, 27 2008); idem, *The Missing Gospels: Unearthing the Truth behind Alternative Christianities* (Nashville: Nelson, 2006).

[10]See Richard R. Melick Jr., *Philippians, Colossians, Philemon*, NAC 32 (Nashville: Broadman, 1991), 95–97, 210–12.

[11]A significant debate exists over whether to call this passage a "hymn" or "exalted prose." For the former view, see Peter T. O'Brien, *Philippians*, NIGTC (Grand Rapids: Eerdmans, 1991), 186–202; for the latter view, see Gordon D. Fee, "Philippians 2:5–11: Hymn or Exalted Pauline Prose?" *BBR* 2 (1992): 29–46.

[12]See the excellent discussion and survey of the debate in O'Brien, *Philippians*, 186–202.

[13]See the discussions in Eduard Lohse, *Colossians and Philemon*, Hermeneia (Philadelphia: Fortress, 1971), 41–46; and Peter T. O'Brien, *Colossians, Philemon*, WBC 44 (Dallas: Word, 1982), 32–37.

parallelism have led many to label the passage as a "hymn," with opinions dividing as to whether the hymn is Pauline or pre-Pauline. Others doubt whether 1:15–20 is a hymn due to the lacking consensus as to a metrical pattern.

In any case, whether Pauline or pre-Pauline, what is remarkable is that these passages are characterized by a very high Christology.[14] Jesus is equated with God (Phil. 2:6; Col. 1:15, 19) and presented as the exalted Lord (Phil. 2:9–11; Col. 1:15–18). These portions also emphasize the importance of the cross as a core component of the gospel (Phil. 2:8; Col. 1:20). That Paul might have been able to draw on these types of materials in his correspondence with the churches under his jurisdiction would attest to the early nature of Christians' worship of Jesus as God and exalted Lord.

Another striking instance of Paul's drawing on antecedent theology is 1 Corinthians 8:4–6, where he applies the most foundational of all Jewish monotheistic texts to Jesus, inserting reference to Jesus into the "one God, one Lord" formula and connecting Jesus with the creative work of God the Father: "We know . . . that 'there is no God but one.' For although there may be so-called gods . . . for us there is one God, the Father, from whom are all things and for whom we exist; *and one Lord, Jesus Christ,* through whom are all things and through whom we exist." As Richard Bauckham notes, "The only possible way to understand Paul as maintaining monotheism is to understand him to be including Jesus in the unique identity of the one God affirmed in the Shema."[15]

Confessional Formulas

Another important indication of early orthodoxy in the New Testament writings is the pervasive presence of confessional formulas. These include "Jesus is Messiah" (Mark 8:29; John 11:27; cf. Matt. 16:16; Acts 2:36; Eph. 1:1); "Jesus is Lord" (Rom. 10:9; Phil. 2:11; Col. 2:6; cf. John 20:28; Acts

---

[14]See Larry W. Hurtado, *How on Earth Did Jesus Become God? Historical Questions about Earliest Devotions to Jesus* (Grand Rapids: Eerdmans, 2005), 83–107.

[15]Richard Bauckham, "Biblical Theology and the Problems of Monotheism," in *Out of Egypt: Biblical Theology and Biblical Interpretation,* ed. Craig G. Bartholomew et al. (Grand Rapids: Zondervan, 2004), 224, cited in Christopher J. H. Wright, *The Mission of God: Unlocking the Bible's Grand Narrative* (Grand Rapids: Eerdmans, 2006), 111–12. See also N. T. Wright, *The Climax of the Covenant: Christ and the Law in Pauline Theology* (Edinburgh: T&T Clark, 1991), 120–36; Richard Bauckham, *God Crucified: Monotheism and Christology in the New Testament* (Grand Rapids: Eerdmans, 1998); Larry W. Hurtado, *Lord Jesus Christ: Devotion to Jesus in Earliest Christianity* (Grand Rapids: Eerdmans, 2003), 123–26; and the discussion in Andreas J. Köstenberger and Scott R. Swain, *Father, Son, and Spirit: The Trinity and John's Gospel,* NSBT 24 (Downers Grove, IL: InterVarsity, 2008), 34–43.

2:36; 1 Pet. 1:3; Jude 17);[16] and "Jesus is the Son of God" (Matt. 14:33; Mark 1:1; 15:39; Luke 1:35; John 20:31; Acts 9:20; 2 Cor. 1:19; Heb. 10:29; 1 John 3:8). These formulas represent a set of core beliefs that center on the person of Jesus Christ.

In the Old Testament, the messianic hope is considerably broader than references to "the LORD's anointed." Moses is one of the earliest proto-types of the Messiah as the miracle-working deliverer (e.g., Deut. 33:5; Isa. 63:11); David is portrayed as a suffering yet ultimately victorious king (e.g., Psalm 22) whose dynasty would endure (2 Sam. 7:14; cf. Jer. 30:9; Ezek. 34:23; 37:25; Hos. 3:5). Other related figures are the suffering Servant of the Lord (see especially Isaiah 53); the smitten shepherd (Zech. 13:7), who is part of a cluster of messianic references in Zechariah; and the Son of Man mentioned in Daniel 7:13.

The New Testament writers universally testify to the belief, pervasive in earliest Christianity, that Jesus was the Messiah and Son of God.[17] In Mat-thew, Jesus is referred to at the outset as "Jesus Christ, the son of David" (Matt. 1:1; cf. 2:1–4). In both Matthew and Mark, Peter confesses Jesus as "the Christ" at a watershed in Jesus' ministry (Matt. 16:16; cf. Mark 8:29), though at that time Jesus did not want this fact openly proclaimed, presumably owing to the likelihood that his messianic nature would be misunderstood in political or nationalistic terms. Later, Jesus was asked directly by the Jewish high priest whether he is the Christ and responds in the affirmative (Matt. 26:63–64; Mark 14:61–62; cf. Dan. 7:13).

In Luke, likewise, early reference is made to the coming of "a Savior, who is Christ the Lord" (Luke 2:11; cf. Acts 2:36). Simeon prophetically links Jesus' coming to "the Lord's Christ" (Luke 2:26). References to Jesus as the Christ in the body of Luke's Gospel closely parallel those in Matthew and Mark. Distinctive Lucan references to Jesus as the Christ predicted in the Hebrew Scriptures are found at the end of his Gospel (24:26–27, 44–47).[18]

---

[16]Of the 740 times the term "Lord" is used in the New Testament, the vast majority occurs with reference to Jesus.

[17]See Stanley E. Porter, ed., *The Messiah in the Old and New Testaments,* McMaster New Testament Studies (Grand Rapids: Eerdmans, 2007). See also Richard N. Longenecker, ed., *The Christology of Early Christianity* (Grand Rapids: Baker, 1981); Donald Juel, *Messianic Exegesis: Christological Interpretation of the Old Testament in Early Christianity* (Philadel-phia: Fortress, 1988); I. Howard Marshall, *The Origins of New Testament Christology,* upd. ed. (Downers Grove, IL: InterVarsity, 1990); Martin Hengel, *Studies in Early Christology* (Edinburgh: T&T Clark, 1995); and Richard N. Longenecker, ed., *Contours of Christology in the New Testament* (Grand Rapids: Eerdmans, 2005).

[18]The various references to "Jesus Christ," "Christ Jesus," or "the Lord Jesus Christ" in the book of Acts largely parallel Paul's usage (see below).

Similar to the Synoptics, John identifies Jesus as the Messiah in keeping with Jewish messianic expectations. In keeping with the purpose statement (20:30–31; cf. 11:27), Jesus' messianic identity is revealed in his encounters with his first followers (1:41; cf. 1:49); a Samaritan woman (4:25, 29); and the crowds (7:25–44; 12:34). This includes the Messiah's uncertain provenance (7:27); his performance of signs (7:31; cf. 20:30–31); his birth in Bethlehem (7:40–44); and his "lifting up" and subsequent exaltation (12:34; cf. 3:14; 8:28). Already in 9:22, confession of Jesus as the Christ leads to synagogue expulsion. When asked directly whether he is the Christ, Jesus responds with an indirect affirmation (10:34–39). The identification of the heaven-sent Son of Man with Jesus the Christ and Son of God is at the center of John's Gospel.

The term "Christ," often as part of the designation "Jesus Christ," "Christ Jesus," or "Lord Jesus Christ," and sometimes absolutely as "Christ" (e.g., Rom. 9:5), is virtually ubiquitous in Paul's writings (almost four hundred of the five hundred New Testament references).

The designation of Jesus as "Lord" implies an equation of Jesus with Yahweh, the Creator and God of Israel featured in the Hebrew Scriptures. Some suggest that the term only reflects the Hellenistic culture and/or a translation of a title (*mārā*) applied to Jesus by the earliest Aramaic-speaking Christians (1 Cor. 16:22; cf. Rev. 22:20). This may be part of the background, but in light of the clear attribution of deity to Jesus in the New Testament (John 1:1–3; 10:30; 20:28; Phil. 2:6–8; Heb. 1:8), not to mention references to Jesus' lordship over the created order (Col. 1:15–20; Heb. 1:3) and over history (1 Cor. 3:6; 15:25–26), the term "Lord" clearly carries divine freight. Thus, the universal New Testament ascription of "Lord" to Jesus attests to an early and pervasive understanding of the orthodox view that Jesus was God.[19]

Theological Standards

Another feature that suggests a sense of orthodoxy among the New Testament writers is their assumed theological standards. Such standards assume criteria with regard to theological orthodoxy. When Paul speaks of the gospel of Christ that differs from a false gospel, he assumes it contains specific content (Gal. 1:6–9), even more so as Paul claims that he received the gospel by divine revelation (Gal. 1:11–12). Paul's command to "stand

---

[19]See also the work of Larry W. Hurtado, who has shown that worship of Jesus as God was historically very early: "Pre-70 C. E. Jewish Opposition to Christ-Devotion," *JTS* 50 (1999): 35–58; idem, *Lord Jesus Christ*.

firm and hold to the traditions" (2 Thess. 2:15) also implies a specific body of Christian teaching. Elsewhere, Paul distinguishes the content of his teaching from false teachings (Rom. 16:17), which likewise implies a standard of accuracy and fidelity.

Jude's reference to "the faith that was once for all delivered to the saints" (Jude 3) also is predicated upon a fixed set of core Christian beliefs since "once for all" implies finality. Finally, John speaks of "the message we have heard from him and proclaim to you" (1 John 1:5). In the context of John's concern for truth (1 John 1:6), it is clear that this message has determinative theological content.[20] Although Bauer suggested that there were no overarching theological standards in the earliest church that were pervasive and orthodox, the above sampling of New Testament references clearly suggests otherwise.

Summary

The New Testament bears credible and early witness to the unified doctrinal core, in particular with regard to Christology, centered on Jesus and his apostles, a core that is, in turn, grounded in Old Testament messianic prophecy. This Christological core, for its part, is in essential continuity with the gospel Paul and the early Christians preached, a gospel that centered on Jesus crucified, buried, and risen according to the Scriptures (1 Cor. 15:3–4). Preexisting liturgical materials (including Christological hymns), confessional formulas acknowledging Jesus as Messiah, Lord, and Son of God, and New Testament references to theological standards (such as Jude's reference to "the faith once for all delivered to the saints") all combine to present early, New Testament Christianity as doctrinally unified and standing in essential continuity with the teaching of the Old Testament Scriptures and the message of Jesus and his apostles.

Diversity in the New Testament

The New Testament writings do not merely reflect an underlying doctrinal unity, especially with regard to the confession of Jesus as Messiah and Lord; they also display a certain degree of legitimate or acceptable diversity, that is, diversity that does not compromise its underlying doctrinal unity but merely reflects different, mutually reconcilable perspectives that are a func-

---

[20]See Decker, "Rehabilitation of Heresy," 32–35, who cites the following passages (in presumed historical order): James 3:1; Gal. 1:6–9; 1:11–12; 2 Thess. 2:15; 1 Cor. 16:13; 2 Cor. 13:5; Rom. 16:7; 1 Tim. 1:3; 2 Tim. 1:13–14; Jude 3; 1 John 1:5; 4:1–2; 2 John 9–10.

tion of the individuality of the New Testament writers.[21] Bauer and those after him tend to magnify the diversity present in the New Testament to the extent that they see conflicting messages and multiple contradictions within its pages.[22] These scholars tend to see the New Testament as a collection of diverse documents that do not represent a unified perspective and allege that any such unity is merely an anachronistic imposition on the part of subsequent interpreters onto the New Testament data.

Further complicating any argument for supposed unity among the New Testament writers are the "heretical" groups within the New Testament. Such groups include the Judaizers, possible precursors of Gnosticism, and various other opponents. These groups apparently professed to be Christian, and references to some of them appear in the earliest strata of the historical evidence. What precludes the possibility, contend Ehrman and others, that these groups "got it right" and that the New Testament writers "got it wrong"? In this section, we examine the diversity, both legitimate (acceptable) and illegitimate (unacceptable), reflected in the writings of the New Testament as we further examine Bauer's thesis that earliest Christianity moved from doctrinal diversity to unity rather than vice versa.

Legitimate Diversity

What is legitimate diversity? To the minds of some, labeling anything "legitimate" may beg the question of what is legitimate or illegitimate. Legitimate in whose eyes? The answer, in historical terms, is that, judging by the New Testament documents themselves, we find a certain degree of latitude with regard to individual vantage points and perspectives, within boundaries which to cross incurred censure ("illegitimate diversity"). Thus if anyone

---

[21]For relevant studies see Andreas J. Köstenberger, "Diversity and Unity in the New Testament," in *Biblical Theology: Retrospect and Prospect,* ed. Scott J. Hafemann (Downers Grove, IL: InterVarsity, 2002), 144–58; D. A. Carson, "Unity and Diversity in the New Testament: The Possibility of Systematic Theology," in *Scripture and Truth,* ed. D. A. Carson and John D. Woodbridge (Grand Rapids: Zondervan, 1983); James D. G. Dunn, *Unity and Diversity in the New Testament: An Inquiry into the Character of Earliest Christianity,* 2d ed. (Philadelphia: Trinity Press International, 1990); Gerhard F. Hasel, "The Nature of Biblical Theology: Recent Trends and Issues," *AUSS* 32 (1994): 203–15; and Craig L. Blomberg, "The Unity and Diversity of Scripture," in *New Dictionary of Biblical Theology,* ed. T. Desmond Alexander and Brian S. Rosner (Downers Grove, IL: InterVarsity, 2000), 64–72.

[22]Arnold Ehrhardt, "Christianity Before the Apostles' Creed," *HTR* 55 (1962): 73–119; Helmut Koester, "*Gnomai Diaphoroi*: The Origin and Nature of Diversification in the History of Early Christianity," *HTR* 58 (1965): 279–318; idem, "Apocryphal and Canonical Gospels," *HTR* 73 (1980): 105–30; James M. Robinson and Helmut Koester, *Trajectories through Early Christianity* (Philadelphia: Fortress, 1971); Dunn, *Unity and Diversity*; and Elaine Pagels, *Beyond Belief: The Secret Gospel of Thomas* (New York: Random House, 2003).

were to ask: Who is to say what was or was not doctrinally acceptable in the first century, and who enforced such supposed doctrinal orthodoxy? we would answer that, historically, this role fell to the apostles who had been appointed by Jesus as his earthly representatives subsequent to his ascension. Luke's reference to the early church's adherence to apostolic teaching (Acts 2:42), Paul's letter to the Galatians (see esp. Gal. 1:6), the Jerusalem Council (Acts 15), and the references to false teachers in the Pastorals and other New Testament letters are all examples of the type of "diversity" that did exist but clearly was not acceptable by the apostolic heirs of Jesus' messianic mission, which in turn, fulfilled Old Testament teaching (see, e.g., Luke 1:1).

Proposed Conflicts

As mentioned, the diversity of earliest Christianity lies at the heart of Bauer's thesis. Some contend that this diversity also extends to the New Testament. Scholars who emphasize the irreconcilable diversity of the New Testament writings generally point to the following four major features of New Testament theology.[23] First, it is often argued that the teachings of Jesus and the theology of Paul are irreconcilably diverse, resulting in the common assertion that Paul, not Jesus, was the true founder of Christianity.[24] This is suggested, as the argument goes, because Paul adds theological layers to Jesus' message, especially in his teachings about the church, the Old Testament, and the inclusion of the Gentiles. Jesus, on the other hand, rarely taught about the church, set forth his own teaching, and focused his mission on Israel (e.g., Matt. 15:24).

Second, since the late 1700s, some see irreconcilable differences between John and the Synoptics.[25] Since John was written later than the Synoptics

---

[23]See Ehrman, *Jesus, Interrupted*, chaps. 3 and 4. The scope of this section allows only a brief sketch of these arguments. For a more developed treatment of these and other related topics see Craig L. Blomberg, *The Historical Reliability of the Gospels*, 2d ed. (Downers Grove, IL: InterVarsity, 2007).

[24]See especially David Wenham, *Paul: Follower of Jesus or Founder of Christianity?* (Grand Rapids: Eerdmans, 1995). For a history of this debate, see Victor Paul Furnish, "The Jesus-Paul Debate: From Baur to Bultmann," in *Paul and Jesus*, ed. A. J. M. Wedderburn, JSNTSup 37 (Sheffield: Sheffield Academic Press, 1989), 17–50, and S. G. Wilson, "From Jesus to Paul: The Contours and Consequences of a Debate," in *From Jesus to Paul: Studies in Honour of Francis Wright Beare*, ed. Peter Richardson and John C. Hurd (Waterloo, ON: Wilfrid Laurier University Press, 1984), 1–21.

[25]See Andreas J. Köstenberger, "Early Doubts of the Apostolic Authorship of the Fourth Gospel in the History of Modern Biblical Criticism," in *Studies in John and Gender: A Decade of Scholarship, Studies in Biblical Literature* (New York: Peter Lang, 2001), 17–47.

and substantially differs in content, many believe that John is less reliable historically. Some suggest that John's chronology stands in contradiction to the Synoptics and/or that he, in presenting Jesus as resolutely divine, presents a more advanced Christology than the Synoptics.[26]

A third irreconcilable New Testament conflict alleged by some is that the Paul of Acts differs from that of the Epistles.[27] The Paul of Acts, they observe, is invincible, intelligent, persuasive in speech, and moves from place to place in victorious procession.[28] The Paul of the Epistles, on the other hand, is weak, frail, perplexed, and unpersuasive in speech.[29]

A fourth proposed irreconcilable difference pertains to alleged developments in Paul's theology.[30] It is suggested that as Paul matured as a theologian, his theology changed, even to the point of self-contradiction. For example, Hans Dieter Betz argues that Paul moved from a more egalitarian (Gal. 3:28) to a more patriarchal view (1 Tim. 2:12).[31] Others claim that he abandoned the libertinism evidenced in his Galatian letter to embrace the "legalism" found in his first letter to the Corinthians before embracing a synthesis of the two in 2 Corinthians and Romans.[32]

Resolution of Alleged Conflicts: A Case for Legitimate Diversity

Each one of these alleged contradictions, however, when scrutinized, turns out to be feasibly reconcilable.[33] With regard to the first question, the rela-

---

[26]For a thorough study of the alleged discrepancies between John and the Synoptics see Blomberg, *Historical Reliability*, 196–240; see also Darrell L. Bock, *Jesus According to Scripture: Restoring the Portrait from the Gospels* (Grand Rapids: Baker, 2002).

[27]For a general treatment, including a taxonomy of views on the issue, see A. J. Mattill Jr., "The Value of Acts as a Source for the Study of Paul," in *Perspectives on Luke-Acts,* ed. Charles H. Talbert (Danville, VA: Association of Baptist Professors of Religion, 1978), 76–98.

[28]Acts 13:9–11, 16–41; 14:15–17, 19–20; 16:40; 17:22–31; 18:9–10; 19:11; 20:10–11, 18–35; 22:1–21; 23:11, 31–34; 24:10–21; 26:2–26, 28–29; 27:43–44; 28:30–31.

[29]1 Cor. 2:1–5; 2 Cor. 10:1, 10–11; 11:16–12:10.

[30]Hans Dieter Betz, *Galatians,* Hermeneia (Philadelphia: Fortress, 1979), 200; Heikki Räisänen, *Paul and the Law*, 2d ed. (Tübingen: Mohr Siebeck, 1987); Udo Schnelle, *Wandlungen im paulinischen Denken* (Stuttgart: Katholisches Bibelwerk, 1989).

[31]Betz, *Galatians,* 200.

[32]Cf. F. F. Bruce, "'All Things to All Men': Diversity in Unity and Other Pauline Tensions," in *Unity and Diversity in New Testament Theology,* ed. Robert Guelich (Grand Rapids: Eerdmans, 1978), 82–83, with reference to John W. Drane, *Paul: Libertine or Legalist?* (London: SPCK, 1975).

[33]Contra Ehrman, *Jesus, Interrupted,* who strenuously maintains that the New Testament represents "a world of contradictions" featuring "a mass of variant views" (the respective titles of chapters 3 and 4 of his work). However, it is rather apparent that Ehrman has an axe to grind and that his arguments on any given issue are predicated upon the underlying notion that in the development of earliest Christianity, diversity preceded unity—the Bauer thesis.

tionship between Jesus and Paul, it should be noted that although Paul's theology legitimately expands Jesus' teachings, it in no way contradicts them. Paul was not the "founder of Christianity," as some have argued; he teased out the major elements of Jesus' life and ministry in the course of his own ministry to various churches in the first century.

Paul's core message was that Christ died for humanity's sin, was buried, and was raised from the dead (1 Cor. 15:3–4). This coheres with Jesus' affirmation that he would die as a ransom for others (Mark 10:45; cf. Matt. 20:28) and rise from the dead (Matt. 20:19; Luke 9:22). Paul, who shows knowledge of some of Jesus' specific teachings (Romans 12–13; 1 Cor. 9:14; 11:23–26; 1 Thess. 4:15), applied Jesus' teachings in the context of his own ministry.

Continuity between Paul and Jesus, however, does not require uniformity. Paul was his own theological thinker.[34] Since Paul's predominantly Gentile audience (Rom. 11:13) differed from Jesus' primarily Jewish audience (Matt. 15:24), Paul did not simply reiterate Jesus' teachings but developed them within the next phase of salvation history.[35] For example, while Jesus rarely spoke of the church (Matt. 16:18; 18:17), Paul significantly expounded on this subject (Rom. 16:25–26; Eph. 3:2–11; Col. 1:25–27).

Also, while Jesus focused his mission on Israel (Matt. 10:5–6; 15:24), Paul, taking the gospel to the ends of the earth (Acts 9:15; Rom. 16:26), explored the salvation-historical "mystery" of believing Gentiles becoming part of God's people (Rom. 16:25–26; Eph. 3:2–11; Col. 1:25–27).[36] Thus "Paul did not limit himself to reiterating the teaching of Jesus but . . . formulated his proclamation in light of the antecedent theology of the OT and on the basis of the apostolic gospel as called for by his ministry context."[37]

With regard to the relationship between John and the Synoptic Gospels, it is true that John's Gospel exhibits a larger degree of profound theological reflection on Jesus' life and ministry, perhaps at least in part because

Indeed, Ehrman reaffirms his commitment to the Bauer thesis in *Jesus, Interrupted* (see pp. 213–16). While conceding that "in many, many details of his analysis Bauer is wrong, or at least that he has overplayed his hand," Ehrman, strikingly, goes on to say that, nonetheless, "Bauer's basic portrayal of Christianity's early centuries appears to be correct." However, this assessment seems to be based on the premise that one should never let the actual evidence get in the way of a good theory.

[34] Wilhelm Heitmüller, "Zum Problem Paulus und Jesus," *ZNW* 13 (1912): 320–37.

[35] Werner G. Kümmel, *The Theology of the New Testament according to Its Major Witnesses, Jesus—Paul—John*, trans. John E. Steely (Nashville: Abingdon, 1973), 246–48.

[36] Andreas J. Köstenberger and Peter T. O'Brien, *Salvation to the Ends of the Earth: A Biblical Theology of Mission*, NSBT 11 (Downers Grove, IL: InterVarsity, 2001).

[37] Köstenberger, "Diversity and Unity," 146.

John wrote a generation later. What obtains with regard to the Jesus-Paul relationship, however, also obtains in the case of John and the Synoptics: theological expansion or further reflection does not equal contradiction.[38] As I (Andreas Köstenberger) note, "the different mode of presentation need not constitute a discrepancy but reflects a theological transposition of the Synoptic tradition into a higher scale."[39]

Specific claims of contradictions between John and the Synoptics include arguments that the crucifixion accounts conflict. For example, some argue that John places the crucifixion on Thursday instead of Friday in light of John's reference to "the day of Preparation" (19:14).[40] "The day of Preparation" usually occurred on Thursdays when the Passover lambs would have been slaughtered in preparation for Passover later that evening. Yet the solution to this apparent dilemma lies close at hand. In John 19:31, it is made clear that Jesus' crucifixion took place on "the day of Preparation," with the very next day being a "high day" (i.e., the Sabbath of Passover week). Thus, even in John the crucifixion takes place on Friday, with "the day of Preparation" in John, as in Mark and Luke, referring, not to the day of preparation for the Passover, but to the Sabbath (Mark 15:42; Luke 22:1; cf. Josephus, *Ant.* 16.163–64). Moreover, since Passover lasted a week (in conjunction with the associated Feast of Unleavened Bread; Luke 22:1), it was appropriate to speak of the day of preparation for the Sabbath as "the day of Preparation of Passover Week" (though not of the Passover in a more narrow sense; cf. John 19:14).[41]

With regard to alleged historical contradictions between John and the Synoptics, there is evidence of "interlocking traditions" between the two, "which mutually reinforce or explain each other, without betraying overt literary dependence."[42] In addition, there are ample similarities, including the Spirit's anointing of Jesus as testified by John the Baptist (Mark 1:10, par.; John 1:32); the feeding of the 5,000 (Mark 6:32–44 par.; John 6:1–15); and Jesus' walking on the water (Mark 6:45–52 par.; John 6:16–21).[43] What

---

[38]Ibid., 148.

[39]Ibid. For an excellent discussion of this topic see Blomberg, *Historical Reliability of the Gospels*, 231–36.

[40]This is Bart Ehrman's "opening illustration" in *Jesus, Interrupted*, "Chapter 3: A World of Contradictions," on pp. 23–28. Ehrman categorically states, "I do not think this is a difference that can be reconciled" (ibid., 27).

[41]The argument is taken and adapted from Köstenberger, "Diversity and Unity," 148.

[42]See D. A. Carson, *The Gospel according to John*, PNTC (Grand Rapids: Eerdmans, 1991), 49–58, esp. 52–55.

[43]For further examples see ibid., 51–52.

is more, John presupposes that his readers are aware of the Synoptic tradition, perhaps even the written Gospels (John 1:40; 3:24; 4:44; 6:67, 71; 11:1–2).[44] All apparent contradictions between John and the Synoptics can be explained without doing historical injustice to the data and without imposing on John a rigidity that sacrifices his literary integrity or defies legitimate diversity.

Third, does the way in which Luke portrays Paul in Acts differ from the way that Paul portrays himself? While there are legitimately different emphases in the portrayal of Paul in the New Testament, they can be integrated into a cohesive picture. At the outset, it should be noted that while Luke was able to portray Paul as the missionary statesman and strategist who led the Gentile mission of the early church, humility dictated that Paul represented his own work in more humble terms.

In addition, the book of Acts and Paul's letters are not meant to be complete biographies. Rather, they are written with larger, missional interests in mind. Luke was concerned to present Paul as the leading proponent of the early church who overcame all obstacles by his complete dependence upon God. Paul set out to portray himself in the shadow of Christ's redeeming work as one who was merely a conduit for Christ and not a celebrity to be admired (Gal. 2:20; 1 Cor. 2:1–5; Rom. 15:18–19).

Apart from these generally differing purposes, which reasonably explain the different emphases of Luke's and Paul's portrayals, there are a number of unintentional convergences between the Lucan Paul and the Paul of the Epistles that suggest that both wrote accurately about the same person.

1) Luke nuanced Paul's claims to impeccable Jewish credentials (Phil. 3:6; cf. Gal. 1:14; 2 Cor. 11:22) by teaching that Paul was educated by one of the most famous Jewish scholars of his day, Gamaliel (Acts 22:3; cf. Acts 5:35; see also Phil. 3:5; Acts 23:6; 26:5).

2) Paul's activity as persecutor of the early church is recounted repeatedly in the book of Acts (Acts 8:3; 9:1); in his letters, the apostle regularly acknowledges this ignominious part of his past (Gal. 1:13, 22–23; 1 Cor. 15:9; Phil. 3:6; 1 Tim. 1:13).

3) The Pauline conversion narratives of Acts (Acts 9; 22; 26) are paralleled by statements in Paul's letters (Gal. 1:15; 1 Cor. 9:1; 15:8; 2 Cor. 4:6), and the location of Paul's conversion at or near Damascus seems confirmed by Galatians 1:17.

---

[44]For a fuller explanation see Andreas J. Köstenberger, *Encountering John,* Encountering Biblical Studies (Grand Rapids: Baker, 1999), 36–37.

4) The Paul of Acts, like the Paul of the letters, is shown to support himself by labor (Acts 20:34; 28:3; 1 Thess. 2:9; 2 Thess. 3:7–8; 1 Cor. 9:18).

5) Acts and the letters reveal Paul's pattern of going first to the Jews and then to the Gentiles (Acts 13:46–48; 28:25–28; cf. Rom. 1:16; 2:9–10; 10:12; 1 Cor. 1:22, 24; 12:13; Gal. 3:28; Col. 3:11).

6) The Paul of Acts who can adapt himself readily to Jew and Gentile as well as a wide variety of audiences is the Paul who speaks in 1 Corinthians 9:19–23.

7) While Luke may be the theologian of salvation history par excellence, salvation history is not an alien concept to Paul, so that he can view the age of law as a parenthesis in salvation history (Gal. 3:15–19; Rom. 5:20).[45]

The Paul of Acts and the Paul of his letters, then, are the same person.

Finally, fourth, we turn to an adjudication of alleged developments, perhaps contradictions, in Paul's theology. Indeed, the apostle's theology likely developed during the span of his lifetime and writing, but one needs to exercise caution in claiming more than what can be proven from the data. D. A. Carson has rightly noted several factors to consider when attempting to trace supposed developments in the theology of the apostle.[46]

To begin with, it is difficult to date precisely Paul's letters, even for those who hold to Pauline authorship and thus an early dating of the material. Thus it is precarious to impose an evolving theological structure on Paul's writings. Also, Paul, far from a novice writer, had been a believer for fifteen years before he wrote his first canonical letter, giving him plenty of time to mature as a theologian. In addition, Paul's extant writings span only about fifteen years. This is a relatively brief time span compared to others who wrote for half a century or more and makes it less likely that Paul significantly altered his theological perspective.

These factors do not negate the fact that Paul grew and developed or, during the course of his ministry, emphasized some theological aspects more than others. After all, Paul perceived himself to be a growing and maturing believer (1 Cor. 13:8–12; Phil. 3:12–16). In addition, his purposes varied from dealing with a set of opponents (Galatians), to setting forth and developing the doctrine of the church (1 Corinthians, Romans, Ephesians, Colossians), to instructions to church leaders (Pastorals). As Carson observes, there is no indication that Paul thought his theology had changed.[47] Since there is no other available data about Paul from the first century, interpreters must

---

[45]Köstenberger, "Diversity and Unity," 150.
[46]Carson, "Unity and Diversity," 84.
[47]Ibid.

be careful to interpret Paul by Paul.[48] "In the end, Paul's writings must therefore be judged to exhibit a considerable degree of theological coherence and unity in the midst of a certain extent of terminological diversity and thoughtful contextualization."[49]

A close study of the New Testament writings, therefore, does not support the argument that the New Testament writers blatantly contradicted one another.[50] What is more, the diversity of perspectives represented in the New Testament proceeds on the basis of a larger, underlying unity. I (Köstenberger) demonstrate three integrative motifs among the New Testament writers: (1) monotheism; (2) Jesus the Christ as the exalted Lord; and (3) the gospel.[51] Apart from this legitimate diversity which is balanced by its underlying unity, however, there is also an illegitimate diversity found in the New Testament, which forms our next subject of discussion.

Illegitimate Diversity

By "illegitimate diversity," in historical terms, we mean doctrinal variance from the apostolic teaching that was unacceptable to the writers of the New Testament, judging by the documents included in the New Testament canon. As mentioned, while the proponents of early orthodoxy were inclusive to some extent in that they allowed for different perspectives on a given issue to be represented, there were clear doctrinal boundaries that incurred sure sanctions. The crossing of such boundaries, from the vantage point of the New Testament writers, constituted illegitimate diversity.[52]

---

[48]Ibid.

[49]Köstenberger, "Diversity and Unity," 152.

[50]As mentioned above, space does not permit addressing all the alleged incongruities. In *Jesus, Interrupted*, chap. 3, Ehrman also cites the following: (1) the genealogy of Jesus (pp. 36–39), on which see D. S. Huffman, "Genealogy," in *DJG*, 253–59; (2) various other minor alleged discrepancies from the life of Jesus (pp. 39–42) including the duration of Jesus' ministry, on which see Köstenberger, Kellum, and Quarles, *The Cradle, the Cross, and the Crown*, 141–42; and the excellent entry on "The Date of Jesus' Crucifixion" in the *ESV Study Bible* (Wheaton, IL: Crossway, 2008), 1809–10; (3) alleged discrepancies in the passion narratives (pp. 43–53), especially regarding the trial before Pilate, on which see the discussion under the heading "The Historicity of John's Account of Jesus' Trial before Pilate" in Andreas J. Köstenberger, "'What Is Truth?' Pilate's Question in Its Johannine and Larger Biblical Context," in Andreas J. Köstenberger, ed., *Whatever Happened to Truth?* (Wheaton, IL: Crossway, 2005), 21–29; and (4) alleged discrepancies involving the life and writings of Paul (pp. 53–58), many of which were discussed in the preceding pages of the present volume.

[51]Ibid., 154–57.

[52]Some might say that the very fact that there was not a structure of orthodoxy in place that could prevent the emergence of alternate viewpoints or successfully define the Christian faith to avoid such controversies proves that there was not as of yet a notion of orthodoxy in the first (few) centuries of the Christian era. But this is surely to set the bar too high. How

Some argue that the presence of "heretics" within the pages of the New Testament proves that diversity was the norm among the first Christians; the early "orthodox" were simply one sect among many.[53] However, as will be seen, while there are elements of legitimate (acceptable) diversity in the New Testament, there were clear boundaries that to cross meant to incur sharp censure by the representatives of early orthodoxy. The following discussion will examine the New Testament data regarding the opponents mentioned in Galatians, Colossians, the Pastorals, Jude, 2 Peter, 1 John, and Revelation.[54]

Galatians

The heretics in Galatia preached a "different gospel" from Paul's (Gal. 1:6) and promoted circumcision for Gentile Christians (Gal. 6:12), most likely under the maxim, "Unless you are circumcised according to the custom of Moses, you cannot be saved" (Acts 15:1).[55] They apparently stressed the importance of observing the Old Testament law (Gal. 2:15–16; 3:19–24) and claimed an especially close association with Jerusalem. They were not originally part of the founding church in Galatia; challenged Paul's apostleship;[56] and may not have been known by Paul by name (Gal. 1:7–9; 3:1; 5:7).[57]

The identity of the opponents in Galatia has been variously identi-fied as zealous Jewish Christians, spiritual radicals, Gentiles who misun-

---

could there ever be a structure in place that would preclude the very possibility of alternate viewpoints arising?

[53]Bart D. Ehrman, *Lost Christianities: The Battles for Scripture and the Faiths We Never Knew* (Oxford: Oxford University Press, 2003).

[54]There is no scholarly consensus regarding the identity and teachings of the "heretics" mentioned in the New Testament. For a list of the heretics/heresies in late first- and early second-century literature and scholarly identifications of them see John J. Gunther, *St. Paul's Opponents and Their Background: A Study of Apocalyptic and Jewish Sectarian Teachings* (Leiden: Brill, 1973), 1–58. For a good overview of the history of the research on Paul's opponents see E. Earle Ellis, *Prophecy and Hermeneutic in Early Christianity* (Grand Rapids: Eerdmans, 1978), 80–115. See also F. F. Bruce, *Paul: Apostle of the Heart Set Free* (Grand Rapids: Eerdmans, 1977). For the most recent examination of Paul's opponents see Stanley E. Porter, ed., *Paul and His Opponents* (Leiden: Brill, 2005).

[55]For an excellent discussion of Paul's opponents in Galatia see Martinus C. De Boer, "The New Preachers in Galatia," in *Jesus, Paul, and Early Christianity: Studies in Honour of Henk Jan de Jonge*, ed. M. M. Mitchell and D. P. Moessner (Boston: Brill, 2008), 39–60.

[56]John C. Hurd, "Reflections Concerning Paul's 'Opponents' in Galatia," in *Paul and His Opponents*, 144.

[57]Paul refers to them as "some" (*tines*) and "anyone" (*tis*; 1:7–9). He asks, "Who has bewitched you?" (3:1) and "Who hindered you from obeying the truth?" (5:7; cf. 5:10). Paul frequently cites the names of his opponents (cf. 1 Tim. 1:20).

derstood Paul's teaching, or Gnostics.[58] Although it is probable, as J. B. Lightfoot suggested, that these opponents came from the mother church in Jerusalem,[59] there is not enough evidence to suggest that the Jerusalem church supported them.[60] It is, therefore, impossible to know whether Paul's opponents in Galatia originated independently or were sent from the Jerusalem church.

It is impossible to know whether or not and to what degree the Judaizers represented a unified group. All that can be known from the available data is that a group from Jerusalem, be it Judaizers or Jewish-Christian missionaries,[61] sought to add additional requirements (i.e., circumcision) to Paul's gospel. What is more, the fact that the Judaizing issue was settled conclusively at the Jerusalem Council (Acts 15) and that Paul does not address the issue in later letters such as Romans points to the temporary, limited, and local nature of the Judaizing heresy.

Colossians

The identity of the "Colossian heresy" has been variously identified, and no scholarly consensus has been achieved.[62] The heresy clearly incorporated elements of Judaism since Paul mentions circumcision, food laws, Sabbaths, and purity regulations (Col. 2:11, 13, 16, 20–21). At the same time, however, the false teaching was not limited to Judaism, since Paul's argument involved other elements. For example, in Colossians 2:1–3:4 Paul uses rare vocabulary that some say were technical Gnostic terms or catchwords. These words include "philosophy" (*philosophia*; Col. 2:8); "fullness" (*plērōma*; Col. 2:9); "going on in detail" (*embateuō*; Col. 2:18); and "knowledge" (*gnōsis*; Col.

---

[58]For a summary of positions held since F. C. Baur, see Richard N. Longenecker, *Galatians*, WBC 41 (Dallas: Word, 1990), lxxxi–xcvi.

[59]J. B. Lightfoot, The *Epistle of St. Paul to the Galatians: With Introductions, Notes and Dissertations* (Grand Rapids: Zondervan, 1957), 292–374. Hurd, "Paul's 'Opponents' in Galatia," 146, agrees.

[60]Longenecker suggests that it is generally agreed that the dissenters were probably "taking a line of their own, and so were unsupported by the Jerusalem apostles" (*Galatians, xciv*).

[61]Hans Dieter Betz, "Heresy and Orthodoxy in the NT," *ABD* 3:145.

[62]For a history of interpretation see O'Brien, *Colossians, Philemon, xxxiii–xxxviii*; and Melick, *Philippians, Colossians, Philemon*, 173–75. In 1973, J. J. Gunther listed forty-four different suggested identifications (*St. Paul's Opponents*, 3–4). For a list of suggestions that have been added since 1973, see Christian Stettler, "The Opponents at Colossae," in Porter, *Paul and His Opponents*, 170–72. For an important recent contribution see Ian K. Smith, *Heavenly Perspective: A Study of Paul's Response to a Jewish Mystical Movement at Colossae*, LNTS 326 (Edinburgh: T&T Clark, 2007), who surveys four major possibilities: Essene Judaism and Gnosticism; Hellenism; paganism; and Judaism; see also the discussion in Köstenberger, Kellum, and Quarles, *The Cradle, the Cross, and the Crown*, chap. 14.

2:18).[63] It is impossible to know, however, whether these words were taken directly from the theology of the heretics.[64]

The opponents' religious practice may also have included elements of astrology, pagan mystery religions, and asceticism. Specific aspects mentioned by Paul are visions (Col. 2:18); food laws (Col. 2:18); special festival days (Col. 2:18); and the elemental spirits of the world (Col. 2:20). The asceticism of Paul's opponents is seen in the apostle's encouragement to the Colossians to ignore the opposing teaching: "Do not handle, Do not taste, Do not touch" (Col. 2:21).

Paul's opponents in Colossae, then, were probably propagating an eclectic amalgamation of Judaism and incipient Gnosticism,[65] including elements of astrology, asceticism, and pagan mystery cults.[66] They were most likely not considered Christians (Col. 2:8: "not according to Christ"). The type of Judaism found at Colossae seems less coherent than that in Galatia.[67] It is unclear whether the proponents of the Colossian heresy were a well-organized group and what affinities, if any, they had to other religious groups in the region.[68]

Titus, 1 and 2 Timothy

Elsewhere I (Andreas Köstenberger) noted, "Paul's primary concern in the PE [Pastoral Epistles] is not to describe the heresy but to refute it."[69]

---

[63]Martin Dibelius, "The Isis Initiation in Apuleius and Related Initiatory Rites," in *Conflict at Colossae*, ed. Fred O. Francis and Wayne A. Meeks, 2d ed., SBLSBS 4 (Missoula, MT: Scholars Press, 1975), 61–121.

[64]Morna D. Hooker, "Were There False Teachers in Colossae?" in *Christ and Spirit in the New Testament: Studies in Honor of Charles Francis Digby Moule*, ed. Barnabas Lindars and Stephen S. Smalley (Cambridge: Cambridge University Press, 1973), 315–31, however, argues that the terms do not reflect the heresy itself but the Colossian situation in general. She suggested that the problem came from within the congregation as the Colossians were in danger of conforming to the beliefs and practices of their pagan and Jewish neighbors. For a similar assessment see N. T. Wright, *Colossians and Philemon*, TNTC (Grand Rapids: Eerdmans, 1986), 23–30.

[65]Bruce, *Paul: Apostle of the Heart Set Free*, 13. If incipient Gnosticism was present, Melick, *Philippians, Colossians, Philemon*, 183, is correct that such was only secondary.

[66]See especially Smith, *Heavenly Perspective*, 206, who proposes the Colossian "philosophy" stood within the stream of apocalyptic Judaism, perhaps incipient or proto-Merkabah mysticism.

[67]O'Brien, *Colossians, Philemon*, xxxii–xxxiii. Melick, however, argues that since "philosophy" (2:8) is articular, the opponents probably had a specific and organized formulation of thought (*Philippians, Colossians, Philemon*, 177).

[68]Hooker, "Were There False Teachers?" 315–31.

[69]Andreas J. Köstenberger, "1–2 Timothy, Titus," in *The Expositor's Bible Commentary*, vol. 12, *Ephesians—Philemon*, rev. ed. (Grand Rapids: Zondervan, 2005), 491; see his entire discussion

Thus a composite picture of the heretics must be reconstructed from the internal clues in the Pastorals.[70] Two regions are represented: the island of Crete (Titus 1:5) and Ephesus (1 Tim. 1:3). In both cases, the teaching appears to have emerged from within the congregations rather than having infiltrated them from the outside (1 Tim. 1:3; 6:2; 2 Tim. 2:14; 4:2; Titus 1:13; 3:10; cf. 1 Tim. 1:20; 2 Tim. 2:17–18), just as Paul had predicted in the case of the Ephesian church (Acts 20:28–31). It is even possible that the heretics were elders in the church.[71] It is possible that there are connections with heresies in other locations, such as in Corinth (e.g., 1 Cor. 15:12, 34), and especially in the Lycus Valley (1 Tim. 4:3; cf. Col. 2:8, 16–23).

With regard to the false teachers in Crete, both Jewish and Gnostic elements can be detected. Paul refers to his opponents as "those of the circumcision party" (Titus 1:10); tells Titus to rebuke the false teachers sharply not to devote themselves to "Jewish myths" (Titus 1:14); and warns him to avoid "foolish controversies, genealogies, dissensions, and quarrels about the law" (Titus 3:9). Apparently, they engaged in an impure lifestyle (Titus 1:15–16) and were "upsetting whole families by teaching for shameful gain what they ought not to teach" (Titus 1:11). The label "the circumcision party" suggests a distinguishable group, perhaps aligned with or at least in affinity with the Judaizing party in Galatia.

Paul's letters to Timothy contain a considerable amount of information about the heretics. The heresy seems to have incorporated both Jewish and Gnostic elements.[72] Regarding the former, the heretics desired to be teachers of the law and had a strong concern for the law of Moses, yet did not truly understand the purpose of the law (1 Tim. 1:7–11; cf. Titus 1:10, 14; 3:9; Col. 2:16–17).[73] Possible (proto-) Gnostic elements are "the irreverent babble and contradictions of what is falsely called 'knowledge'" (1 Tim. 6:20); asceticism, including the prohibition of marriage and the eating of certain foods (1 Tim. 4:1–5; cf. 1 Tim. 2:15; Titus 1:15; Col. 2:18–23); and

---

"The False Teachers" on pp. 491–92. See also the articles by Oskar Skarsaune, "Heresy and the Pastoral Epistles," *Them* 20/1 (1994): 9–14; and Robert J. Karris, "The Background and Significance of the Polemic of the Pastoral Epistles," *JBL* 92 (1973): 549–64.

[70]See especially William D. Mounce, *Pastoral Epistles*, WBC 46 (Nashville: Nelson, 2000), lxix–lxxxiii.

[71]See Gordon D. Fee, *1 and 2 Timothy, Titus*, NIBCNT 13 (Peabody, MA: Hendrickson, 1988), 7–9.

[72]Mounce adds a third element, Hellenism (*Pastoral Epistles, lxxi*).

[73]See ibid., lxx.

the teaching that the resurrection had already taken place (2 Tim. 2:17–18; cf. 1 Tim. 1:19–20; 1 Cor. 15:12).[74]

The practice of forbidding marriage is attested in both Judaism (especially among the Essenes; cf. Philo, *Hypoth.* 11.14) and later Gnosticism (Irenaeus, *Haer.* 1.24.2). George Knight identifies the heresy in question as a "Gnosticizing form of Jewish Christianity"; Fee speaks of "Hellenistic-Jewish speculation"; others call it "a form of aberrant Judaism with Hellenistic/ Gnostic tendencies," "Jewish proto-Gnosticism," or "Judaism crossed with Gnosticism."[75] I concluded that "what Paul seems to be opposing here is an appeal to the Mosaic law in support of ascetic practices that at the root were motivated by Gnostic thinking."[76] It is unclear whether the opposition was well organized or not.[77] In the end, "owing to the limited extent of our present understanding of first-century heresies, certainty remains elusive."[78]

Jude

It appears that the false teachers mentioned in Jude's epistle cannot be identified with any of the other heretics mentioned in the New Testament.[79] Jude indicates that "certain people have crept in unnoticed" (v. 4; cf. Gal. 2:4). They may have been itinerant teachers who went from church to church and were dependent on the hospitality of local believers (cf. 1 Cor. 9:5; 2 John 10; 3 John 5–10). These godless individuals denied "our only Master and Lord, Jesus Christ" (v. 4), pursuing unfettered freedom in the sense of complete ethical autonomy (vv. 4, 8). As in the case of the heretics mentioned

---

[74]Köstenberger, "1–2 Timothy, Titus," 491, observes that this "may point to a Greek-style dualism that prized spirituality over the natural order." Cf. Philip H. Towner, "Gnosis and Realized Eschatology in Ephesus (of the Pastoral Epistles) and the Corinthian Enthusiasm," *JSNT* 31 (1987): 95–124.

[75]George W. Knight, *The Pastoral Epistles,* NIGTC (Grand Rapids: Eerdmans, 1992), 27–28; Fee, *1 and 2 Timothy, Titus,* 8–9; Mounce, *Pastoral Epistles,* lxix–lxxvi; Raymond F. Collins, *Letters That Paul Did Not Write* (Wilmington, DE: Michael Glazier, 1988), 100; and E. Earle Ellis, "Pastoral Letters," *DPL,* 663.

[76]Köstenberger, "1–2 Timothy, Titus," 492, with reference to Stephen Westerholm, "The Law and the 'Just Man' (1 Timothy 1:3–11)," *ST* 36 (1982): 82.

[77]Mounce suggests that their views do not appear to represent a well-thought-out or cohesive system (*Pastoral Epistles,* lxix).

[78]Köstenberger, "1–2 Timothy, Titus," 492.

[79]Köstenberger, Kellum, and Quarles, *The Cradle, the Cross, and the Crown,* chap. 18. See also Richard Bauckham, "The Letter of Jude: An Account of Research," *ANRW:* 2.25.5 (Berlin: de Gruyter, 1988), 3809–12; Gerhard Sellin, "Die Häretiker des Judasbriefes," *ZNW* 76–77 (1985–86): 206–25; and Hermann Werdermann, *Die Irrlehrer der Judas- und 2. Petrusbriefe,* BFCT 17/6 (Gütersloh: C. Bertelsmann, 1913).

in the Pastorals, these false teachers may have espoused an over-realized eschatology, emphasizing believers' present enjoyment of the benefits of salvation (cf. 2 Tim. 2:17–18).

Jude classifies the heretics as "people . . . relying on their dreams" (v. 8), that is, mystics who claimed to enjoy privileged access to esoteric knowledge. Perhaps they were charismatics, whose claims of visionary experiences may have led to lack of respect for angels (vv. 9–10). It is even possible that people were said to have an angel-like nature, resulting in a blurring of the distinction between humans and angelic creatures. Jude makes clear that the heretics do not possess the Spirit and thus are not Christians (v. 19; cf. Rom. 8:9).

According to Jude, the false teachers were feasting with the believers at the church's "love feasts" (i.e., *agapē* meals, including communal meals and the Lord's Supper; v. 12; cf. vv. 8, 23; Acts 2:42; 1 Cor. 11:20–22). The false teachers were shepherds who nurtured only themselves (v. 12). They were self-seeking (v. 11), unreliable, and unstable (vv. 12–13) and misled people (v. 6). They were divisive (v. 19; cf. 1 Cor. 1:10–4:7; James 3:14) and earthly minded (v. 19; cf. 1 Cor. 2:14; James 3:15; 4:5).

2 Peter

The opponents mentioned in 2 Peter appear to have considered themselves Christian teachers (2 Pet. 2:1, 13), though Peter associated them with the false prophets of old. At the core, their teaching seems to have involved eschatological skepticism. Apparently, they denied the second coming, arguing that Peter and the other apostles espoused "cleverly devised myths" when they preached that Christ would return (2 Pet. 1:16). The heretics' eschatological skepticism seems also to have extended to the notion of divine judgment. According to the heretics, the world would always remain as it had been (2 Pet. 3:4). Thus they indulged in fleshly fulfillment in pursuit of freedom (2 Pet. 2:13, 19; cf. 2:10, 14).

Many have sought to tie the opponents in 2 Peter to Gnosticism,[80] but this is improbable since the letter was most likely written prior to the emergence of Gnosticism. Others have suggested parallels with Epicurean philosophy,[81] though this identification is doubtful as well.[82] Most likely, the opponents

---

[80]E.g., Werdermann, *Irrlehrer*; Charles H. Talbert, "2 Peter and the Delay of the Parousia," *VC* 20 (1966): 141–43.

[81]E.g. Richard Bauckham, *Jude, 2 Peter*, WBC 50 (Waco, TX: Word, 1983), 156, following Jerome H. Neyrey, "The Form and Background of the Polemic in 2 Peter," *JBL* 99 (1980): 407–31.

[82]Thomas R. Schreiner, *1, 2 Peter, Jude*, NAC 37 (Nashville: Broadman, 2003), 280; see also Peter H. Davids, *The Letters of 2 Peter and Jude*, PNTC (Grand Rapids: Eerdmans, 2006), 133–36;

advocated a philosophy that is otherwise not attested in the New Testament or extant extrabiblical literature, similar to the "Colossian heresy," which likewise appears to have been unique and local. Strangely enough, the opponents' philosophy seems to have precluded divine intervention in the world (2 Pet. 3:3–4), whether by sending a flood (which denied the veracity of the Hebrew Scriptures, see Genesis 6–9) or by Jesus' return at the end of time (involving a denial of Jesus' own words and of the apostles' witness).

1 John

John's first epistle was apparently written to reassure believers shortly subsequent to the departure of false teachers, who, John makes clear, turned out not to be true believers (1 John 2:19). While John presupposes that his readers know the issues that were at stake, the precise nature of the false teaching is difficult to determine due to the oblique nature of the references in his letter. Some, with reference to Irenaeus, believe that the letter was written to oppose Cerinthus, an early Gnostic teacher who taught that the "Christ spirit" came upon Jesus at the occasion of his baptism and left him at the cross.[83] But while nascent Gnosticism was certainly afoot, and some form of it may have influenced the secessionists' departure, wholesale identification of the false teachers with the followers of Cerinthus seems unwarranted.[84]

The clearest indication of the teaching of those who departed from the congregation is provided by references to their denial that Jesus is the Messiah (1 John 2:22–23; cf. John 20:30–31). The secessionists, or a group distinguished from them, also denied that Jesus had come in the flesh (1 John 4:2–3; cf. 2 John 7; 1 Tim. 3:16). This may reflect a Docetic Christology, involving denial of the full humanity of Jesus. Yet in what follows, rather than reinforcing the humanity of Jesus, John simply defines the denial as failure to confess Jesus (see also 4:15; 5:1, 5). Thus the main emphasis seems to lie not so much on refuting a Docetic Christology but on rejection versus confession of Jesus.[85] In any case, the underlying denial, in 1 John as well as in John's Gospel, was that Jesus was the Messiah. As to the exact nature

---

Frank Thielman, *Theology of the New Testament: A Canonical and Synthetic Approach* (Grand Rapids: Zondervan, 2005), 526.

[83]See Irenaeus, *Haer.* 3.11.1 (though Irenaeus related Cerinthus to the writing of John's Gospel, not his first epistle).

[84]See Rudolf Schnackenburg, *The Johannine Epistles: A Commentary* (New York: Crossroad, 1992), 21–23. Terry Griffith, *Keep Yourselves from Idols: A New Look at 1 John* (London: Sheffield Academic Press, 2002), believes that the secessionists were reverting to Judaism.

[85]So Daniel R. Streett, "'They Went Out from Us': The Identity of Opponents in First John" (PhD diss., Wake Forest, NC: Southeastern Baptist Theological Seminary, 2008).

and background of the denial, it is hard to be certain. In addition, it is also possible that the secessionists denied the atoning merit of the cross. This is hinted at in 1 John 5:6, "He is the one who came by water and blood; not by water only, but by water and by blood."

In sum, the secessionists seem to have rejected the apostolic witness, including that borne by John's Gospel (1 John 1:1–5); denied that Jesus was the Messiah (1 John 2:22–23); and most likely also denied the atonement rendered by Christ (1 John 5:6). It is unclear whether they were Gnostics, whether followers of Cerinthus or Docetists or some other variety of early gnosis, or simply people (Jews) who denied that Jesus was the Messiah.

Revelation

The letters to the seven churches in Revelation 2 and 3, which are addressed to a series of congregations in Asia Minor, make reference to several heresies. The letters to the churches in Ephesus and Pergamum mention a group called "the Nicolaitans" (2:6, 15).[86] These are maligned as particularly detestable and compared to Balaam, who led Israel to stumble by eating things sacrificed to idols and to commit acts of sexual immorality (2:14; cf. 2:20).[87] Most likely, the Nicolaitans urged believers to take part in pagan rituals.[88] Hemer concludes:

> Nicolaitanism was an antinomian movement whose antecedents can be traced in the misrepresentation of Pauline liberty, and whose incidence may be connected with the special pressures of emperor worship and pagan society. The important "Balaam" simile may point to a relationship with similar movements facing the church elsewhere, but the nature of such relationship is a matter of speculation in default of explicit data. There may have been a

---

[86]See especially Colin J. Hemer, *The Letters to the Seven Churches of Asia in Their Local Setting*, JSNTSup 11 (Sheffield: JSOT, 1986), 87–94. The reference to the Nicolaitans by Irenaeus, *Haer.* 1.26.3, is of doubtful value. According to Irenaeus, this group followed Nicolaus, one of the seven deacons mentioned in Acts 6:5, and was linked to the Gnostic heretic Cerinthus (*Haer.* 3.11.7).

[87]See Num. 25:1–2; 31:16. It is of interest that Balaam was the subject of elaborate midrashic tradition in the first century AD. See Philo, *Vit. Mos.* 1.54.295–99. Josephus, *Ant.* 4.6.6.126–30. See also Jude 11 and 2 Pet. 2:15 (though see Hemer's comment that "we cannot assume that the opposition in Jude and in 2 Peter necessarily represented the same movement or time"; *Letters to the Seven Churches*, 93; and later *Pirke Aboth* 5.2. On eating food sacrificed to idols, cf. 1 Cor. 8:1–13; 10:20–30. See also Acts 15:20, 29.

[88]Adolf Harnack, *JR* 3 (1923): 413–22, argued that the Nicolaitans were Gnostics, but, as Hemer (*Letters to the Seven Churches*, 93) notes, some of Harnack's assumptions are unwarranted.

Gnostic element in Nicolaitanism, but in our primary texts it is a practical error and not Gnosticism *qua* Gnosticism.[89]

The church in Thyatira even had allowed a false prophetess to gain a following (2:20–21). She was called "Jezebel" because, like the infamous queen in Israel's history, this heretical female teacher had led God's people into idolatry as well as immorality and encouraged a syncretistic blend of pagan religion and Christianity.[90] While attempts at identifying a specific individual behind the designation "Jezebel" are pure conjecture, this unknown woman apparently commanded undue influence in the Thyatiran church and addressed the issue of Christian membership in trade guilds with "permissive antinomian or Gnostic teaching."[91]

The common denominator between the designations "Balaam" and "Jezebel" is that both had led Israel into idolatry.[92] Also, like Balaam of old, the woman called "Jezebel" in Thyatira called herself a prophetess (2:20) and abused her supposed prophetic office to lead God's people astray. By way of background, it is interesting to note that Lydia, Paul's first convert in Philippi, was a businesswoman, a "seller of purple goods," who dealt in products of a guild that was prominent in her native Thyatira (Acts 16:14). After her conversion, she may have faced problems in her participation of the guild.

The reference to "the deep things of Satan" in Revelation 2:24 raises the question of whether there is any connection with similar terminology used by later Gnostic groups. Possibly, their claim to be privy to "the deep things of God" is here reversed. Hemer provisionally accepts the common assumption that the teaching of Jezebel and the Nicolaitans are linked, albeit in a different setting.[93] In Jezebel's case, this popular female teacher may have wrongly allowed Christians participating in trade guilds to compromise their faith by taking part in practices that involved them in idolatry.[94]

---

[89]Hemer, *Letters to the Seven Churches*, 94.

[90]Ibid., 117–23. See 1 Kings 16:31–33; 18:4, 13; 19:1–2; 21:25–26; 2 Kings 9:30–37.

[91]Hemer, *Letters to the Seven Churches*, 117. Hemer chronicles several unpersuasive attempts at identifying this person as an Asiarch, Lydia, the Sibyl Sambathe, or some other woman (pp. 117–19).

[92]See esp. Num. 25:1; 31:16; 1 Kings 16:31–33; 21:25–26.

[93]Hemer, *Letters to the Seven Churches*, 123.

[94]Hemer (ibid.) rightly sees certain parallels with earlier challenges faced by Paul and the apostles, but argues that "under the new tensions induced by Domitianic policy the issues were being fought on rather different ground." He adds that the uncertain data do not permit an adjudication of the matter if the error in question was related to Gnosticism.

Summary

The New Testament writings reveal the presence of various opponents who were denounced in a variety of ways. Different heresies are found in different geographical locations. One important question was the role of circumcision and of keeping the law in salvation. Various challenges came from various combinations of proto-Gnosticism, Judaism, Hellenism, mysticism, and asceticism.

It is unclear whether the heretics of the first century engaged in literary activity of their own. Our main source, the New Testament writings, does not allow us to reconstruct a complete or entirely coherent picture of the various first-century groups. On the whole, it seems that most of these heresies were local and fragmented, though certain common elements can be discerned.[95]

In the end, the only group of early Christians that possessed demonstrable theological unity around a core message that goes back to Jesus and is rooted in the Old Testament was the movement represented by the New Testament writers. The available evidence does not suggest that other groups during this era were equally widespread or unified.

Conclusion

As we have seen, the New Testament writings display a certain amount of legitimate theological diversity. In addition, these documents also bear witness to illegitimate doctrinal diversity in the form of heresy, expressed particularly in aberrant Christological teaching. It must be remembered, however, that the question is not whether there was diversity in earliest Christianity; this is not seriously in dispute. Rather, the question is whether there were an infrastructure and mechanisms in place by which authentic, original Christianity could be confidently passed down by eyewitnesses and others in form of creedal statements, Christological confessions, and other set doctrinal formulations.

The question is also whether heresy was as widespread in the first century as Bauer and others allege while orthodoxy was as late and sporadic as they contend. Our investigation of the New Testament thus far has shown that,

---

[95]I. Howard Marshall, in "Orthodoxy and Heresy in Earlier Christianity" (*Them* 2 [1976]: 5–14), writes, "There appears to be an organized opposition against the Pauline position" (p. 10). Gunther also argues for a unified anti-Pauline front (*St. Paul's Opponents and Their Background*). Elisabeth Schüssler Fiorenza rightly notes, however, that the opponents' diversity outweighs any supposed unity (review of Gunther, *St. Paul's Opponents and Their Background*, *CBQ* 39 [1977]: 435–36). See also Mounce (*Pastoral Epistles, lxxiii*), who lists parallels between the heretics in the Pastorals and those in Colossians.

to the contrary, orthodoxy was considerably more widespread and pervasive than Bauer allowed. Conversely, as we have seen, heresy was considerably more limited and local than Bauer suggested. Thus orthodoxy and heresy were not evenly matched, nor did they exert equally legitimate claims to represent authentic Christianity. What is more, it is important to distinguish between legitimate diversity, in the form of varying theological emphases and mutually complementary perspectives, and illegitimate diversity, striking at the core of the earliest Christological affirmations made by the apostles and other New Testament writers.

Legitimate diversity does not detract from the presence of core beliefs in early Christianity; it simply bears witness to the presence of different personalities and perspectives among the New Testament writers (such as the Synoptics and John, Paul, Peter, and James, and so on). Illegitimate diversity differs in the critical core affirmation of Jesus as crucified, buried, and risen according to the Scriptures, and of Jesus as Messiah, Savior, Lord, and Son of God (see, e.g., the teachings propagated by the opposing groups mentioned in Colossians, 2 Peter, Jude, and 1 John). *This* kind of "diversity," while claiming to be "Christian" by its adherents, is soundly denounced and renounced in the pages of the New Testament.

The reason for this, contra the Bauer-Ehrman thesis, is not that one segment of Christendom acquired sufficient political ecclesiastical clout to impose its will on others; it is the belief that the gospel, as mentioned above, is not of human origin at all; it is a product of divine revelation, from ages past. This is why Paul can oppose a fellow apostle, Peter (Gal. 2:11–14), and why he can say that even if he himself were to preach another gospel—which would be no gospel, in the sense of being a life-saving message, at all—he would be accursed (Gal. 1:6–9). Indeed, the authority of the gospel was considered to be inherent, not in any human messenger, but in the message *itself*, which was deemed to be divine in origin and therefore unchanging and essentially immutable. To cast the history and beliefs of early Christianity therefore primarily, or even exclusively, in terms of human ecclesiastical power fails to do justice to this demonstrable tenet of early Christians.

In essence, the gospel had become a way of reading and understanding the Hebrew Scriptures in light of the conviction that Jesus was both Messiah and exalted Lord. Bauer and his followers also fail to do justice to the massive Old Testament substructure of New Testament theology and vastly underestimate the pivotal significance of Jesus (who was both the primary subject and object of the gospel message) in linking Old Testament messianic prophecy organically with the gospel of the early Christians. The Old Testament message, the preaching and messianic consciousness of Jesus, and the gospel of the apostles, including Paul, were integrally related and stood in close continuity to one another.

There is one more vital and regularly overlooked element in this discussion: the New Testament notion of apostolic authority. Paul claimed to have authority—apostolic authority—that extended not only to matters of congregational polity but also to questions of doctrine. He derived this authority directly from his commissioning by the risen Jesus, as did the other apostles, the Twelve. Thus authority was not vested in an *ecclesiastical body* (as Roman Catholics hold) but in the *quality of Christological confession made possible by divine revelation* (see Matt. 16:13–19). The Bauer-Ehrman thesis insufficiently recognizes that at the core, power was a function of divine truth, appropriately apprehended by selected human messengers, rather than truth being a function of human power.

This, in turn, reveals an anti-supernatural bias in Bauer's historical method and underscores the importance of using the proper philosophical grid in the study of Christian origins. In the end, arriving at the truth of the matter is not just a matter of sifting through data, but of making sense of the data in light of one's worldview. In light of the current stalemate regarding the interpretation of the data, the question of the underlying paradigm assumes utmost importance. This is why, in the final analysis, the present investigation serves as a case study in scholarly paradigms. What we are arguing, then, is that the Bauer-Ehrman thesis is wrong not just because these scholars' *interpretation of the data* is wrong, but because their interpretation proceeds *on the basis of a flawed interpretive paradigm.*

PART 2

PICKING THE BOOKS

Tracing the Development of the New Testament Canon

4

Starting in the Right Place

The Meaning of Canon in Early Christianity

The impact of Walter Bauer's *Orthodoxy and Heresy in Earliest Christianity* has been felt in numerous areas related to the study of early Christianity, but perhaps no area has felt the impact more than the study of the New Testament canon. As we have seen, Bauer argued that early Christianity was far from a monolith but was found in a number of divergent forms, none of which represented the obvious majority over the others. There was no "orthodoxy" or "heresy" within earliest Christianity, but rather there were various "Christianities," each competing for dominance. Thus, argued Bauer, we should not evaluate early Christian literature only on the basis of the views of the eventual theological winners but should consider all early Christian writings as equally valid forms of Christianity.

Bauer's thesis has reshaped many aspects of canonical studies, but, in particular, it has impacted scholarly discussions about the meaning and definition of "canon."[1] As a result of Bauer's influence, scholars have

---

[1]Regarding the word itself, it comes from the Greek word *kanōn* (borrowed from the Hebrew *qāneh*) which can mean "rule" or "standard." Paul uses this term, "As for all who walk by this rule [*kanoni*], peace and mercy be upon them" (Gal. 6:16)—a clear allusion to the message of the gospel. It was picked up by the early church fathers, such as Irenaeus and Clement of

more readily viewed "canon" as a concept that derives entirely from the period of early church history—a phenomenon that arose well *after* the books of the New Testament were written. The idea of "canon" is not something that *preceded* (and led to) the production of the New Testament books within the early centuries of Christianity but is an idea retroactively imposed upon books by the later theological winners. Thus, it is argued, the existence of a New Testament canon could not have been anticipated or expected ahead of time but finds its roots squarely in the theological and political machinations of later Christian groups. Harry Gamble represents this approach:

> During the first and most of the second century, it would have been impossible to foresee that such a collection [of NT Scriptures] would emerge. Therefore, it ought not to be assumed that the existence of the NT is a necessary or self-explanatory fact. Nothing dictated that there should be a NT at all.[2]

James Barr makes a similar claim:

> Jesus in his teaching is nowhere portrayed as commanding or even sanctioning the production of a written Gospel, still less a written New Testament. . . . The cultural presupposition suggested that committal to writing was an unworthy mode of transmission of the profoundest truth . . . The idea of a Christian faith governed by Christian written holy scriptures was not an essential part of the foundation plan of Christianity.[3]

In addition to these sorts of statements, scholars also argue that the New Testament books were not written intentionally as canonical Scripture but rather that such a category, again, was imposed on them at a later date. Lee McDonald notes:

Alexandria, to refer to the "Rule of Faith," and eventually began to be used to refer to the collection of Christian Scriptures (Irenaeus, *Haer.* 1.9.4; 1.10.1; Clement of Alexandria, *Strom.* 6.15.125; Eusebius, *Hist. eccl.* 6.25.3.). For further discussion of this term see Bruce M. Metzger, *The Canon of the New Testament: Its Origin, Development, and Significance* (Oxford: Clarendon, 1987), 289–93; Eugene Ulrich, "The Notion and Definition of Canon," in *The Canon Debate*, ed. Lee Martin McDonald and James A. Sanders (Peabody, MA: Hendrickson, 2002), 21–35; and Hermann Beyer, "κανών," *TDNT* 3:596–602.

[2]Harry Y. Gamble, *The New Testament Canon: Its Making and Meaning* (Philadelphia: Fortress, 1985), 12.

[3]James Barr, *Holy Scripture: Canon, Authority and Criticism* (Philadelphia: Westminster, 1983), 12.

No conscious or clear effort was made by these [New Testament] authors to produce Christian scriptures. It is only at a later stage in the second century, when the literature they produced began to take on the function of scripture within the Christian community, that its status as scripture began to be acknowledged.[4]

Gamble makes the same general argument:

None of the writings which belong to the NT was composed as scripture. . . . The documents which were eventually to become distinctively Christian scriptures were written for immediate and practical purposes within the early churches, and only gradually did they come to be valued and to be spoken of as "scripture."[5]

These citations make it clear that Bauer's conception of the canon as a later, after-the-fact concept imposed upon the New Testament books is quite widespread among modern scholarship.[6] As a result, when scholars attempt to define the term "canon" more formally, there is inevitable confusion.[7] If the canon is merely the product of ecclesiastical maneuverings in the later centuries of Christianity, then are we able to legitimately use the term prior to that time period? Is it anachronistic to speak of a New Testament "canon" prior to, say, the fourth century? A. C. Sundberg has addressed this question and insists that the answer is yes; we cannot speak of the idea of canon until at least the fourth century or later.[8] Sundberg draws a sharp distinction between "scripture" and "canon," arguing that canon, by definition, is a fixed, final, closed list of books and therefore we cannot use the term "canon" to speak of any second- (or even third-) century historical realities. The meaning of canon, according to Sundberg, has very little to do with the New Testament books themselves (or factors

---

[4]Lee M. McDonald, *The Formation of the Christian Biblical Canon* (Peabody, MA: Hendrickson, 1995), 142.

[5]Gamble, *New Testament Canon*, 18.

[6]D. Moody Smith, "When Did the Gospels Become Scripture?" *JBL* 119 (2000): 3–20, acknowledges that there is a widespread conviction among scholars that the New Testament books were not written to be Scripture: "The presumption of a historical distance, and consequent difference of purpose, between the composition of the NT writings and their incorporation into the canon of scripture is representative of our discipline" (p. 3).

[7]John Barton has written a very helpful comparison and contrast of the different definitions of canon, including Sundberg's, Harnack's, and Zahn's. See J. Barton, *The Spirit and the Letter: Studies in the Biblical Canon* (London: SPCK, 1997), 1–34.

[8]A. C. Sundberg, "Towards a Revised History of the New Testament Canon," *Studia Evangelica* 4 (1968): 452–61.

leading to their production), but instead should be understood only as the result of decisions of the later church.

Given this overall trend of modern scholarly opinion on canon, it seems that the idea of a "New Testament" is an idea very much in trouble. As the influence of Bauer has continued to redefine canon and push it further into the realm of church history—and therefore more the result of human, rather than divine, activity—the critical question ceases to be about the boundaries of the canon (which books), but now is about the very legitimacy of canon (should there be one at all). We might be tempted to agree with Ernest Best when he declares, "No matter where we look there are problems and it may therefore be simpler at this stage to cut our losses and simply dispense with the concept of canon."[9]

However, there is a way forward. While the Bauer model is myopically focused on the time well *after* the writing of the New Testament books, it has overlooked the critical time *before* the writing of these books and has even overlooked the New Testament books themselves. There has been too little attention given to the historical and theological influences on the earliest Christians and how these factors may have shaped and determined their expectations regarding whether God would give more revelatory books. This chapter will explore three of these critical areas: (a) canon and covenant; (b) canon and redemptive history; and (c) canon and community. When these considerations are taken into account, it will become clear that the idea of a "canon" was not an after-the-fact development with roots solely in church history[10] but rather a natural, early, and inevitable development with roots in redemptive history.[11]

---

[9]Ernest Best, "Scripture, Tradition, and the Canon of the New Testament," *BJRL* 61 (1979): 258–73.

[10]This is not to suggest that the time period after the production of the New Testament books is irrelevant to the development of the canon. Indeed, as we shall see below, the church plays a vital role, by the help of the Holy Spirit, receiving and recognizing the books God has given. The point here is simply that the concept of a New Testament canon was not born from the post–New Testament church and retroactively imposed upon documents originally written with a wholly other purpose.

[11]Given that this chapter will argue the concept of "canon" precedes any formal decisions of the church about books, then we will not follow Sundberg's definition which restricts "canon" to a final closed list. Canon here will be used simply to denote "a collection of scriptural books" whether or not that collection is formally "closed." Although one is free to adopt Sundberg's terminology voluntarily, this does not seem to be required historically—indeed, it would be difficult to show that the earliest Christians would have made such a sharp distinction between the concepts of "scripture" and "canon" (regardless of what terms they used). For more discussion on this point see E. Ferguson, "Review of Geoffrey Mark Hahneman, *The Muratorian Fragment and the Development of the Canon*," *JTS* 44 (1993): 691–97.

Canon and Covenant

A fundamental missing piece in most prior studies of the New Testament canon is an understanding of the overarching covenantal backdrop of the New Testament itself. The New Testament canon does not exist in a biblical or historical vacuum but finds its proper context within the larger covenantal structure laid down by the Old Testament.[12]

The Concept of Covenant

Simply put, a covenant (*berith*) is an arrangement or contract between two parties that includes the terms of their relationship, covenant obligations (stipulations), and blessings and curses. Although covenants are made between humans in Scripture (1 Sam. 18:3; 20:16), the dominant biblical concept of covenant focuses on the relationship between God and man (Gen. 15:18; 17:2; Ex. 34:28; Isa. 55:3; Luke 1:72; 22:20; Heb. 8:6–13). Indeed, all human-divine relationships in Scripture can be subsumed under and understood within the concept of covenant. Immediately after the fall, God made provision to save a particular people for himself by grace through the shed blood of the promised seed who would crush the head of the serpent (Gen. 3:15). Jesus Christ, the second Adam (1 Cor. 15:21–22), acting as the federal representative of this agreement, kept its obligations perfectly and took the curse for disobedience upon himself at the cross, securing blessings for all those he represented.

This brief description suggests that the concept of covenant forms the overall structural backdrop to the entire redemptive story of the Scriptures. To tell the story of how God has redeemed his people is to simply tell the story of God's covenantal relationship with them. Thus, the archetypal macro-story of God's redeeming work is told by way of the covenantal structure of Scripture. This structure provides the "nuts and bolts" of the redemptive message of the gospel and puts much-needed flesh on an otherwise bare biblical skeleton. We can agree with Horton, who notes that the covenantal concept is "an architectonic structure, a

---

[12]Some helpful studies on covenant include O. Palmer Robertson, *The Christ of the Covenants* (Phillipsburg, NJ: P&R, 1980); idem, *Covenants: God's Way With His People* (Philadelphia: Great Commission, 1978); Meredith G. Kline, *Treaty of the Great King* (Grand Rapids: Eerdmans, 1963); idem, *Kingdom Prologue: Genesis Foundations for a Covenantal Worldview* (Overland Park, KS: Two Age Press, 2000); Thomas Edward McComiskey, *The Covenants of Promise: A Theology of the Old Testament Covenants* (Grand Rapids: Baker, 1985); William J. Dumbrell, *Covenant and Creation* (Grand Rapids: Baker, 1984); Steven L. McKenzie, *Covenant* (St. Louis, MO: Chalice, 2000); and most recently, Michael Horton, *God of Promise: Introducing Covenant Theology* (Grand Rapids: Baker, 2006).

matrix of beams and pillars that hold together the structure of biblical practice."[13]

The Structure of the Covenant

Now that we have seen how central the covenantal concept is within the fabric of Scripture, its connection to the issue of canon becomes clear when we examine the covenantal structure in more detail. The covenantal structure of the Old Testament is illumined by the realization that it is patterned after the treaty covenants of the ancient near Eastern world from which it came.[14] Within these extrabiblical treaties, a suzerain king would address the terms of his relationship with the vassal king over whom he ruled, laying out the stipulations of their agreement, including blessings and curses. These ancient treaties—particularly Hittite ones—had a clearly defined structure:

1) *Preamble.* The opening line of Hittite treaty covenants included the name of the great suzerain king who was issuing the covenant and often listed his many titles and attributes.[15]

2) *Historical prologue.* This portion of the treaty laid forth the history of the relationship between the suzerain king and the vassal. If the suzerain king had rescued the vassal king in the past, then this would provide the grounds for loyalty and love towards the suzerain. Hillers notes, "The history had a function to perform: it was meant to place the relation on a basis other than that of sheer force."[16]

3) *Stipulations.* Ancient treaty covenants set forth the terms of the covenant arrangement and the obligations that each party had agreed to fulfill. Among other things, such stipulations would include the loyal behavior of the vassal king and faithful protection offered by the suzerain king if any foreign armies would threaten his vassal.

4) *Sanctions (blessings and curses).* Hittite treaties also included the various punishments that either party would endure if they broke the terms of the covenant. Although the suzerain would protect his vassal from foreign armies, he would attack his vassal himself and administer discipline if he proved disloyal.

---

[13]Horton, *God of Promise*, 13.
[14]Delbert R. Hillers, *Covenant: The History of a Biblical Idea* (Baltimore: Johns Hopkins University Press, 1969); George E. Mendenhall, *Law and Covenant in Israel and the Ancient Near East* (Pittsburgh: The Biblical Colloquium, 1955), 24–50; and Meredith G. Kline, *The Structure of Biblical Authority*, 2d ed. (Eugene, OR: Wipf & Stock, 1997), 27–44.
[15]Hillers, *Covenant*, 29–30.
[16]Ibid., 31.

5) *Deposit of written text of the covenant.* The final component of ancient Hittite treaty-covenants—and most important for our purposes here—was that a deposit of a *written* copy of the covenant documents would be given to each party to place in their holy shrines. Not only was each party to receive a written copy of the covenant terms, but there were provisions to have the covenant documents read publicly at regular intervals.

When we look at the structure of key portions of the Mosaic covenant—such as Deuteronomy and the Decalogue—we see that it is clearly patterned after the same structure of these treaty-covenants from the Near Eastern world.[17] The Ten Commandments given at Sinai, clearly the core of God's covenant with Israel, had a preamble (Ex. 20:2a: "I am the Lord your God"); a historical prologue (Ex. 20:2b: "who brought you out of the land of Egypt"); a list of stipulations (Ex. 20:3–17); a list of blessings and curses (Ex. 20:5, 6, 7, 11, 12); and, most notably, two copies of the covenant in *written* form deposited in the holy place of worship (Ex. 31:18; Deut. 10:2).[18] As Meredith Kline notes, "The duplicate tables of the covenant at Sinai reflect the custom of preparing copies of the treaty for each covenant party."[19] Just as these ancient treaties created covenant documents as permanent witnesses to the covenant arrangement between the suzerain king and his vassal, so God supplies covenant documents to bear witness to the terms of the arrangement between him and his people.[20] Kline proceeds to argue that the entire Old Testament structure, and all the books therein, reflect various aspects of these ancient extrabiblical treaties.[21] In particular, he observes that ancient treaties included an "inscriptional curse" that pronounced judgment on all those who changed the wording of the covenant documents.[22] Likewise, such an inscriptional curse is evident through the biblical witness from Deut. 4:2: "You shall not add to the word that I command you, nor take from it, that you may keep the commandments of the Lord your God."

The new covenant documents are no exception to this overall pattern. The religious world of Judaism had already anticipated the reality of

---

[17]Other passages that reflect this structure include Joshua 24; see Mendenhall, *Law and Covenant*, 41ff. Hillers, *Covenant*, 59–62; and Horton, *God of Promise*, 34, 39–40.
[18]Kline, *Treaty of the Great King*, 13–26.
[19]Kline, *Structure of Biblical Authority*, 35.
[20]Hillers, *Covenant*, 35; Mendenhall, *Law and Covenant*, 34.
[21]Kline, *Structure of Biblical Authority*, 45–75; see also Hillers, *Covenant*, 120–42, as he demonstrates the covenantal function of the prophetical books.
[22]Kline, *Structure of Biblical Authority*, 29–34; F. C. Fensham, "Common Trends in Curses of the Near Eastern Treaties and Kudurru-Inscriptions Compared with Maledictions of Amos and Isaiah," *ZAW* 75 (1963): 155–75.

another future covenant whereby Israel would be redeemed: "Behold the days are coming, declares the LORD, when I will make *a new covenant* with the house of Israel and the house of Judah" (Jer. 31:31). Certainly any first-century Jew, when confronted with the term "covenant" (*berith*) in Jeremiah 31, would have understood that term within his own historical and biblical context—a context patterned after the treaty covenants of the Near Eastern world. Thus, there would have been clear expectations that this new covenant, like the old covenant, would be accompanied by the appropriate *written texts* to testify to the terms of the new arrangement that God was establishing with his people. Kline shows that the New Testament documents themselves, from Gospel to Epistle to Revelation, all reflect the formal covenantal structure already laid forth in the Old Testament pattern.[23] Moreover, we again see the "inscriptional curse" in Revelation 22:18–19, "I warn everyone who hears the words of the prophecy of this book: If anyone adds to them, God will add to him the plagues described in this book, and if anyone takes away from the words of the book of this prophecy, God will take away his share in the tree of life and in the holy city, which are described in this book." Thus, the New Testament canon, at its core, is a covenantal document.

In light of such a historical reality, it is clear that canon is inherent to and derives its function from the concept of covenant. The canonical writings are God's documentation, as it were, of his covenantal relationship with his people, laying out the nature of their relationship, the terms and conditions, and the blessings and curses. Just as the ancient extrabiblical treaty covenants would not have a covenant without a written document as a witness to the relationship between the two parties, so the biblical covenants would not exist without a written witness to the relationship between God and his people. Canon, therefore, is the *inevitable result of covenant*. Kline declares, "Biblical canon is covenantal canon."[24]

Once the covenantal nature of canon is understood, then we can see that conceptions of canon as merely a product of the early church fundamentally miss what the canon really is. As noted above, Gamble declared, "Nothing dictated that there should be a NT at all."[25] And Barr claimed that "writing was an unworthy mode of transmission" for new covenant

---

[23]Kline, *Structure of Biblical Authority*, 68–74; Meredith G. Kline, "The Old Testament Origins of the Gospel Genre," *WTJ* 38 (1975): 1–27.

[24]Kline, *Structure of Biblical Authority*, 75.

[25]Gamble, *New Testament Canon*, 12.

truth.[26] However, in light of the above discussions of canon and covenant, these statements are simply not historically or biblically accurate. In fact, we have seen that the concept of a written canon of Scripture is woven into the very covenantal fabric of both the Old Testament and the New Testament. Far from being an "unworthy mode of transmission," written texts were the central manner in which God testified to the terms of his covenant relationships within ancient Israel, and thus would be the expected means of communication in the context of the new covenant. As soon as early Christians recognized that God's redemptive acts in Jesus Christ were the beginnings of the new covenant—and they recognized this very early—then they naturally would have anticipated *written documents* to follow that testified to the terms of that covenant.[27] The canon is not simply an idea created by fourth-century Christians or some "after-the-fact" concept that the church devised to battle early heretics like Marcion.[28] Rather, the canon is a concept that has been indelibly part of the life of God's people from the very start of the nation of Israel, and thus continues to be part of his people in the life of the church.

Canon and Redemptive History

As we continue to explore the meaning of canon, it is clear that one of the primary functions of canon is to attest to (and interpret) God's redemptive activity.[29] The two main covenants of Scripture—the old (Sinaitic) covenant and the new covenant—are both established in written form *after* God's special (and powerful) redemptive work was accomplished. Before God formed his people Israel into a theocratic nation and gave them covenant documents, he first delivered them from the hand of Pharaoh in Egypt, in what is undoubtedly the archetypal redemptive event of the old covenant era.[30] When God delivers the Decalogue, the core of the written canon of the Old Testament, to his people on Mount Sinai, he first recounts this

---

[26]Barr, *Holy Scripture*, 12.

[27]Matt. 26:28; Mark 14:24; Luke 22:20; 1 Cor. 11:25; 2 Cor. 3:6, 14; Heb. 7:22; 8:6.

[28]The idea that Marcion "created" the canon, though originally suggested by Harnack, was popularized and expanded by Hans von Campenhausen, *The Formation of the Christian Bible* (London: Adam & Charles Black, 1972); German title *Die Entstehung der christlichen Bibel* (Tübingen: Mohr, 1968). For other assessments of Marcion's influence on the canon see R. Joseph Hoffmann, *Marcion: On the Restitution of Christianity: An Essay on the Development of Radical Paulist Theology in the Second Century* (Chico, CA: Scholars Press, 1984); Barton, *The Spirit and the Letter*, 35–62; and Robert Grant, *The Formation of the New Testament* (New York: Harper & Row, 1965), 126.

[29]Mendenhall, *Law and Covenant*, 32; Kline, *Structure of Biblical Authority*, 76–78.

[30]1 Sam. 8:8; 12:6; 2 Sam. 7:23; Neh. 9:9–10; Pss. 78:12–14; 135:9; Isa. 11:16; Hos. 11:1.

deliverance from Pharaoh: "I am the LORD your God, who brought you out of the land of Egypt, out of the house of slavery" (Ex. 20:2). Thus, we see here in this Old Testament pattern that canonical documents are distinctively the *result* of God's redemptive activity on behalf of his people and function to proclaim that redemptive activity to his people (and to the nations). Canonical books, therefore, are redemptive books. They are a "divine word of triumph."[31]

Inasmuch as early Christians were immersed in the Old Testament and the redemption-revelation pattern that it contained, and inasmuch as they viewed the deliverance from Egypt as simply typological and anticipatory of the ultimate deliverance through Jesus Christ, we would expect that this same function of canon would naturally hold true in the new covenant time period. Indeed, Jesus himself draws a parallel between the deliverance he would bring and the deliverance of Israel from Egypt by instituting the new covenant meal at the Passover itself (Luke 22:20). Thus, in both covenants, God's people are delivered by "the lamb of God" (Ex. 12:1–7; John 1:29). In addition, Jesus is portrayed as leading his own "exodus" from Egypt when in Matthew 2:15 he leaves Egypt in fulfillment of Hosea 11:1: "Out of Egypt I called my son." Similarly, in Luke's Gospel, Jesus is speaking to Moses and Elijah about his "exodus" (*exodon*), which "he was about to accomplish at Jerusalem" (Luke 9:31).

So, just as covenant documents were delivered to Israel after the deliverance from Egypt by Moses, so it would seem natural to early Christians that new covenant documents would be delivered to the church after deliverance from sin by the second Moses, Jesus Christ.[32] If Israel received written covenant documents to attest to their deliverance from Egypt, how much more would the church expect to receive written covenant documents to attest to their deliverance through Christ? Thus, it is the dawning of God's long-awaited redemptive triumph in the person of Jesus that is the foundation for the giving of canonical documents, and not later fourth-century ecclesiastical politics. As D. Moody Smith declared, "The early Christian claim that the narrative and prophecies of old are fulfilled and continued

[31]Kline, *Structure of Biblical Authority*, 79.
[32]Moses-Jesus typology is a well-established theme throughout the New Testament. See Vern S. Poythress, *The Shadow of Christ in the Law of Moses* (Phillipsburg, NJ: P&R, 1991), and Kline, "Old Testament Origins of the Gospel Genre," 1–27. For a broader look at images of Moses in the New Testament see John Lierman, *The New Testament Moses* (Tübingen: Mohr Siebeck, 2004).

in Jesus and the church prefigures, perhaps even demands, *the production of more scripture.*"[33]

Redemptive History and the Apostolic Office

The link between the redemptive activities of God and the giving of the canon is further established by the fact that God gave the office of apostle to the church to be the guardian, preserver, and transmitter of the message of redemption.[34] God did not simply perform redemptive acts and then leave the announcement and promulgation of those redemptive acts to chance or to the random movements of human history. Instead, God established the authority structure of his apostolate to be the foundation of his church for generations to come. It is the apostolic office that forms the critical connection between the redemptive work of God and God's subsequent announcement of that redemption.

That the earliest Christians would have understood the authoritative role of the apostles is made clear by the way it is affirmed in the New Testament writings. Jesus had commissioned his apostles "so that they might be with him and he might send them out to preach and have authority to cast out demons" (Mark 3:14–15). Thus, the apostles were his mouthpiece to the nations, his authoritative witnesses. In John 20:21, Jesus declares to the apostles, "As the Father has sent me, even so I am sending you." Peter testifies to the fact that the apostles were "chosen by God as witnesses . . . to preach to the people and to testify that [Christ] is the one appointed by God to be judge of the living and the dead" (Acts 10:41–42). As Christ's spokesmen, the apostles bore his full authority and power: "The one who hears you hears me, and the one who rejects you rejects me" (Luke 10:16). Their message, therefore, was binding on all those who heard it. The book of 2 Peter makes it clear that the words of the apostles are the words of Jesus and are on par with the authority given to the Old Testament prophets: "You should remember the predictions of the holy prophets and the commandment of the Lord and Savior through your apostles" (2 Pet. 3:2). Likewise, the author of Hebrews argues that the message of the apostles is the same message of salvation that was announced by the Lord Jesus himself and

---

[33]Smith, "When Did the Gospels Become Scripture?" 12 (emphasis added).

[34]For a look at the unique authority of the apostles as bearers of authentic Christian tradition, see Oscar Cullman, "The Tradition," in *The Early Church*, ed. A. J. B. Higgins (London: SCM, 1956), 59–99; and C. K. Barrett, *The Signs of an Apostle* (Philadelphia: Fortress, 1972). For a survey of prior literature on the subject see F. Agnew, "The Origin of the NT Apostle-Concept: A Review of Research," *JBL* 105 (1986): 75–96.

thus bears his full authority and weight—more weight even than the Old Testament message borne by angels (Heb. 2:2–3).

The Apostolic Tradition and Written Texts

It is clear from our earliest Christian documents, the New Testament itself, that the apostolic message would have borne the authority of Christ and therefore would have been seen as a divine message with the same authority as (if not more than) the Old Testament Scriptures. Although this apostolic oversight was certainly exercised orally through preaching, teaching, and visiting churches (2 Thess. 2:15), it was ultimately preserved and passed along in *written* form. It must be remembered that the apostles functioned within the backdrop of Old Testament covenantal patterns that suggested that the inauguration of a new covenant would be accompanied by new written covenantal documents (as discussed above). Given the explicit teachings of Jesus about his inauguration of a new covenant, and given the Jewish identity of the apostles and their immersion in the covenantal structure of the Old Testament, and given the authority that the apostles had been given directly by Jesus Christ to speak on his behalf, it would have been quite natural to pass along the apostolic message through the medium of the written word. The apostolic message was put into textual form so that it would be God's abiding testimony to his church regarding the terms of the new covenant.

In addition, the movement toward a written text would have been driven by the very mission of the apostles given by Christ himself (Matt. 28:19). As the church continued to spread throughout the world into further geographic regions, it became evident that the apostolic authority could only be effectively communicated and accurately maintained in written form. Obviously, the apostles were not able to provide personal attention to every church within the ever-expanding range of missionary influence. Moreover, their limited life span made it clear that they could never bring the apostolic message to the ends of the earth in person but would need a way to preserve their message for future generations.[35] Thus, the mission of the apostles to bring the message of Christ to all nations would have made the enscripturation of their message a virtual inevitability. One is reminded of when Isaiah is exhorted, "And now, go, write it before them on a tablet and inscribe it in a book, that it may be for the time to come as a witness forever" (Isa. 30:8).[36]

---

[35]Cullmann, "Tradition," 90.
[36]C. E. Hill, "The New Testament Canon: *Deconstructio Ad Absurdum?*" *JETS* 52 (2009): 111.

As a result, not only did the apostles themselves write many of these New Testament documents but, in a broader sense, they would have presided over the general production of such material even by non-apostolic authors.[37] The function of the apostolate was to make sure that the message of Christ was firmly and accurately preserved for future generations, through the help of the Holy Spirit, whether written by its members directly or through a close follower of theirs. In the end, the New Testament canon is not so much a collection of writings by apostles, but rather a collection of apostolic writings—writings that bear the authoritative message of the apostles and derive from the foundational apostolic era (even if not directly from their hand). The authority of the New Testament books, therefore, is not so much about the "who" as it is about the "when." It is about the place of a particular book within the scope of redemptive history.

In this way, a written New Testament was not something the church formally "decided" to have at some later date, but rather it was the natural outworking of the redemptive-historical function of the apostles. Inasmuch as that text was deemed to be an embodiment of the apostolic message, it would have retained the authority of the apostles and thereby the authority of Christ himself. It is here that we see the vivid contrast with the Bauer-influenced approaches noted above. Those approaches suggest that *the writing down of these Jesus traditions took place before they were seen as authoritative* (the latter happening at a much later date), whereas the historical evidence suggests that *the traditions were seen as authoritative before they were written down* (due to their apostolic connections). Thus, it is not difficult to see why early Christians would have regarded some texts as authoritative from the very start. The idea of a New Testament canon was not something developed in the second century (or later) when the church was faced with pressing needs, but rather it was something that was handed down to and inherited by the early church from the beginning. It was the foundation *for* the church, not the consequence *of* the church. The idea of canon, therefore, does not belong formally in *church* history, but is more accurately understood as a central plank in *redemptive* history.

When we examine the New Testament books more closely, their content confirms that they are to be understood as bearing apostolic (and therefore divine) authority in written form. In other words, there seems to be an

---

[37]See especially Richard Bauckham, *Jesus and the Eyewitnesses: The Gospels as Eyewitness Testimony* (Grand Rapids: Eerdmans, 2006).

awareness amongst the New Testament authors that they are producing authoritative documents that would function as canonical books for the church.[38] Although there is not space to enter into detailed exegesis of New Testament passages here,[39] consider the following passage in 1 Corinthians 14:37–38: "If anyone thinks that he is a prophet, or spiritual, he should acknowledge that the things I am writing to you are a command of the Lord. If anyone does not recognize this, he is not recognized." Paul not only equates his authority with that of Jesus Christ but specifically applies such authority to the *written* words of his letter, employing the term *graphō*, which is often used elsewhere to refer to the written Scriptures. Moreover, Paul deems his spiritual authority to be so clear that he offers a "prophetic sentence of judgment" on all those who refuse to acknowledge it.[40] In light of a text such as this, it is difficult to imagine that McDonald is being fair with the New Testament data when he declares that Paul "was unaware of the divinely inspired status of his own advice."[41] N. T. Wright sums it up well:

> It used to be said that the New Testament writers "didn't think they were writing 'scripture.'" That is hard to sustain historically today. The fact that their writings were, in various senses, "occasional" . . . is not to the point. At precisely those points of urgent need (when, for instance, writing Galatians or 2 Corinthians) Paul is most conscious that he is writing as one authorized, by the apostolic call he had received from Jesus Christ, and in the power of the Spirit, to bring life and order to the church by his words.[42]

Canon and Community

As already noted above, Bauer's influence on canonical discussions has led many scholars to suggest that the existence of the New Testament canon—its raison d'étre, if you will—is to be attributed directly to the actions of later Christian communities. Such an approach often gives the impression that the early church not only "created" the canon but also consciously "chose"

---

[38]Peter Balla, "Evidence for an Early Christian Canon (Second and Third Century)," in *The Canon Debate*, 372–85.

[39]There are many passages that indicate the New Testament authors were aware of the authoritative status of their own writings, e.g., Mark 1:1; Luke 1:1–4; John 21:24; Gal. 1:1; 1 Cor. 7:12; Col. 4:16; 1 Thess. 2:13; 2 Pet. 3:16; 1 John 1:3–5; and Rev. 1:1–3; 22:18–19.

[40]Gordon D. Fee, *The First Epistle to the Corinthians* (Grand Rapids: Eerdmans, 1987), 712.

[41]McDonald, *Formation of the Christian Biblical Canon*, 9.

[42]N. T. Wright, *The Last Word: Beyond the Bible Wars to a New Understanding of the Authority of Scripture* (San Francisco: Harper, 2005), 51.

the books that were to be included therein.[43] However, we must again ask whether early Christians would have understood the relationship between canon and community in this manner. Would they have been inclined to think of themselves, the Christian community, as the "impelling force"[44] behind the canon's existence? As the ones who determined its shape? It is to these questions we now turn.

Canon Shapes Community

When we again turn to the Old Testament background—the immediate canonical context for the earliest Christians—we see a very different approach to the relationship between canon and community than the one offered by Bauer. The manner in which God established the old covenant at Sinai demonstrates that covenant documents not only attest to God's redemptive activity (as noted above), but they subsequently function to then provide the structural and organizational principles to govern God's people so that God can fellowship with them and dwell among them. In other words, the canon does not simply announce God's redemptive acts, but serves to *shape* a community of people with whom God can unite himself. This pattern can be observed in how God's initial revelation to Moses, right after redemption from Egypt and the establishment of the old covenant at Sinai, bore commands about divine house building—how his "house" (sanctuary) should be organized and operated (Exodus 26–40).[45] Although in one sense this sanctuary was God's dwelling place, it was symbolic of the fact that his real dwelling place was in the hearts of his people, the community of faith, the "house of Israel" (Ex. 40:34–38). Thus we see a biblical pattern in which God triumphs over his enemies by redeeming his people; then he gives his canonical documents that function to structure, organize, and transform God's people into a dwelling place suitable for him. According to the Old Testament paradigm, then, canon constitutes and shapes community, not the other way around.

When we look to the earliest Christian writings, we see that this pattern is unchanged. James notes the power of God's word to constitute, transform, and shape his people into his dwelling place: "He *brought us forth* by the word of truth. . . . Therefore put away all filthiness and rampant wickedness

---

[43]E.g., Helmut Koester, *Introduction to the New Testament,* vol. 2: *History and Literature of Early Christianity* (Philadelphia: Fortress, 1982), 10; and Elaine Pagels, *Beyond Belief: The Secret Gospel of Thomas* (New York: Random House, 2003), 114–42.

[44]Koester, *Introduction to the New Testament,* 8.

[45]Kline, *Structure of Biblical Authority,* 79–88.

and receive with meekness the implanted word which is able to save your souls" (James 1:18, 21).[46] Likewise, Paul speaks of the word shaping the church: "Christ loved the church and gave himself up for her, that he might sanctify her, having cleansed her by the washing of water with the word" (Eph. 5:25–26).[47] As John Webster notes, "The church exists in the space that is made by the Word . . . ; it is brought into being and carried by the Word."[48] Moreover, the theme of divine house building continues in these early Christian texts, reminding us that in the new covenant God is still engaged in building, shaping, and forming people into his divine "temple." For instance, 1 Peter 2:5 refers to the church in temple language: "You yourselves like living stones are being built up as a spiritual house, to be a holy priesthood, to offer spiritual sacrifices acceptable to God through Jesus Christ." Numerous other New Testament texts function to lay out the terms for how God's spiritual "house" (the church) should function and operate (e.g., Romans 12–15; 1 Corinthians 5–12; 2 Corinthians 6–9; 1 Timothy 3–6) so that God may be glorified there. Indeed, the New Testament itself ends with a final description of the dwelling place of God, his consummate house, when the great temple, the new city of God, is unveiled in the new heavens and earth (Revelation 21–22).

Thus, according to the earliest Christian conceptions, canonical documents (God's Word) are understood as God's building plan, the means by which he structures and molds the community of faith to be his dwelling. If so, then it is clear that they would have viewed *the community of faith to*

---

[46]The context of James 1 and 2 makes it clear that the "word" in view here is primarily the gospel message in conjunction with the Old Testament law (cf. 1:23–25; 2:10–12). See D. J. Moo, *The Letter of James* (Grand Rapids: Eerdmans, 2000), 84–85. Although the "word" in this passage (and the one below) is obviously not a reference to the completed New Testament canon, it still establishes the principle carried over from the Old Testament, namely that God's word-revelation (whether oral or written) constitutes and shapes the believing community and is not determined by that community. Moreover, it is worth noting that the oral proclamation of the "word" during this time period would eventually form the essential content of the New Testament canon; one could say that the canon is the oral apostolic message in written form.

[47]The "word" here is likely a reference again to the gospel message; see Harold Hoehner, *Ephesians: An Exegetical Commentary* (Grand Rapids: Baker, 2002), 754–57. It demonstrates that early Christians like Paul would not have conceived of the Word of God (whether oral or written) as being created by the church, but as something that shapes the church and makes the church what it is (by sanctifying her). Such a conviction about the relationship between word and community would have reasonably applied to any new covenant documents that began to be regarded as scriptural.

[48]John Webster, *Holy Scripture: A Dogmatic Sketch* (Cambridge: Cambridge University Press, 2003), 44.

be, in some sense, the result of the canon, rather than the canon being the result of the community of faith.[49] Thus, any suggestion that the church creates the canon, or that the canon is simply and solely the outcome of a long period of "choosing" by the established church, would not only unduly reverse the biblical and historical order but would have been an idea foreign to the earliest Christians.[50] This is why the early church fathers speak consistently of "recognizing"[51] or "receiving"[52] the books of the New Testament, not creating or picking them.[53] In their minds, scriptural authority was not something they could give to these documents but was something that was (they believed) *already* present in these documents—they were simply receiving what had been "handed down" to them.[54] This pattern of "receiving" what is handed down is reflected even earlier in the writings of Paul where he also confesses that "I delivered to you . . . what I also received [*parelabon*]" (1 Cor. 15:3) and even praises the Thessalonians for doing likewise: "And we also thank God . . . that when you received [*paralabontes*] the word of God, which you heard from us, you accepted it not as the word of men but as what it really is, the word of God" (1 Thess. 2:13). Although modern scholars like to impute more sinister moves to the leaders of early Christian communities (such as political power grabs), we can at least acknowledge that this is foreign to their own conception of their role and the way they understood the relationship between canon and community.

Horton sums it up well: "It should be beyond doubt that the people of God are constituted such by the covenant, not vice versa. To say that the community creates the canon is tantamount to saying that it also creates the

---

[49]Stephen B. Chapman, "The Old Testament Canon and Its Authority for the Christian Church," *Ex Auditu* 19 (2003): 125–48, makes a very similar statement, "The biblical canon is not a creation of the church, the church is instead a creation of the biblical canon" (141).

[50]Craig D. Allert, *A High View of Scripture? The Authority of the Bible and the Formation of the New Testament Canon* (Grand Rapids: Baker, 2007), has labored to show that "the Bible grew in the cradle of the church, but also that the leaders of the institutional church had a significant hand in forming our New Testament canon" (p. 77). To a large extent, we can agree with this, depending on what is meant. If he simply means that the church plays an important role in receiving and recognizing canonical books, and that through the Holy Spirit God providentially led the church, then we have little objection. However, if his point is that the canon is somehow determined and/or created by the church in a fundamental sense, and that the canon of the Scripture does not have roots beyond the church's own activity and authority, then we would disagree. The church's role, though vital, is primarily a responsive one, not a foundational one.

[51]E.g., *Muratorian Fragment*, l. 14; Irenaeus, *Haer.* 3.12.12.

[52]E.g., *Muratorian Fragment*, l. 66–67; Serapion cited in Eusebius, *Hist. eccl.* 6.12.3.

[53]See discussion in Hill, "The New Testament Canon," 118.

[54]E.g., Irenaeus, *Haer.* 1.27.2; 3.1.1; 3.4.1; 3.11.9; see also 1 Cor. 11:23; 15:3; Gal. 1:9, 12.

covenant. Such a view would seem to approach the height of institutional hubris."[55] Thus, again we see that Bauer-influenced approaches to canon miss the meaning of canon in a fundamental way when they consider canon to be an idea emerging merely from the period of church history. Understanding the relationship between canon and community can help us recognize that canon, at least in the minds of the earliest Christians, is an idea inherent to these documents and not something retroactively imposed upon them.

Canon Connects to Community

If God has designed canon to transform, organize, and change a people to be the dwelling place for their covenant Lord (2 Tim. 3:16), then the covenant community must rightly recognize these books in order for them to function as God intended.[56] The purpose of covenant documents is not fully realized without a covenant community to which they are connected.[57] If covenant documents and covenant community go hand in hand in this manner, then we should expect that there would be some connection between the community and these documents that would allow the documents to be rightly recognized for what they are.

Put differently, we should expect that there would be something about the manner in which God constitutes the covenant community, and the way he constitutes these covenantal books, that would allow them to "connect" with one another. Indeed, it would be contrary to the character of a covenant-making God to issue covenantal documents, with the purpose of fashioning a believing community for himself, and then establish no means by which such documents could be recognized and adopted by that community. Theologians have historically affirmed that the critical link between the covenant books and the covenant community is the work of the Holy Spirit.

First, as far as the covenant books are concerned, the work of the Holy Spirit produced these books and therefore they are books that are living, active, and powerful (Heb. 4:12). Since these books are from God, they bear God's attributes, so to speak, and are identified by these attributes. Second, as far as the covenant community is concerned, it is also the result of the work of the Holy Spirit. The Holy Spirit has regenerated the hearts and minds of God's people so that they are now attuned to his voice: "My sheep

---

[55]Michael S. Horton, *Covenant and Eschatology: The Divine Drama* (Louisville, KY: Westminster, 2002), 207.
[56]Kline, *Structure of Biblical Authority*, 90–91.
[57]Ibid.

hear my voice . . . and they follow me" (John 10:27). It is the operation of the Holy Spirit, then, that allows members of the covenant community to see the voice of God speaking in the covenant books.[58]

It is this theological paradigm—a paradigm shared by the earliest Christians—that, once again, helps transform our conceptions concerning the origin of the canon within early Christianity. Rather than the canon being something that is formally "chosen" by the later generations of the church (and thus a primarily human construction), it seems instead that the books, in a manner of speaking, imposed themselves on the church through the powerful testimony of the Holy Spirit within them. If the Spirit of God was at work in both these books and in the early Christian communities that received them, then we should expect that the concept of a canon was quite an early and natural development within early Christianity.

Thus the canon is a phenomenon that developed not so much because of formal church decisions (though the vital role of the church cannot be discounted), but because of something that was *already* inherent to these particular books—the power of the Holy Spirit. As Cullmann aptly stated, "Among the numerous Christian writings the books which were to form the future canon *forced themselves on the Church by their intrinsic apostolic authority*, as they do still, because the *Kyrios* Christ speaks in them."[59] Because of the activity of the Holy Spirit, we can agree with Dunn when he declares, "In a very real and important sense the major NT documents chose themselves; the NT canon chose itself!"[60]

Conclusion

It has been the intent of this chapter to explore the meaning of canon in a manner that is distinctive from the variety of modern approaches that are committed to Bauer's reconstruction of early Christianity. Under the Bauer model, any early evidence for the emergence of canonical books would be discounted as "premature" and anachronistic, guilty of importing later (i.e., fourth-century) canonical ideas back into these early stages of the church. But, if the concept of canon is not simply a product of the early church but rooted in the very structure of the canonical documents themselves, then

---

[58]R. C. Sproul, "The Internal Testimony of the Holy Spirit," in *Inerrancy*, ed. Norman Geisler (Grand Rapids: Zondervan, 1980), 337–54.

[59]Cullmann, "Tradition," 91 (emphasis original).

[60]James D. G. Dunn, *Unity and Diversity in the New Testament: An Inquiry into the Character of Early Christianity*, 2d ed. (London: SCM, 1990), xxxi.

we have a new context in which to analyze the historical evidence. This context includes the following.

First, the entire covenantal structure of the Bible (New Testament and Old Testament alike) suggests that written texts are the natural, and even inevitable, consequence of God's covenantal activity. Thus, the earliest Christians would have had a disposition toward, and an expectation of, written documents to attest to the covenant activities of God.

Second, it is clear that God's decisive act of redemption in Jesus Christ would have led to the expectation of a new word-revelation documenting that redemption. It is through Christ's authoritative apostles that this new revelation comes to us, not as part of church history, but as part of redemptive history. Thus, apostolic books were written with the intent of bearing the full authority of Christ and would have been received in such an authoritative manner by its original audiences.

Third, early Christians did not conceive of themselves (or their communities) as those who created or determined canonical books, but merely as those who "received" or "recognized" them. The Holy Spirit was at work in both the canonical documents and the communities that received them, thus providing a means by which early Christians could rightly recognize these books. It is the work of the Spirit that brings about the unity between covenant community and covenant books.

All these considerations, then, cast an entirely new light upon how we should understand early evidence for an emerging canon. Instead of following the Bauer model and discounting early references to canonical books on the grounds that they had not yet *become* Scripture, we are now free to consider the possibility that they are being read, used, and copied by early Christians because of what they *already* are—covenantal documents. Indeed, with these three factors in mind, we would expect that canonical books would have begun to be recognized as such at quite an early point within the development of Christianity. Perhaps, then, we can move beyond the practice of studying the canon simply by starting in the period of the early church and then moving *backward* toward the New Testament. Instead, we can start our studies of canon with the New Testament itself and then move *forward* to the time of the early church.

5

Interpreting the Historical Evidence

The Emerging Canon in Early Christianity

In the previous chapter, we examined how the Bauer thesis has led many modern scholars to understand the canon as a concept that arose solely from within the life of the early church and then was retroactively applied to books not originally written for that purpose (and thus, in principle, could have been applied to *any* set of books within the early centuries of Christianity). What ended up as the "canon" was determined solely by the actions of human beings—as one Christian group battled for supremacy and dominance over competing Christian groups—and had nothing to do with any divine purpose or activity. Such a paradigm has reigned unchallenged within the world of modern biblical studies for generations and has affected the manner in which the historical evidence for an emerging canon is evaluated.

As a result, many in modern canonical studies have interpreted the historical evidence in a manner that places the origin of the New Testament canon well into the late second century (and even beyond). Harnack famously argued that the canon was the result of the church's reaction to the heretic Marcion, thus placing the canon in the mid to late second century. This position was also defended by the very influential work of von

Campenhausen as he continued to argue for the latter half of the second century as the critical time of canonical formation.[1] Such a position is well exemplified by Helmut Koester who declared, "The New Testament canon of Holy Scripture . . . was thus essentially *created* by Irenaeus" in the late second century.[2] Elaine Pagels, in her recent book *Beyond Belief*, follows Koester's argument and virtually lays the entire creation of the New Testament canon at the feet of Irenaeus.[3]

In the midst of this commitment to a later date for the "creation" of a New Testament canon, much earlier evidence has been routinely overlooked or dismissed. After all, if one engages the historical data already convinced that the canon was an after-the-fact development in later centuries of the church, then it is hardly surprising that any earlier evidence for a canon would be considered anachronistic and inconclusive.

Thus, it is the purpose of this chapter to reevaluate the evidence within early Christianity for an emerging Christian canon. When the historical evidence for an emerging canon is viewed in light of the conclusions from the prior chapter—a predisposition toward written texts, acknowledged authority of the apostles, and the operation of the Holy Spirit—substantially different interpretations can result. Since most scholars who follow the Bauer model of canonical history place the origins of the canon in the mid to late second century, we want to explore whether there is evidence for an emerging canon that precedes this date. Thus, we will narrow down our discussion to the time prior to AD 150. Within this timeframe, our attention will be devoted to two areas that are often misinterpreted or, in some cases, ignored entirely: (1) evidence from the New Testament itself;[4] and (2) evidence from the apostolic fathers.

As we examine these texts, the concern is rather narrow: did the *concept* of a New Testament canon (i.e., an understanding that God had given a new collection of scriptural books[5]) exist before c. AD 150, or was it the invention

---

[1]Hans von Campenhausen, *The Formation of the Christian Bible* (London: Adam & Charles Black, 1972).

[2]E.g., Helmut Koester, *Introduction to the New Testament*, vol. 2: *History and Literature of Early Christianity* (Philadelphia: Fortress, 1982), 10 (emphasis added).

[3]Elaine Pagels, *Beyond Belief: The Secret Gospel of Thomas* (New York: Random House, 2003), 114–42.

[4]E.g., two important New Testament passages bearing on the canon, 2 Peter 3:16 and 1 Timothy 5:18, are barely mentioned in Craig D. Allert, *A High View of Scripture? The Authority of the Bible and the Formation of the New Testament Canon* (Grand Rapids: Baker, 2007). The former receives only five lines (p. 127), and the latter is only listed in a footnote (p. 152 n.18).

[5]Allert, *A High View of Scripture?* might object, along with Sundberg, that one cannot use the term "canon" until the boundaries are finally and fully decided (pp. 44–47). But, as the

of the late second-century church? The issue here is not the boundaries of the canon (that is not solidified until later), but whether the early Christian communities had a *theological category* for a New Testament canon. There are a number of other questions related to this issue: Is there evidence that Christians had an interest in written accounts and not just oral tradition? Is there evidence that Christians began to view some of our New Testament books as authoritative from an early time? Are there indications that the apostles, and their writings, would have been viewed alongside the prophets and the Old Testament writings? Of course, with such limited space, our historical survey can take place only on a cursory level. However, the cumulative overview is intended to demonstrate that the concept of a New Testament canon existed before c. AD 150, revealing that much of the historical data is being misread through the predetermined lens of the Bauer model.

The New Testament
When we begin to look for evidence of an emerging canon within early Christianity, some of our best (and earliest) evidence comes from the New Testament itself. However, as we shall see, such evidence is often too quickly dismissed by those committed to the Bauer model of canonical origins. Let us consider several examples here.

Early Collections of Canonical Books
One of the earliest expressions of an emerging canon comes from the well-known passage in 2 Peter 3:16 where Peter proclaims that Paul's letters are "Scripture" on par with the authority of the Old Testament. Most notably, this passage does not refer to just one letter of Paul, but to a *collection* of Paul's letters (how many is unclear) that had already begun to circulate throughout the churches—so much so that Peter could refer to "all his [Paul's] letters" and expect that his audience would understand that to which he was referring.[6] The implications of this verse are multifaceted: (1) Peter's reference to

---

prior chapter argued, the use of the term in this manner does not seem to be required, either practically or historically. Given the Old Testament canonical background of early Christians, as seen above, we ought to be able to look for evidence of a Christian canon earlier than the fourth century, even if it is not "closed." The argument of this chapter is not that the boundaries of the canon are resolved in the second century, but that the canonical concept has clearly begun by the second century.

[6] Regarding Pauline letter collections see S. E. Porter, "When and How Was the Pauline Canon Compiled? An Assessment of Theories," in *The Pauline Canon*, ed. S. E. Porter (Leiden: Brill, 2004), 95–127; and D. Trobisch, *Paul's Letter Collection: Tracing the Origins* (Minneapolis: Fortress, 1994).

the letters of Paul as "Scripture" is made quite casually, as if he expected his readers would have already known about Paul's writings and would agree they are Scripture; he offers no defense or explanation of this idea. (2) Peter does not give any indication that Paul would have objected to the idea that his letters would be considered "Scripture." Moreover, Peter himself does not seem to think it is odd that a letter from an apostle would be considered authoritative Scripture by the communities that received it. Indeed, since Peter also introduced himself as an apostle (1:1), the implications are that his own letter ought to be taken with the same authoritative weight as Paul's. (3) If some of Paul's letters were already considered "Scripture" by many early Christians, then we can reasonably suppose that other written documents were also being recognized as such by this time. Thus, any suggestion that the idea of a written New Testament canon was a late ecclesiastical decision does not comport with the historical testimony found here.

The primary objection leveled against the testimony of 2 Peter as evidence for an emerging canon is the claim that it is a pseudonymous epistle from the early second century.[7] However, three responses are in order here. First, it is curious to note that the reference to Paul's letters in 2 Peter 3:16 is often put forth as a reason for why 2 Peter is a late, pseudonymous epistle.[8] After all, if the reigning Bauer paradigm suggests that collections of canonical literature developed much later in the life of the church, then 2 Peter 3:16 must be evidence of pseudonymity. But, there appears to be some circularity in this sort of approach. One cannot use the reference to Paul's letters as evidence of pseudonymity and then use pseudonymity as evidence for why the reference to Paul's letter collection is inauthentic. Such circularity is yet another example of how the reigning scholastic paradigm functions, at the same time, as both the presupposition and the conclusion.

Second, it is also important to note that the pseudonymous status of 2 Peter has not gone unchallenged.[9] There are numerous historical consider-

---

[7]E.g., J. N. D. Kelly, *A Commentary on the Epistles of Peter and of Jude* (New York: Harper & Row, 1969), 235–37; Richard Bauckham, *Jude, 2 Peter*, WBC (Waco, TX: Word, 1983), 158–63; Bart D. Ehrman, *Lost Christianities: The Battles for Scripture and the Faiths We Never Knew* (New York: Oxford University Press, 2002), 234.

[8]E.g., Kelly, *Epistles of Peter and of Jude*, 235, declares that such explicit concern for apostolic tradition "smacks of emergent 'Catholicism.'" See also this argument used by James Moffatt, *An Introduction to the Literature of the New Testament* (Edinburgh: T&T Clark, 1961), 363; Werner G. Kümmel, *Introduction to the New Testament* (London: SCM, 1975), 432.

[9]Michael J. Kruger, "The Authenticity of 2 Peter," *JETS* 42 (1999): 645–71; E. M. B. Green, *2 Peter Reconsidered* (London: Tyndale, 1960); Donald Guthrie, *New Testament Introduction* (Downers Grove, IL: InterVarsity, 1990), 805–42.

ations—that we cannot delve into here—that suggest the author was likely the apostle Peter himself. At a minimum, it ought to be acknowledged that the authorship of 2 Peter is still an open question and thus not grounds, in and of itself, for too quickly dismissing this text.

Third, even if one grants a late date for 2 Peter, that still puts a collection of Paul's epistles as "Scripture" at a remarkably early date.[10] Those who regard 2 Peter as pseudonymous typically date the epistle to the early second century (c. 100–125),[11] and some scholars have suggested an earlier time of 80–90.[12] Such a collection would show that by the end of the first century Christians already had a clear conception of an emerging canon on par with the Old Testament.

If the internal authorial claims of 2 Peter are given the benefit of the doubt, then by the mid to late sixties of the first century, Paul's letters (or at least some of them) are already being received as Scripture and formed into a collection. Not only does such a historical scenario fit with what we know of Paul's own claims to authority (Gal. 1:1; 1 Thess. 2:13; 1 Cor. 7:12), but it also fits quite well with the conclusions of the prior chapter concerning the nature of early Christian communities—a disposition toward written texts, acknowledged authority of the apostolic writings, and the operation of the Holy Spirit.

Early Citations of Canonical Books

Another New Testament passage routinely dismissed in canonical discussion is 1 Timothy 5:18: "For the Scripture says, 'You shall not muzzle an ox when it treads out the grain,' and, 'The laborer deserves his wages.'" Paul introduces the double citation with the introductory formula, "For the Scripture says," making it clear that both citations bear the same authoritative scriptural status. Some have attempted to argue that the "Scripture"

---

[10]Bauckham, who accepts the pseudonymity of 2 Peter, suggests a date of AD 75–100 (*Jude, 2 Peter,* 158).

[11]Kelly, *Commentary on the Epistles of Peter and of Jude,* 237; C. E. B. Cranfield, *I & II Peter and Jude: Introduction and Commentary* (London: SCM, 1960), 149; J. B. Mayor, *The Epistle of St. Jude and the Second Epistle of St. Peter* (London: Macmillan, 1907), *cxxvii*; D. J. Harrington, *Jude and 2 Peter* (Collegeville, MN: Liturgical Press, 2003), 237. Some have tried to push its date as late as the middle of the second century (e.g., Lee M. McDonald, *The Formation of the Christian Biblical Canon* [Peabody, MA: Hendrickson, 1995], 277), but this position is decidedly in the minority and there seems to be little evidence to justify it. Of course, even if such a date were correct, then we still have a substantive collection of New Testament books that was viewed as Scripture by c. 150 (and even earlier given that such a collection would not pop into existence overnight).

[12]E.g., Bauckham, *Jude, 2 Peter;* and B. Reicke, *The Epistles of James, Peter, and Jude* (New York: Doubleday, 1964).

refers only to the first citation and not the second.[13] However, the manner in which Paul joins the two with the simple *kai*, and the manner in which one citation follows immediately after the other, compels us to understand "Scripture" to apply to both. Indeed, other New Testament examples of double citations have both citations included in the introductory formula (e.g., Matt. 15:4; Mark 7:10; Acts 1:20; 1 Pet. 2:6; 2 Pet. 2:22).[14] Marshall declares, "Both quotations are envisaged as coming from 'Scripture.'"[15]

The first citation is clearly derived from Deuteronomy 25:4, and the second is virtually identical in wording to Luke 10:7 where it is found on the lips of Jesus.[16] Although the natural conclusion would be that Paul is citing from Luke's Gospel, this has been resisted by some modern scholars on the grounds that Luke would not have been considered canonical Scripture by this point in time—such a scenario could not have happened until late in the second century (or beyond). However, there are a number of good reasons to take the text at face value:

1) Suggestions that Paul is merely alluding to oral tradition of Jesus does not fit with the fact that he places this citation alongside an Old Testament citation and refers to both as "Scripture."[17] Marshall again notes, "A *written* source is surely required, and one that would have been authoritative."[18] Thus, regardless of which book Paul is citing, it is clear that he considered *some* book to be Scripture alongside the Old Testament. That fact alone should reshape our understanding of canonical origins.

2) Insistence that Paul is using some other written source besides Luke (such as Q or an apocryphal gospel[19]) seems strange when Luke 10:7 provides such a clear and obvious source for this citation. Indeed, not only is the Greek identical in these two texts, but it is *only* in these two texts that this passage occurs in this form.[20] When faced with such a historical scenario, why would we unnecessarily insist upon hypothetical and conjectural sources? Moreover,

---

[13]E.g., J. N. D. Kelly, *A Commentary on the Pastoral Epistles* (Peabody, MA: Hendrickson, 1960), 126; Martin Dibelius and Hans Conzelmann, *The Pastoral Epistles* (Philadelphia: Fortress, 1972), 79.

[14]George W. Knight, *The Pastoral Epistles: A Commentary on the Greek Text*, NIGTC (Grand Rapids: Eerdmans, 1992), 234.

[15]I. Howard Marshall, *A Critical and Exegetical Commentary on the Pastoral Epistles*, ICC (Edinburgh: T&T Clark, 1999), 615.

[16]Though note that the conjunction *gar* ("for") is found in Luke 10:7 but not in 1 Timothy.

[17]That Paul is using oral tradition here is suggested by Lorenz Oberlinner, *Kommentar zum ersten Timotheusbrief* (Freiburg im Breisgau: Herder, 1994), 254.

[18]Marshall, *Pastoral Epistles*, 616 (emphasis added).

[19]Kelly, *Pastoral Epistles*, 126; Dibelius and Conzelmannm, *The Pastoral Epistles*, 79.

[20]The similar phrase in Matt. 10:10 is still different from Luke 10:7 and 1 Tim. 5:18.

such conjecture misses an obvious point. If a gospel was used and endorsed by the apostle Paul, is it more likely to end up being lost or forgotten (as would be the case if he were citing an apocryphal text), or is it more plausible that it would end up being widely known and recognized as authoritative (as would be the case if he were citing Luke)? Clearly the latter is more likely.

3) The idea that Paul is citing Luke in 1 Timothy 5:18 is also more plausible when one considers his relationship with Luke. Luke was not only a frequent traveling companion of Paul's throughout the book of Acts, but Paul also refers to Luke a number of times in his epistles (Col. 4:14; 2 Tim. 4:11; Philem. 24). Moreover, there is a regular link between Paul and Luke's Gospel in the writings of the early church fathers.[21] Some have even suggested that Luke was Paul's amanuensis for 1 Timothy.[22] Such a strong historical connection between these two individuals makes Paul's citation from Luke 10:7 all the more likely.

4) Although the date of Luke's Gospel is often considered to be in the 70s, there are a number of scholars that place the gospel somewhere in the 60s.[23] Most noteworthy in this regard is the abrupt and incomplete ending to Acts, suggesting that Acts was written sometime in the late 60s on the eve of Paul's death.[24] Since Luke preceded Acts, this would put Luke into the early 60s, and certainly early enough to have been known by Paul when he composed 1 Timothy, likely sometime in the mid to late 60s. In the end, we can agree with John Meier when he declares, "The only interpretation that avoids contorted intellectual acrobatics or special pleading is the plain, obvious one. [First Timothy] is citing Luke's Gospel alongside Deuteronomy as normative Scripture for the ordering of the church's ministry."[25]

Of course, a primary objection raised here is that 1 Timothy, like 2 Peter, is considered by many scholars to be a late pseudonymous work. However, it needs to be acknowledged that this argument has also not gone unchallenged. An impressive case has been made over the years for the authenticity

---

[21]E.g., Irenaeus (*Hist. eccl.* 5.8.3); Origen (*Hist. eccl.* 6.25.6); and the Muratorian Fragment.
[22]C. F. D. Moule, "The Problem of the Pastoral Epistles: A Reappraisal," *BJRL* 47 (1965): 430–52.
[23]D. A. Carson and Douglas J. Moo, *An Introduction to the New Testament* (Grand Rapids: Zondervan, 2005), 207–8; Leon Morris, *The Gospel According to St. Luke: An Introduction and Commentary*, TNTC (Grand Rapids: Eerdmans, 1974), 22–26; and I. Howard Marshall, *The Gospel of Luke* (Grand Rapids: Eerdmans, 1978), 33–35.
[24]John Wenham, *Redating Matthew, Mark, and Luke: A Fresh Assault on the Synoptic Problem* (Downers Grove, IL: InterVarsity, 1992), 223–30; and J. A. T. Robinson, *Redating the New Testament* (Philadelphia: Westminster, 1976), 88–92.
[25]John P. Meier, "The Inspiration of Scripture: But What Counts as Scripture?" *Mid-Stream* 38 (1999): 77.

of this epistle (although there is not room here to engage the question).[26] Beyond this, it is important to recognize that if 1 Timothy were pseudonymous and placed, as many do, around AD 100, then by this time it would be even *more* likely that the author is citing from Luke's Gospel. And thus it would still show that Luke's Gospel was received as authoritative Scripture alongside the Old Testament by the turn of the century—remarkably early on anyone's reckoning. Meier, who accepts the pseudonymity of 1 Timothy, agrees: "The very thought of Luke's gospel being on such a fast track toward canonization boggles the mind, but we do not see any explanation that offers a viable alternative."[27]

Allusions to a Bi-covenantal Canon

As the canon emerges within the early church, questions arise as to when Christians began to conceive of something like a "New Testament" alongside the Old. However, the New Testament evidence is again overlooked. Peter alludes to just such a scenario in 2 Peter 3:2 where he asks his audience to submit to "the predictions of the holy prophets and the commandment of the Lord and savior through your apostles." Several observations are worth making here:

1) Peter places the testimony of the apostles alongside the testimony of the Old Testament prophets, revealing that each has equal and divine authority to speak the Word of God.

2) The fact that he refers first to the Old Testament Scripture, and then juxtaposes it with the teaching given "through your apostles," suggests that he views divine revelation in two distinct phases or epochs—perhaps an allusion to the beginnings of a bi-covenantal canon. The fact that he refers to plural "apostles" is noteworthy as an acknowledgment that any emerging "New Testament" would be composed of more than just one apostle's teaching (thus making it clear that Paul is not the only author in view).[28]

3) Given that the reference to the "holy prophets" is clearly a reference to *written* texts,[29] it seems that 2 Peter 3:2 brings up the possibility that the teaching given "through your apostles" may also refer (at least in part) to

---

[26]See discussion in Guthrie, *New Testament Introduction*, 607–49.
[27]Meier, "The Inspiration of Scripture," 78.
[28]The reference in 2 Pet. 3:2 to the singular "commandment" of the apostles has confused some. Daniel J. Harrington, *Jude and 2 Peter*, sums it up well when he declares, "[The command] refers not so much to one commandment (e.g., the love command) but rather to the substance of the Christian faith proclaimed by the apostles" (pp. 281–82).
[29]Attempts to make "prophets" here refer to New Testament prophets has been roundly rejected; see Bauckham, *Jude, 2 Peter*, 287.

written texts. In fact, 2 Peter 3:16 refers to a particular example of *written* texts of at least one of the apostles. Since 2 Peter 3:16 shows that Peter understood some of the apostolic testimony to be preserved in written form, then 2 Peter 3:2 begins to appear like a possible reference to the Old Testament canon and the (beginnings of a) New Testament canon.

4) 2 Peter 3:2 (NIV) is a good example of how written texts are often referred to with "oral" language. Notice that Peter asks his audience to "recall" (*mnēsthēnai*) the words of the prophets "spoken" in the past (*proeirēmenōn*). If we did not know better, we might conclude that Peter's mention of "holy prophets" was not referring to a written text. Likewise, in light of 2 Peter 3:16, we cannot be too sure that the reference to "apostles" in 3:2 does not have a written text in mind.

Whether one takes 2 Peter 3:2 as an allusion to written apostolic texts or not, this verse clearly lays a critical foundation for the future emergence of the New Testament collection alongside the Old. It reveals that early Christians had a theological conviction that apostolic teaching (and writings; cf. 3:16) were the next phase of God's covenantal revelation. Even if one considers 2 Peter as pseudonymous, such a conviction would have been widespread by the end of the first century.

Public Reading of Canonical Books

A number of Paul's epistles include commands that they be read publicly at the gathering of the church. Colossians 4:16 declares, "After this letter has been read to you, see that it is also read in the church of the Laodiceans" (NIV). Also, in 1 Thessalonians 5:27 Paul strongly exhorts his audience, "I charge you before the Lord to have this letter read to all the brothers" (NIV). In 2 Corinthians 10:9, in the context of Paul defending his apostolic authority, he mentions the public reading of his letters and expresses concern over their impact: "I do not want to appear to be frightening you with my letters."

The book of Revelation also anticipates that it will be read publicly in that it pronounces a blessing on "the one who reads aloud the words of this prophecy, and . . . those who hear" (1:3).[30] This practice of reading Scripture in worship can be traced back to the Jewish synagogue where portions from the Old Testament were routinely read aloud to the congregation (Luke 4:17–20; Acts 13:15; 15:21).[31] Others have suggested that the Gospels of

---

[30]Harry Y. Gamble, *Books and Readers in the Early Church* (New Haven, CT: Yale University Press, 1995), 206.

[31]Ibid., 209–11.

Matthew and Mark were written with a liturgical structure that implied they were used for year-round public reading in worship.[32]

Paul's insistence that his letters be publicly read, coupled with his own overt claims to apostolic authority, combined with the fact that many of his readers understood what public reading would mean within a synagogue context, provide good reasons to think that his letters would have been viewed as being in the same category as other "Scripture" read during times of public worship. Indeed, Paul himself makes this connection clear when he exhorts Timothy, "Devote yourself to the public reading of *Scripture*" (1 Tim. 4:13).

The practice of reading canonical books in worship—though visible only in seed form in the books of the New Testament—is more explicitly affirmed as commonplace by the time of Justin Martyr in the middle of the second century:

> And on the day called Sunday, all who live in cities or in the country gather together to one place, and the memoirs of the apostles or the writings of the prophets are read, as long as time permits; then, when the reader has ceased, the president verbally instructs, and exhorts to the imitation of these good things.[33]

Not only does Justin put the "memoirs of the apostles" (a clear reference to the Gospels) on par with the Old Testament prophets, but he mentions them first, showing that by this time the reading of New Testament Scriptures had in some ways superseded the reading from the Torah.[34] Remarkably, Justin's twofold source of scriptural revelation—the prophets and the apostles—is precisely the twofold source affirmed by 2 Peter 3:2 as discussed above. Again, it seems that the emerging structure of the New Testament canon was already present during the time of Peter and Paul, though more fully realized during the time of Justin.

The primary objection raised by some scholars is that such public reading does not prove a book was considered authoritative because non-canonical literature—e.g., the *Gospel of Peter*, the *Shepherd of Hermas*,

---

[32]G. D. Kilpatrick, *The Origins of the Gospel according to St. Matthew* (Oxford: Clarendon, 1950), 72–100; Michael D. Goulder, *Midrash and Lection in Matthew* (London: SPCK, 1974), 182–83; Phillip Carrington, *The Primitive Christian Calendar: A Study in the Making of the Marcan Gospel* (Cambridge: Cambridge University Press, 1952).

[33]*1 Apol.* 67.3.

[34]Martin Hengel, "The Titles of the Gospels and the Gospel of Mark," in *Studies in the Gospel of Mark* (London: SCM, 1985), 76.

1 Clement—was occasionally read in the churches as well.[35] However, this objection does not negate our point here for a number of reasons. First, it needs to be noted that simply because there was disagreement in some areas of the church concerning the content of these public readings does not mean that public readings in the church meant nothing about a book's perceived authority. The question of which books were to be read regularly in worship was integrally related to the question of which books were considered to bear scriptural authority for the church. The lack of unanimity over the scope of these readings does not change that fact. Gamble declares, "Liturgical reading was the concrete setting from which texts acquired theological authority, and in which that authority took effect."[36]

Second, aside from differences here and there, the vast majority of books read in early Christian worship were the very books that eventually found a home in the New Testament canon. Indeed, it was precisely *for this reason* that they eventually found a home in the canon—they were the books most commonly acknowledged and affirmed in public worship. Eusebius even acknowledges that the books that are received as authoritative Scripture are the ones that "had been publicly read in all or most churches."[37]

Third, it cannot be forgotten that early churches (not unlike the church today) had a category in their public worship for reading that which was deemed helpful and edifying but still known by all *not* to be scriptural. Such reading included letters from important Christian leaders, accounts of the death of martyrs, and other readings considered beneficial to the congregation.[38] Given that a book like the *Shepherd of Hermas*, though quite popular and considered to be orthodox, was widely known to be a non-apostolic, second-century production, it seems it may also have been read within the same category.[39]

In summary, we have seen in this first section that there is much evidence within the New Testament itself concerning an emerging canon of Scripture: references to Paul's letter collection as "Scripture," a citation from the Gospel of Luke as "Scripture," allusions to a twofold canonical authority in the prophets and apostles, and the reading of New Testament books—books understood to be bearing apostolic authority—in the public worship of the church. Although any one of these points may not be conclusive in and of

---

[35] *Hist. eccl.* 6.12.2; 3.3.6; 4.23.11.
[36] Gamble, *Books and Readers*, 216.
[37] *Hist. eccl.* 3.31.6; English translation from Gamble, *Books and Readers*, 216.
[38] *Hist. eccl.* 4.23.11; and Canon 36 of the Council of Carthage.
[39] The *Shepherd* is expressly rejected by the second-century Muratorian Fragment.

itself, their cumulative weight becomes significant. This historical evidence for an emerging canon becomes even more compelling when one remembers the overall context within which to interpret this evidence as established by the prior chapter: an early Christian community with a disposition toward written texts, acknowledged authority of the apostolic writings, and the operation of the Holy Spirit.

The Apostolic Fathers

We have seen that by the end of the first century, contra to the expectations of the Bauer theory, there is already substantial evidence for an emerging New Testament canon composed of written apostolic texts, of both epistles and gospels, and considered authoritative alongside the Old Testament. As we move out of the New Testament period and into the early second century we will explore whether this trend is substantiated by the writings of the apostolic fathers. Needless to say, this is an enormous field of study, and we must restrict ourselves to the mention of only a few selected texts here.[40]

1 Clement

The epistle of *1 Clement* circulated around AD 95 and was attributed to a prominent Christian leader in Rome by the name of Clement. The epistle was quite popular in early Christianity and widely received as orthodox. Most noteworthy for our purposes is the following statement:

> Take up the epistle of that blessed apostle, Paul. What did he write to you at first, at the beginning of his proclamation of the gospel? To be sure he sent you a letter in the Spirit (πνευματικῶς) concerning himself and Cephas and Apollos.[41]

This citation has a number of notable features that are consistent with what was observed in the New Testament evidence above.

First, it is immediately apparent that Clement, a prominent leader in Rome, acknowledges the apostolic authority of Paul and refers to him as "blessed apostle." Indeed, Paul's authority is so certain that Clement is calling his readers to submit to it. Second, Clement makes a clear reference

---

[40]For more on this enormous subject see Andrew Gregory and Christopher Tuckett, eds., *The Reception of the New Testament in the Apostolic Fathers* (Oxford: Oxford University Press, 2005); and Andrew Gregory and Christopher Tuckett, eds., *Trajectories through the New Testament and the Apostolic Fathers* (Oxford: Oxford University Press, 2005).

[41]*1 Clem.* 47.1–3.

to Paul's letter 1 Corinthians and assumes his audience was familiar with it, showing again that Paul's letter collections (or at least parts thereof) seem to be widely known throughout the empire by this time.[42] Clement also makes reference to other epistles of Paul including Romans, Galatians, Philippians, Ephesians, and Hebrews (depending on whether one considers it Pauline).[43] Third, Clement refers to 1 Corinthians as a "letter in the Spirit," a clear acknowledgment that it was written under the inspiration of the Holy Spirit. These sorts of phrases are a common biblical reference to a prophet's authority to deliver the inspired word of God (e.g., Ezek. 37:1; Matt. 22:43; Rev. 1:10).[44]

The objection is often made that *1 Clement* and some of the other apostolic Fathers do not expressly call the New Testament books "Scripture" and therefore these books could not have had such status in the early Christian communities. However, the absence of any particular term is not definitive for a number of reasons.

1) The apostolic fathers often expressly acknowledge the distinctive authority of the apostles to speak for Christ, making apostolic writings implicitly equal to (if not even superior to) the authority of the Old Testament. For example, Clement says elsewhere, "The apostles were given

---

[42]Those arguing for a clear reference to 1 Corinthians include Andreas Lindemann, *Paulus im Ältesten Christentum: Das Bild des Apostels und die Rezeption der paulinischen Theologie in der frühchristlichen Literatur bis Marcion* (Tübingen: Mohr, 1979), 190–91; Andrew F. Gregory, "1 Clement and the Writings That Later Formed the New Testament," in *Reception of the New Testament*, 144; and D. A. Hagner, *The Use of the Old and New Testaments in Clement of Rome* (Leiden: Brill, 1973), 196–97.

[43]Bruce M. Metzger, *The Canon of the New Testament: Its Origin, Development, and Significance* (Oxford: Clarendon, 1987), 42.

[44]Allert, *A High View of Scripture?* is correct to point out that inspiration-like language is occasionally used to refer to other works outside the New Testament writings, and is even used by Clement in reference to his own letter; e.g., 63.2, 59.1 (p. 61). However, this reality does not seem to negate the implications of 47.1–3 for the following reasons: (1) The fact that different early writers designated different sets of books as being "in the Spirit" is beside the point here; we are not asking whether the boundaries of the New Testament books were fixed at this point but simply whether the preliminary concept of a New Testament is starting to emerge (a proto-canon if you will). (2) Allert's study demonstrates that the "in the Spirit" language seems to have some flexibility of use in the apostolic Fathers; sometimes it is used to speak of general ecclesiastical authority (e.g., *1 Clem.* 59.1) but other times it is a clear reference to the authority of Scripture (e.g., *Barn.* 14.2). Thus, it is overly simplistic to think the terminology is always being used in the same manner; the context must determine which is being done. (3) Given the broader context of *1 Clement*, it is difficult to believe that the author is using such language to place his own writings on the same level of the apostle Paul's since, as noted below, Clement draws a sharp distinction between his own authority and that of the apostles (42.1–2), and then expressly refers to Paul as the "blessed apostle."

the gospel by the Lord Jesus Christ, and Jesus Christ was sent forth from God. Thus Christ came from God, and the apostles from Christ."[45] This understanding of apostolic authority—an understanding likely shared in the broader church due to the popularity of *1 Clement*—suggests that an apostolic book would have been considered equally authoritative with "Scripture" even if it was not called such.[46]

2) When one insists that the term "Scripture" must be explicitly used in order for a particular book to be authoritative, the larger issue is being missed. The question is less about the *terminology* used for these writings and more about the *function* of these writings in early Christian communities. What does their *use* indicate about the authority they were given? John Barton notes:

> Astonishingly early, the great central core of the present New Testament was already being treated as the main authoritative source for Christians . . . the core of the New Testament mattered more to the church of the first two centuries than the Old [Testament], if we are to judge by the actual *use* of the texts.[47]

Barton concludes that it would be "mistaken to say that [in the early second century] 'there was no Christian Scripture other than the Old Testament' for much of the core already had as high a status as it would ever have."[48]

3) As we will see below, some apostolic fathers *do* refer to New Testament books explicitly as "Scripture." Moreover, as we have already observed, passages such as 1 Timothy 5:18 and 2 Peter 3:16 refer to New Testament books as "Scripture." Thus, it would be misleading to say that neither the apostolic fathers, nor their predecessors, had a category in their thinking for viewing these books as, in some sense, scriptural. The fact that the term "Scripture" was not always used in certain instances, therefore, does not mean the concept was not already present.

If, indeed, Clement viewed Paul's epistles as bearing the authority of Scripture, then it is probable that he did the same for other apostolic

---

[45] *1 Clem.* 42.1–2.

[46] There are numerous examples of apostolic fathers acknowledging the distinctive authority of the apostles. For an example of such references in Ignatius see Charles E. Hill, "Ignatius and the Apostolate," in *Studia Patristica*, ed. M. F. Wiles and E. J. Yarnold (Leuven: Peeters, 2001), 226–48.

[47] John Barton, *The Spirit and the Letter: Studies in the Biblical Canon* (London: SPCK, 1997), 18 (emphasis original).

[48] Ibid., 19.

books—particularly given his high view of the apostolic office. There are numerous gospel citations in Clement that seem to come from Matthew and Luke (and possibly Mark), and some scholars have noted allusions to Acts, James, and 1 Peter. Thus, Clement provides hints of an emerging canon at the end of the first century.

The Didache

The *Didache* is an early Christian manual of church practice probably from around the turn of the century (c. AD 100). At one point this manual declares, "Nor should you pray like the hypocrites, but as the *Lord commanded in his gospel*, you should pray as follows, 'Our Father in heaven . . .'"[49] The citation goes on to recite the Lord's prayer and is a clear reference to Matthew 6:9–13. What is noteworthy here is that the *Didache* indicates this citation comes from the "gospel," a reference to a *written* text that is "without doubt the gospel according to Matthew."[50] Thus, by the turn of the century we are continuing to see evidence of an emerging written canon, as the apostolic fathers look to gospel texts like Matthew as authoritative sources for the life of Jesus. By this time it is clear that the Lord not only offers his commands through the Old Testament writings, but now it can be said that the Lord offers his commands also through a new set of writings, one of which the *Didache* calls a "gospel." Note also that the author assumes his readers have access to the Gospel of Matthew and would have already been familiar with the book. This assumption becomes more evident later when the author declares, "Engage in all your activities as you have learned in the gospel of our Lord."[51]

There are further confirmations that the *Didache* views the commandments of the Lord as being deposited in *written* texts. The manual declares,

---

[49]*Didache* 8.2 (emphasis added).

[50]Metzger, *Canon of the New Testament*, 51. Christopher Tuckett, "The Didache and the Writings That Later Formed the New Testament," in *Reception of the New Testament*, 83–127, takes a similar position to Metzger and argues that "it seems hard to resist the notion that there is some relationship between the *Didache* and Matthew here" (p. 106). Other scholars disagree, and some have argued that Matthew is either dependent upon the Didache or that both depend on a common source; see H. Koester, *Synoptische überlieferung bei den apostolischen Vätern* (Berlin: Akademie, 1957); R. Glover, "The Didache's Quotations and the Synoptic Gospels," *NTS* 5 (1958): 12–29; J. S. Kloppenborg, "The Use of the Synoptics or Q in Did. 1.3b–2.1," in *The Didache and Matthew: Two Documents from the same Jewish-Christian Milieu?* ed. H. van de Sandt (Minneapolis; Fortress, 2005), 105–29; A. Milavec, "Synoptic Tradition in the Didache Revisited," *JECS* 11 (2003): 443–80; and A. J. P. Garrow, *The Gospel of Matthew's Dependence on the Didache* (London: T&T Clark, 2004).

[51]*Didache* 15.4.

"Do not abandon the commandments of the Lord [*entolas kyriou*], but guard [*phylaxeis*] what you have received, neither adding to them [*prostitheis*] nor taking away [*aphairōn*]."[52] It is probable that the author is drawing an express parallel to Deuteronomy 4:2 (LXX): "You shall not add [*prosthēsete*] to the word that I command you, nor take from it [*apheleite*], that you may keep [*phylassesthe*] the commandments of the Lord [*entolas kyriou*]." The text of Deuteronomy 4:2 originally functioned as an "inscriptional curse" warning the reader of the old covenant documents not to add or take away from the texts before them (see discussion above about the structure of the covenant).

However, in this passage from the *Didache*, the "commandments of the Lord" are no longer a reference to the Old Testament texts, but now the "commandments of the Lord" refer to the teachings of Jesus. The implication of the parallel to Deuteronomy 4:2 now becomes clear: the teachings of Jesus that have been received by the readers of the *Didache* now have a new "inscriptional curse" attached to them—the people must be careful that they are "neither adding to them [n]or taking away." This suggests that the teachings of Jesus (these "commandments of the Lord") are now viewed by the *Didache* as teachings found in authoritative *written* form. In particular, as we already noted above, these commandments of Jesus are found in a book called a "gospel," which was a reference to the Gospel of Matthew (*Didache* 8:2). And if this Gospel of Matthew warrants an inscriptional curse, then this implies that it has been received as a covenant document from God, bearing the type of authority in which the reader must be careful to be "neither adding to them [n]or taking away." In short, the allusion to Deuteronomy 4:2 would have indicated to any reader with a Jewish background that the Gospel of Matthew shares the same authoritative status as the Old Testament books.

If our analysis is correct, then we see that the pattern begun in 2 Peter 3:16, 1 Timothy 5:18, and 1 *Clement*, continues on naturally in the *Didache*. By c. AD 100, written texts were being received as new, authoritative covenant documents.

Ignatius

Ignatius was the bishop of Antioch at the turn of the century and wrote a number of epistles en route to his martyrdom in Rome in about AD 110. Although there is much in Ignatius worthy of our attention, we will limit our discussion to this quote from his letter to the Ephesians:

---

[52]Ibid., 4.13.

Paul, who was sanctified, who gained a good report, who was right blessed, in whose footsteps may I be found when I shall attaint to God, who in *every epistle* makes mention of you in Christ Jesus.[53]

Most noteworthy here is that Ignatius, writing to the Ephesians, makes reference to multiple letters of Paul, "every epistle." It is not clear exactly which of Paul's letters he is referring to—Paul references the Ephesians in numerous New Testament epistles, or he may be referring to the way Paul generally addresses the saints in his letters—but there is a good possibility that Ignatius assumes his readers already know about a series (possibly collection) of Paul's letters and have received it as from an apostle. Such a reference to a widely known Pauline corpus is particularly significant when coupled with a number of other key factors.

1) Ignatius offers repeated and overt references elsewhere to the absolute and unparalleled authority of the apostles.[54] Charles Hill draws the natural implications from such a fact when he notes that any apostolic texts known by Ignatius would have "held an extremely if not supremely high standing with him."[55] Thus, there is no need for Ignatius to explicitly use the term "Scripture" in reference to Paul's letters—his opinion of such texts would have already been clear to the reader.

2) Ignatius gives indications that he knows of other apostolic writings besides just those from Paul. He refers numerous times to the "decrees" and "ordinances" of the apostles,[56] terms that were often used of *written* texts such as the Old Testament.[57] The fact that he uses the plural "apostles" gives indication that he is thinking of a larger corpus of writings beyond Paul, perhaps including Peter, John, and others. Moreover, Ignatius assumes his readers (in various locations) already know about these "decrees" and "ordinances," implying again some sort of corpus of apostolic texts that was widely known beyond Ignatius himself.

3) There are allusions in Ignatius to some of the canonical Gospels, particularly Matthew, Luke, and John.[58] Inasmuch as Ignatius considered these Gospels to be "apostolic" books, we would expect that he

---

[53]Ign. *Eph.* 12.2 (emphasis added).
[54]Hill, "Ignatius and the Apostolate," 226–48.
[55]Ibid., 234.
[56]E.g., Ign. *Magn.* 13.1; Ign. *Trall.* 7.1.
[57]Hill, "Ignatius and the Apostolate," 235–39.
[58]W. R. Inge, "Ignatius," in *The New Testament in the Apostolic Fathers*, ed. A Committee of the Oxford Society of Historical Theology (Oxford: Clarendon, 1905), 63–83; Metzger, *Canon of the New Testament*, 44–49.

would have attributed to them the same authority he gave to Paul's letter collection.

Given that Ignatius was a well-known bishop of an influential Christian city (Antioch), we would expect that his views of apostolic authority and the apostolic letter collections (particularly Paul's) would have been representative of larger segments of early Christianity. He gives no indication that these concepts would be new or controversial to the churches receiving his epistles.

Polycarp

Polycarp was the bishop of Smyrna and wrote an epistle to the church at Philippi around AD 110. He was said to have known the apostle John himself, and was the teacher of Irenaeus.[59] He cites extensively from the New Testament—over one hundred times compared to only twelve for the Old Testament.[60] In this letter he declares, "As it is written in these Scriptures, 'Be angry and do not sin and do not let the sun go down on your anger.'"[61] The first part of this quote could come from Psalm 4:5, but the two parts together clearly come directly from Ephesians 4:26. Thus, we can agree with Metzger when he declares, "[Polycarp] calls Ephesians 'Scripture.'"[62] Of course, some have sought other explanations for this statement in Polycarp.[63] In particular, Koester suggests that Polycarp simply made a mistake here and thought (erroneously) that the entire phrase in Ephesians 4:26 came from Psalm 4:5.[64] Thus, argues Koester, Polycarp meant to use the term "Scripture" to refer only to the Old Testament. However, there is no evidence within the text that Polycarp had made such a mistake. Polycarp's knowledge of Paul's writing is well established and he has demonstrated a "very good memory" regarding Pauline citations.[65] Consequently, Dehandschutter considers such a mistake by Polycarp to be "very unlikely" and argues that Polycarp is clearly referring to the book of

---

[59]Eusebius, *Hist. eccl.* 5.20.4–7.
[60]Metzger, *Canon of the New Testament*, 60.
[61]Pol. *Phil* 12.1.
[62]Metzger, *Canon of the New Testament*, 62.
[63]For a survey of the different attempts see Kenneth Berding, *Polycarp and Paul: An Analysis of their Literary and Theological Relationship in Light of Polycarp's Use of Biblical and Extra-Biblical Literature* (Leiden: Brill, 2002), 204ff.; and Paul Hartog, "Polycarp, Ephesians, and 'Scripture,'" *WTJ* 70 (2008): 255–75.
[64]Koester, *Synoptische*, 113.
[65]Berding, *Polycarp and Paul*, 118.

Ephesians as "scripture."[66] Even McDonald agrees that Polycarp calls both Psalms and Ephesians "scripture."[67] In light of this scenario, the insistence that Paul must have made a mistake raises the question of whether such a conclusion is being driven by the historical evidence or more by a prior commitment to the Bauer thesis.

In Polycarp, then, we again have a reference to one of Paul's letters as a written text of Scripture on par with the Old Testament. Polycarp also references other epistles of Paul including Romans, 1 Corinthians, Galatians, Philippians, 2 Thessalonians, and 1 and 2 Timothy.[68] There is no reason to think Polycarp would not have acknowledged that these other letters of Paul bear the same authority as Ephesians. After all, Polycarp acknowledges that the apostles bear the same authority as Christ and the Old Testament prophets: "And so we should serve as [Christ's] slaves, with reverential fear and all respect, just as he commanded, as did the apostles who proclaimed the gospel to us and the prophets who preached in advance."[69]

In addition to Paul's epistles, Polycarp quotes from some of the canonical Gospels, just as was done in Clement, the *Didache*, and (as we will see below) the *Epistle of Barnabas*. Polycarp declares, "Remembering what the Lord said when he taught, 'Do not judge lest you be judged.'"[70] This passage being quoted by Polycarp is identical in Greek wording to Matthew 7:1, demonstrating possible knowledge of Matthew's Gospel. Polycarp appears to cite from either Matthew or Mark when he declares, "Just as the Lord says, 'For the spirit is willing but the flesh is weak.'"[71] The Greek wording here is identical to Matthew 26:41 and Mark 14:38. In addition, Polycarp may know Luke's Gospel when he says, "Remembering what the Lord said when he taught . . . 'the amount you dispense will be the amount you receive in return.'"[72] Again the wording here is nearly identical to the Greek text of Luke 6:38.[73] Although Polycarp does not directly cite the Gospel of John,

---

[66]Boudewijn Dehandschutter, "Polycarp's Epistle to the Philippians: An Early Example of 'Reception,'" in *The New Testament in Early Christianity*, ed. J.-M. Sevrin (Louvain: Leuven University Press, 1989), 282.

[67]Lee Martin McDonald, *The Biblical Canon: Its Origin, Transmission, and Authority* (Peabody, MA: Hendrickson, 2007), 276.

[68]Paul Hartog, *Polycarp and the New Testament: The Occasion, Rhetoric, Theme, and Unity of the Epistle to the Philippians and Its Allusions to New Testament Literature* (Tübingen: J.C.B. Mohr (P. Siebeck), 2001), 195.

[69]Pol. *Phil* 6.3.

[70]Ibid., 2.3.

[71]Ibid., 7.2.

[72]Ibid., 2.3.

[73]The only difference in the Greek is that Polycarp does not include the word *gar* ("for").

the fact that he sat under John's teaching and knew him personally suggests that it was likely he knew John's Gospel.

However, such possible references to the canonical Gospels prove to be unpersuasive to some scholars, because Polycarp groups these citations from Matthew and Luke into one larger paragraph and does not explicitly distinguish his sources. Moreover, sometimes Polycarp cites the Gospels more loosely and even combines Gospel citations together.[74] The loose and harmonized wording in these references has led some to argue that they derive from some earlier written or oral source and not from the canonical Gospels themselves.[75] While the possibility of such earlier sources must seriously be considered—especially since we know they existed from Luke 1:1—the following considerations suggest we should be hesitant to invoke them too quickly.

1) When the wording of a particular citation can be adequately explained on the basis of a *known* text, this is a methodologically preferable option to making conjectures about oral tradition or an *unknown* (and hypothetical) written source. Metzger concurs, "It is generally preferable, in estimating doubtful cases, to regard variation from a canonical text as a free quotation from a document known to us than to suppose it to be a quotation from a hitherto unknown document, or the persistence of primitive tradition."[76]

2) Even in situations where a written text is known and highly regarded, it must be remembered that it is encountered by most people in the ancient world primarily in *oral* forms (public readings, recitations and retelling of stories, etc.) due to the fact that society was largely nonliterate. Thus, as people would make oral *use* of the gospel texts, drawing from memory, loose and conflated citations would be a natural occurrence. Such a practice does not suggest there is no written text behind this activity. Barton comments:

> The often inaccurate quotations in the Fathers, it is argued, show that they were drawing on "synoptic tradition" but not actually on the Synoptic Gospels. Such a theory cannot be ruled out absolutely, but it is not the only or, probably, the best explanation for loose quotation. . . . The explanation is to be found not in oral transmission in the strict sense, but in the oral *use* of texts which were already available in written form.[77]

---

[74]At the end of *Phil* 2.3 he combines Luke 6:20 and Matt. 5:10.
[75]E.g., Helmut Koester, "Written Gospels or Oral Tradition?" *JBL* 113 (1994): 293–97.
[76]Metzger, *Canon of the New Testament*, 73 n.47.
[77]Barton, *Spirit and the Letter*, 92 (emphasis original).

3) The loose citations of the Gospel material in the church fathers should be compared to the manner in which the church fathers cite Old Testament books. Citations from the Old Testament are also characteristically loose and drawn from memory despite the fact there are obvious written sources behind them. Barton again notes, "We should remember instead how loose are quotations from the *Old* Testament in many patristic texts, even though the Old Testament was unquestionably already fixed in writing."[78] One can even see such a pattern in the New Testament itself as it cites passage from the Old Testament. Mark 1:2–3, for example, is a composite citation of Exodus 23:20, Malachi 3:1, and Isaiah 40:3, even though Mark only acknowledges the use of Isaiah.[79]

4) Even church fathers who certainly knew the canonical Gospels in written form often cite them loosely and without indicating from which Gospel the citation is taken. Irenaeus, who knew the fourfold Gospel intimately, often makes general statements like, "the Lord said," or "the Lord declared," when introducing a Gospel quote, and often conflates and abbreviates citations.[80] It is this phenomenon that led Graham Stanton to declare:

> The fact that these various phenomena are found in a writer for whom the fourfold gospel is fundamental stands as a warning sign for all students of gospel traditions in the second century. Earlier Christian writers may also value the written gospels highly even though they appeal directly to the words of Jesus . . . or even though they link topically sayings of Jesus taken from two or more gospels.[81]

In the end, with these considerations in mind, Polycarp provides a noteworthy confirmation of the trend we have been observing all along. By a very early point—in this case around AD 110—New Testament books were not only called but were also functioning as authoritative Scripture. Given Polycarp's connections to the apostle John, his friendship with Papias, and his instruction of Irenaeus, it is reasonable to think that his beliefs concerning the canon of Scripture would be fairly widespread by this time.

---

[78]Ibid. (emphasis original).

[79]For more discussion on how Old Testament texts were often cited loosely within the New Testament itself see Christopher D. Stanley, *Paul and the Language of Scripture: Citation Technique in the Pauline Epistles and Contemporary Literature* (Cambridge: Cambridge University Press, 1992).

[80]E.g. *Haer.* 3.10.2–3.

[81]Graham Stanton, "The Fourfold Gospel," *NTS* 43 (1997): 321–22.

The Epistle of Barnabas

The *Epistle of Barnabas* was a theological treatise written as a letter in the early second century (c. AD 130) that proved to be quite popular with early Christians. At one point the epistle declares, "It is written, 'many are called, but few are chosen.'"[82] This citation finds its only parallel in Matthew 22:14 and in nearly identical Greek, leading Köhler and Carleton-Paget to suggest Matthew is the most likely source.[83] Although some have suggested Barnabas is pulling from some oral tradition, this option does not fully account for the phrase "it is written." While the possibility that Barnabas is drawing upon another written gospel source cannot be definitively ruled out, there is again no need, methodologically speaking, to insist on hypothetical sources when a known source can adequately account for the data. Carleton-Paget comments on those who make arguments for other sources:

> But in spite of all these arguments, it still remains the case that the closest existing text to *Barn* 4.14 in all known literature is Matt 22.14, and one senses that attempts to argue for independence from Matthew are partly motivated by a desire to avoid the implications of the *formula citandi* ["it is written"] which introduces the relevant words: namely, that the author of *Barnabas* regarded Matthew as scriptural.[84]

If Barnabas is citing from the Gospel of Matthew with the phrase "it is written" (*gegraptai*)—which was normally reserved for Old Testament passages—it is clear that Barnabas was not, in principle, opposed to or unfamiliar with the idea that a written New Testament text could be considered "Scripture" on par with the Old.[85] There is no reason to think this

---

[82]*Barn.* 4.14.

[83]W.-D. Köhler, *Die Rezeption des Matthäusevangeliums in der Zeit vor Irenäus* (Tübingen: Mohr, 1987), 113; James Carleton-Paget, "The Epistle of Barnabas and the Writings That Later Formed the New Testament," in *Reception of the New Testament in the Apostolic Fathers*, 232–33.

[84]Carleton-Paget, "The Epistle of Barnabas and the Writings That Later Formed the New Testament," 233.

[85]The fact that Barnabas cites other literature outside the Old and New Testaments as "Scripture" (e.g., 16.5 cites *1 Enoch* 89 with "For Scripture says") is beside the point being made here for two reasons: (1) The question is not whether there was agreement amongst early Christians on the extent of "Scripture," but simply whether early Christians understood that new scriptural books had been given under the administration of the new covenant. Disagreements over which books does not change this fact, contra to Allert, *A High View of Scripture?* 88. (2) Although early patristic writers do occasionally cite sources outside of our current canon, it must be acknowledged that the vast majority of books they regard as "Scripture" are ones that are inside our current canon. Thus, one must be careful not to overplay the

is a new or innovative idea with him. Thus, it is quite likely that he would have regarded other apostolic books in the same manner that he regarded Matthew. There is evidence elsewhere in *Barnabas* that he may have also used the Gospel of Mark, the Gospel of John, a number of Paul's epistles, and the book of Revelation.[86] Again, we see that concept of a bi-covenantal canon, already present in seed form within the New Testament (2 Pet. 3:2), is continuing to be manifest within the apostolic Fathers.

Papias

Perhaps the most important figure during the time of the apostolic fathers is Papias, bishop of Hierapolis, who, according to Irenaeus, was known to have been a friend of Polycarp and who had heard the apostle John preach.[87] Papias declares, "The Elder used to say: Mark became Peter's interpreter and wrote accurately all that he remembered. . . . Matthew collected the oracles in the Hebrew language, and each interpreted them as best he could."[88] Although Papias is writing around AD 125 (which is quite early[89]), the time period to which he is referring is actually earlier, namely AD 90–100 when "the Elder" would have shared these traditions with him.[90] Thus, the testimony of Papias allows us to go back to one of the most crucial junctures in the history of the canonical Gospels, the end of the first century.[91] It is clear that Papias receives Mark's Gospel as authoritative on the basis of its connections with the apostle Peter and receives Matthew's

citations from non-canonical books as if they are the norm or majority. There still seems to be an agreed-upon core, though there is disagreement about the borders in various places. It is misleading to use the occasional citation of non-canonical books as grounds for denying there is any canonical consciousness at all.

[86]See, e.g., *Barn.* 1.6 (Titus 1:2; 3:7); 5.6 (Mark 2:17); 6.10 (Eph. 2:10; 4:22–24); 7.2 (2 Tim. 4:1), 9 (Rev. 1:7, 13); 20.2 (Rom. 12:9).

[87]Irenaeus, *Haer.* 5.33.4. For discussion of Papias as a source see S. Byrskog, *Story as History–History as Story: The Gospel Tradition in the Context of Ancient Oral History* (Leiden: Brill, 2002), 272–92; R. H. Gundry, *Matthew: A Commentary on His Handbook for a Mixed Church under Persecution* (Grand Rapids: Eerdmans, 1994), 1026–45; and M. Hengel, *Studies in the Gospel of Mark* (London: SCM, 1985), 47–53.

[88]Eusebius, *Hist. eccl.* 3.39.15–16.

[89]Some have argued for an even earlier date around 110; see V. Bartlet, "Papias's 'Exposition': Its Date and Contents," in H. G. Wood, ed., *Amicitiae Corolla* (London: University of London Press, 1933), 16–22; R. W. Yarbrough, "The Date of Papias: A Reassessment," *JETS* 26 (1983): 181–91.

[90]R. Bauckham, *Jesus and the Eyewitnesses: The Gospels as Eyewitness Testimony* (Grand Rapids: Eerdmans, 2006), 202–39.

[91]This is precisely the point that Bart Ehrman misses in his recent book *Jesus, Interrupted: Revealing the Hidden Contradictions in the Bible* (San Francisco: HarperOne, 2009), when he too quickly dismisses the witness of Papias (pp. 107–10).

Gospel presumably on the same basis, namely Matthew's apostolic status. As for John's Gospel, the fact that Papias sat under John's preaching and knew the book of 1 John makes it probable that he knew and used it.[92] Metzger declares, "Papias knew the Fourth Gospel."[93] If so, then there are good reasons to think he would have accepted it as authoritative apostolic testimony alongside of Matthew and Mark. Whether Papias knew Luke's Gospel is less clear, but Charles Hill has made a compelling case that he did.[94] If so, then Papias provides evidence for a fourfold gospel in the first half of the second century (maybe as early as c. AD 125).[95]

Not surprisingly, there have also been attempts to minimize Papias's witness to the reception of the canonical Gospels. Some have argued that Papias still preferred oral tradition over written texts, thus showing he did not consider Matthew, Mark, or the other Gospels to bear any real authority. This argument is based on the statement by Papias where he declares, "I did not suppose that information from books would help me so much as the word of the living and surviving voice."[96] However, not only would such an interpretation be out of sync with the trends in the early second century that we have already observed in this chapter, but, as Bauckham has shown, it misses what Papias is really trying to say. Papias is not even addressing *oral tradition* at all but is simply noting a truth that was commonplace in the ancient world at this time: historical investigations are best done when one has access to an actual eyewitness (i.e., a *living* voice). Bauckham declares, "Against a historiographic background, what Papias

---

[92]Charles E. Hill, "What Papias Said about John (and Luke): A New Papias Fragment," *JTS* 49 (1998): 582–629.

[93]Metzger, *Canon of the New Testament*, 55.

[94]Hill, "What Papias Said about John (and Luke)," 625–29.

[95]A date for the fourfold gospel in the first half of the second century is also affirmed by: Theo K. Heckel, *Vom Evangelium des Markus zum viergestaltigen Evangelium* (Tübingen: Mohr, 1999), (c. AD 110–120); C. B. Amphoux, "La finale longue de Marc: un épilogue des quatre évangiles," in *The Synoptic Gospels: Source Criticism and the New Literary Criticism*, ed. Camille Focant (Leuven: Leuven University Press, 1993), 548–55 (early second century); T. C. Skeat, "The Origin of the Christian Codex," *ZPE* 102 (1994): 263–68 (early second century); Stanton, "The Fourfold Gospel," 317–46 (c. AD 150); James A. Kelhoffer, *Miracle and Mission: The Authentication of Missionaries and Their Message in the Longer Ending of Mark* (Tübingen: Mohr Siebeck, 2000) (early second century). Older works include Theodor Zahn, *Geschichte des neutestamentlichen Kanons* (Erlangen: A. Deichert, 1888–1892) (early second century); Adolf von Harnack, *Origin of the New Testament and the Most Important Consequences of a New Creation* (London: Williams & Northgate, 1925), 68–83 (early second century); and Edgar J. Goodspeed, *The Formation of the New Testament* (Chicago: University of Chicago Press, 1926), 33–41 (c. AD 125).

[96]Eusebius, *Hist. eccl.* 39.4.

thinks preferable to books is not oral tradition but access, while they are still alive, to those who were direct participants in the historical events—in this case 'disciples of the Lord.'"[97]

As the evidence of Papias is assessed, it must be remembered that he was an influential bishop who can be connected directly to Polycarp, may have known the apostle John, and was a noteworthy influence in the writings of Irenaeus, Eusebius, and many others. It is reasonable to think, therefore, that his reception of Matthew, Mark, and John (and possibly Luke) would not have been an isolated event but part of a larger trend within early Christianity—such a trend that has been borne out by all the evidence we have seen thus far.

Conclusion

It is the contention of those who follow the Bauer paradigm that the concept of a canon did not emerge until (at least) the late second century and that prior to this time the New Testament books were not received as authoritative scriptural documents. As a result, evidence from the New Testament and the apostolic Fathers has been routinely dismissed or overlooked. However, this chapter has demonstrated that the concept of canon not only existed before the middle of the second century, but that a number of New Testament books were already received and being used as authoritative documents in the life of the church. Given the fact that such a trend is evident in a broad number of early texts—2 Peter, 1 Timothy, *1 Clement*, the *Didache*, Ignatius, Polycarp, *Barnabas*, and Papias—we have good historical reasons to think that the concept of a New Testament canon was relatively well established and perhaps even a widespread reality by the turn of the century. Although the borders of the canon were not yet solidified by this time, there is no doubt that the early church understood that God had given a new set of authoritative covenant documents that testified to the redemptive work of Jesus Christ and that those documents were the beginning of the New Testament canon.

Such a scenario provides a new foundation for how we view the historical evidence *after* c. AD 150. For example, the Muratorian Fragment reveals that by c. AD 180 the early church had received all four Gospels, all thirteen epistles of Paul, the book of Acts, Jude, the Johannine epistles (at least two of them), and the book of Revelation. Yet, in light of the evidence viewed here, some of these books had *already* been received and used long before

---

[97]Bauckham, *Jesus and the Eyewitnesses*, 24.

the middle of the second century and viewed as part of the revelation of the new covenant (though we do not know how many). Thus, the Muratorian Fragment does not appear to be establishing or "creating" a canon but is expressly affirming what has already been the case within the early church. Again, the contention of the Bauer thesis that all books within the Christian world were on equal footing until the later centuries of Christianity just does not match the evidence as we have seen it here. Not only did Christians conceive of a New Testament canon before the later second century, but some of the specific books therein were already recognized before the early church made any public declarations about them.

6

Establishing the Boundaries

Apocryphal Books and the Limits of the Canon

In the previous chapter we explored how the concept of a new written collection of scriptural books—a New Testament canon—was well established within the Christian movement by the late first and early second century, contrary to the expectations of the Bauer thesis. Moreover, our historical investigations indicated that many of our New Testament books were already received and being used as authoritative Scripture by this time period, much earlier than some scholars previously allowed. However, while the *concept* of a New Testament canon was already established by this point, the *boundaries* of the canon were not yet solidified in their entirety. Inevitably, there were some differences amongst various early Christian groups concerning which books they considered authoritative Scripture and which books they did not. Some of these differences centered upon apocryphal (or non-canonical) books that never made it into the final New Testament canon. And so it is here that we come to the central challenge posed by the Bauer thesis: on what basis can we say that the twenty-seven books of the New Testament represent the "true" version of Christianity when there are so many other apocryphal books that represent other versions of Christianity? Why should these apocryphal books not be considered equally valid forms of the faith?

It is these sorts of questions about apocryphal literature that have dominated canonical studies in the last few generations. Ever since the discovery of the "Gnostic Gospels" at Nag Hammadi, Egypt, in 1945, there has been an ever-increasing fascination with the role of apocryphal literature in the origins of early Christianity. In recent years, Bart Ehrman has published *Lost Christianities: The Battles for Scripture and the Faiths We Never Knew*, cataloging rival factions in the early church and the apocryphal books used to bolster their cause.[1] Elaine Pagels has published *Beyond Belief: The Secret Gospel of Thomas* and argues that Thomas was one of the earliest gospels, even preceding the gospel of John.[2] The recent discovery of the *Gospel of Judas* has continued to bolster interest in apocryphal materials and whether there are other lost stories of Jesus waiting to be discovered.[3] Indeed, it seems there are new books every year about "secret" or "lost" or "forgotten" apocryphal writings. Thus it is the purpose of this chapter to explore the role of apocryphal material in the development of early Christianity and the implications of such books for establishing the boundaries of the New Testament canon. Of course, the story of how the boundaries of the canon were finally and fully established is a long and complicated one that cannot be addressed fully here. Instead, our concern will be more narrowly whether the diversity of apocryphal literature threatens the integrity of the twenty-seven-book canon as we know it.

Canonical Diversity in Early Christianity

For adherents of the Bauer thesis, the most important fact of early Christianity is its radical diversity. The reason there were different collections of Christian books is that there were different versions of Christianity to produce them. Thus much attention has been given to all the different sects, divisions, and factions within the early church and the battles waged between them. The implication of this diversity among followers of Bauer is quite evident. If early Christianity is radically diverse, then there is no single version of Christianity that can be considered normative or "original."

---

[1]Bart D. Ehrman, *Lost Christianities: The Battles for Scripture and the Faiths We Never Knew* (New York: Oxford University Press, 2002).

[2]Elaine Pagels, *Beyond Belief: The Secret Gospel of Thomas* (New York: Random House, 2003).

[3]James M. Robinson, *The Secrets of Judas: The Story of the Misunderstood Disciple and His Lost Gospel* (San Francisco: Harper, 2006); Herbert Krosney, *The Lost Gospel: The Quest for the Gospel of Judas Iscariot* (Hanover, PA: National Geographic Society, 2006).

After all, what if some other faction in the church had "won" the theological wars? We may have found ourselves with a very different New Testament. Ehrman is representative of this position:

> But where did [the New Testament] come from? It came from the victory of the proto-orthodox. What if another group had won? What if the New Testament contained not Jesus' Sermon on the Mount but the Gnostic teachings Jesus delivered to his disciples after his resurrection? What if it contained not the letters of Paul and Peter but the letters of Ptolemy and Barnabas? What if it contained not the gospels of Matthew, Mark, Luke, and John but the Gospels of Thomas, Philip, Mary, and Nicodemus?[4]

At first glance one can see how such an argument can appear quite compelling to the modern reader. Ehrman overwhelms his reader by painting a picture of seemingly endless varieties of "Christianities" in the ancient world, all supposedly on equal historical footing, causing the reader to wonder, "How can I be sure that the books that came out of this theological mess are, in fact, the right ones?" However, despite the rhetorical appeal of such an argument, it does not quite tell the whole story. Although this is not the place to probe the limits of literary diversity in early Christianity, there are a number of considerations that temper such a pessimistic version of canonical origins.

The Relevance of Diversity

Although Ehrman, Pagels, and others lean heavily on Bauer's thesis, at points they are willing to admit it has been substantively critiqued in regard to its core claims.[5] What is remarkable, however, is their willingness to maintain loyalty to Bauer's thesis despite these admissions. After conceding that Bauer was mistaken about the extent of orthodoxy in early Christianity (Bauer underestimated it) and mistaken about the early presence of orthodoxy in various geographical regions (Bauer vastly overplayed the argument from silence), Ehrman seems unfazed in his commitment to Bauer: "Even so . . . Bauer's intuitions were right. If anything, early Christianity was even less tidy and more diversified than realized."[6] In other words, despite the fact

---

[4]Ehrman, *Lost Christianities*, 248; see also Bart D. Ehrman, *Jesus, Interrupted: Revealing the Hidden Contradictions in the Bible (And Why We Don't Know About Them)* (New York: Harper Collins, 2009), 191–223.

[5]Ehrman, *Lost Christianities*, 176; Elaine Pagels, *The Gnostic Gospels* (New York: Random House, 1979), *xxxi*.

[6]Ehrman, *Lost Christianities*, 176.

that Bauer was wrong in his particulars, we can still affirm that Christianity was very diverse, even more than we thought. We see here a remarkable shift in the way modern scholars use Bauer. The particulars are (generally) abandoned and now the mere *existence* of diversity itself becomes the argument.[7] All one must do is trumpet the vast disparity of views within early Christianity and, by definition, no one version of Christianity can be considered "original" or "orthodox." To readers immersed in a postmodern world where tolerance of various viewpoints requires that no one viewpoint be correct, such an argument can prove quite compelling. Indeed, the idea that diversity trumps exclusivity is more or less a modern-day truism.

The problem is that modern-day truisms do not necessarily function as good historical arguments, nor can they be substituted for such. At the end of the day, the mere existence of diversity within early Christianity proves nothing about whether a certain version can be right or true. Ehrman's extensive cataloging of diversity makes for an interesting historical survey but does not prove what he thinks it does, namely that apocryphal books have an equal claim to originality as the books of the New Testament. The only way that the mere existence of diversity could demonstrate such a thing is if there was nothing about the New Testament books to distinguish them from the apocryphal books. But that is an enormous assumption that is slipped into the argument without being proven. Such an assumption includes the following elements.

1) It assumes that the New Testament books and apocryphal books are (and were) indistinguishable in regard to their *historical merits*. Indeed, Ehrman does this very thing in the quote above, when he lists the *Gospel of Mary* alongside the Gospel of Matthew, implying that there was no substantive difference in their historical credentials and that it was only due to the random flow of history that one was accepted and one was not. Of course, nothing could be further from the truth (as we shall discuss further below).

2) It assumes that there is no means that *God* has given by which his books can be identified. As argued in chapter 4, God has not only constituted these books by his Holy Spirit but also constituted the covenant community by his Holy Spirit, allowing his books to be rightly recognized even in the midst of substantial diversity and disagreement. Ehrman's approach already

---

[7]Frederick W. Norris, "Ignatius, Polycarp, and 1 Clement: Walter Bauer Reconsidered," *VC* 30 (1976): 23–44. Norris actually warns against this exact problem when he declares, "Therefore, in assessing Bauer's work, even though details are conceded as incorrect, it should not be asserted that the major premise of the book stands" (p. 42).

assumes that the formation of the canon is a purely human event—neither the books nor the community have God working in their midst. But, again, such an anti-supernatural assumption must be demonstrated, not merely assumed.

As we recognize the manner in which such assumptions are imported into the debate without expressly being proven, it reveals once again how the Bauer thesis is less a conclusion *from* the evidence and more a control *over* the evidence. The central tenet of Bauer's reconstruction of Christianity is that the reason one set of books "wins" and another does not has nothing to do with the characteristics of the books themselves or their historical connections to an apostle and certainly has nothing to do with any activity of God, but is the result of a political power grab by the victorious party. It is to this tenet that all the historical evidence must be adjusted to fit. Thus, in the cause of making sure all views are equally valid, Ehrman must present the *Gospel of Mary* and the Gospel of Matthew as if they are on equal footing.

In the end, the incessant focus on the diversity within early Christianity proves to be a red herring, distracting us from the real issues at hand. It discourages us from asking the hard questions about what distinguishes books from one another, and insists that all versions of Christianity *must* have equal claim to originality. Ironically, then, commitment to the Bauer thesis serves not to encourage careful and nuanced historical investigation but actually serves to stifle such historical investigation by insisting that only the random flow of history can possibly account for why some books were received and others were not. Thus, it is this philosophical devotion to "no-one-view-is-the-right-view" that explains why so many scholars still affirm Bauer's thesis despite the fact that his particular arguments have been refuted. The siren song of pluralism will always drown out the sober voice of history.

The Extent of Diversity

Another factor often overplayed by adherents to the Bauer thesis is the extent of canonical diversity in the period of early Christianity. Indeed, one might get the impression from some scholars that the boundaries of the canon were a free-for-all of sorts where everyone had an entirely different set of books until issues were finally resolved in the fourth-century councils. However, again, this is a substantial mischaracterization of the way the canon developed. Although there was certainly some dispute about some of the "peripheral" books—e.g., 2 Peter, 2 and 3 John, James, Jude—a "core" set of books were well established by the early to middle second century.

Although it is often overlooked, a part of this core set of books is the *Old* Testament, which was received as Scripture by Christians from the very start. Aside from the numerous examples of such acceptance within the New Testament itself, quotations from the Old Testament are abundant within the writings of the apostolic fathers and other early Christian texts.[8] Thus, right from the outset, certain "versions" of Christianity would have been ruled out of bounds. For example, any Gnostic version of the faith that suggests the God of the Old Testament was not the true God but a "demiurge"—as in the case of the heretic Marcion—would have been deemed unorthodox on the basis of these Old Testament canonical books alone. As Ben Witherington has observed, "Gnosticism was a non-starter from the outset because it rejected the very book the earliest Christians recognized as authoritative—the Old Testament."[9] So the claim that early Christians had no Scripture on which to base their declarations that some group was heretical and another orthodox is simply mistaken. The Old Testament books would have provided that initial doctrinal foundation.

Also, as was noted in the prior chapter, there was a core collection of New Testament books being recognized as Scripture and used as such at the end of the first and beginning of the second century. In particular, this core New Testament collection was composed of the four canonical Gospels and the majority of Paul's epistles. Again, Barton notes:

> Astonishingly early, the great central core of the present New Testament was already being treated as the main authoritative source for Christians. There is

---

[8] John Barton, *The Spirit and the Letter: Studies in the Biblical Canon* (London: SPCK, 1997), 74–79; Larry W. Hurtado, *Lord Jesus Christ: Devotion to Jesus in Earliest Christianity* (Grand Rapids: Eerdmans, 2003), 496; Pheme Perkins, "Gnosticism and the Christian Bible," in *The Canon Debate*, ed. Lee Martin McDonald and James A. Sanders (Peabody, MA: Hendrickson, 2002), 355–71; Harry Gamble, "Literacy, Liturgy, and the Shaping of the New Testament Canon," in *The Earliest Gospels*, ed. Charles Horton (London: T&T Clark, 2004), 27–39.

[9] Ben Witherington, *The Gospel Code: Novel Claims about Jesus, Mary Magdalene, and Da Vinci* (Downers Grove, IL: InterVarsity, 2004), 115. In his recent book *Jesus, Interrupted*, Ehrman ignores the foundational role of the Old Testament when he declares, "These different [Christian] groups were completely at odds with each other over some of the most fundamental issues [such as] *How many gods are there?*" (p. 191, emphasis added). But the question of "how many gods" was not a genuine option for early Christians as Ehrman suggests, because it would have been ruled out of bounds by the unequivocal monotheism of the Old Testament. The fact that Marcion rejected the Old Testament does not prove Ehrman's point but affirms precisely the opposite, namely that the Old Testament was so foundational to Christianity that anyone who rejected it was branded a heretic.

little to suggest that there were any serious controversies about the Synoptics, John, or the major Pauline epistles.[10]

Although much is made of apocryphal gospels in early Christianity, the fact of the matter is that no apocryphal gospel was ever a serious contender for a spot in the New Testament canon. In fact, by the time of Irenaeus (c. AD 180), the four Gospels had become so certain that he can declare they are entrenched in the very structure of creation: "It is not possible that the gospels can be either more or fewer than the number they are. For, since there are four zones of the world in which we live and four principle winds . . ."[11] The firm place of the canonical Gospels within the church of the second century is corroborated by the fact that the Muratorian Fragment—our earliest extant canonical list (c. AD 180)—also affirms these four and only these four.[12] As a result, a number of modern scholars have argued that the fourfold gospel would have been established sometime in the early to middle second century.[13]

Likewise, there was impressive unity around Paul's epistles. Not only was Paul used extensively in the apostolic Fathers (as sampled in the prior chapter), but Irenaeus affirms virtually all of Paul's epistles (except perhaps Philemon) and uses them extensively. Moreover, Paul's dominance is also confirmed in the Muratorian Fragment (c. AD 180) where all thirteen epistles of Paul are listed as authoritative Scripture. As a result, scholars

[10]Barton, *Spirit and the Letter*, 18.

[11]*Haer.* 3.11.8.

[12]The date of the Muratorian Fragment has recently been disputed by Geoffrey Mark Hahneman, *The Muratorian Fragment and the Development of the Canon* (Oxford: Clarendon, 1992). See response from Charles E. Hill, "The Debate over the Muratorian Fragment and the Development of the Canon," *WTJ* 57 (1995): 437–52; and Everett Ferguson, "Review of Geoffrey Mark Hahneman, *The Muratorian Fragment and the Development of the Canon*," *JTS* 44 (1993): 691–97.

[13]E.g., Theo K. Heckel, *Vom Evangelium des Markus zum viergestaltigen Evangelium* (Tübingen: Mohr, 1999) (c. AD 110–120); C. B. Amphoux, "La finale longue de Marc: un épilogue des quatre évangiles," in *The Synoptic Gospels: Source Criticism and the New Literary Criticism*, ed. Camille Focant (Leuven: Leuven University Press, 1993), 548–55 (early second century); T. C. Skeat, "The Origin of the Christian Codex," *ZPE* 102 (1994): 263–68 (early second century); Graham Stanton, "The Fourfold Gospel," *NTS* 43 (1997): 317–46 (c. AD 150); James A. Kelhoffer, *Miracle and Mission: The Authentication of Missionaries and Their Message in the Longer Ending of Mark* (Tübingen: Mohr Siebeck, 2000) (early second century). Older works include Theodor Zahn, *Geschichte des neutestamentlichen Kanons* (Erlangen: A. Deichert, 1888–92) (early second century); Adolf von Harnack, *Origin of the New Testament and the Most Important Consequences of a New Creation* (London: Williams & Northgate, 1925), 68–83 (early second century); and Edgar J. Goodspeed, *The Formation of the New Testament* (Chicago: University of Chicago Press, 1926), 33–41 (c. AD 125).

have suggested that Paul's letter collections were assembled and used at a very early time.[14]

The implications of this historical scenario are clear. The vast majority of "disagreements" about the boundaries of the New Testament canon focused narrowly on only a handful of books, while the core of the New Testament was intact from a very early time period. If so, then this core—including the Old Testament itself—would have provided the theological and doctrinal foundation for combating the onslaught of apocryphal literature and heretical teachings. Regardless of the outcome of the debates about books such as 2 Peter and 3 John, or even the *Apocalypse of Peter* or the *Epistle of Barnabas*, the fundamental direction of Christianity had *already* been established by these core books and would not be materially affected by future decisions. Thus, claims that the canon was not finalized until the fourth century may be true on a technical level, but they miss the larger and more important point—the core of the canon had already been in place and exhibiting scriptural authority for centuries. Metzger declares:

> What is really remarkable . . . is that, though the fringes of the New Testament canon remained unsettled for centuries, a high degree of unanimity concerning the greater part of the New Testament was attained within the first two centuries among the very diverse and scattered congregations not only throughout the Mediterranean world but also over an area extending from Britain to Mesopotamia.[15]

Bauer's thesis that there was no ability to distinguish between heresy and orthodoxy until the fourth century (or later) fails on the basis of this fact alone.

Expectations of Diversity

In the midst of discussions about canonical diversity within early Christianity, rarely is consideration given to what we should *expect* early Christianity to be like. Modern scholars eager to trumpet the vast diversity within early Christianity often present their findings as if they are scandalous,

---

[14]See David Trobisch, *Paul's Letter Collection: Tracing the Origins* (Minneapolis: Fortress, 1994); idem, *The First Edition of the New Testament* (Oxford: Oxford University Press, 2000). For an overview of the various views of how Paul's letter collection emerged, see Stanley E. Porter, "When and How Was the Pauline Canon Compiled? An Assessment of Theories," in *The Pauline Canon*, ed. Stanley E. Porter (Leiden: Brill, 2004), 95–127.

[15]Bruce M. Metzger, *The Canon of the New Testament: Its Origin, Development, and Significance* (Oxford: Clarendon, 1987), 254.

unexpected, and sure to shake the foundations of faith. However, the mere existence of diversity would only produce such a reaction if one had reasons to expect there to be very little diversity within early Christianity. Indeed, it seems that Ehrman has presented the existence of diversity as if it were *contrary* to what we would expect if an original, apostolic version of Christianity really existed. But is this a reasonable assumption to make? Ehrman simply slips this assumption into the debate, expecting everyone would agree that high levels of diversity *must* mean that no version of Christianity is the apostolic and original one. Thus his argument succeeds only if he sets the bar artificially high for the traditional view—it is only if there are very few (if any) dissenters, and virtually immediate and universal agreement on all twenty-seven canonical books, that we can believe we have found the original and true version of Christianity. But such an artificial standard decides the debate from the outset, before any evidence is even considered. After all, no historical religion could ever meet such an *unhistorical* standard. Ehrman never bothers to tell us what amount of diversity is "too much" or what amount is "reasonable." One gets the impression that he has challenged Christianity to vault over a bar where he gets to control (and can quickly change) the height.

Aside from the fact that diversity within early Christianity is often exaggerated (as Bauer did) and the unity often minimized (as Bauer also did), we still have very good reasons to expect that early Christianity would have been substantially diverse, leading to inevitable disagreements over the boundaries of the canon. A number of considerations bear this out.

1) *The controversial nature of Jesus of Nazareth*. If near-universal agreement about the person of Jesus is required before we can affirm the truth of his teachings, then such truth will never be affirmed. Even during his own earthly ministry there were disagreements about this man from Nazareth, who he was, and the validity of his teachings. The Pharisees and chief priests considered him to be a mere man, some considered him to be Elijah, and others just a prophet (Mark 9:28). Thus it is no surprise that after Jesus' departure the churches faced heretical teachers and false doctrines nearly from the very start. Paul fought the Judaizers in Galatians (3:1) and the "super-apostles" in 2 Corinthians (11:5), and other heretics are battled in 1 John, 2 Peter, Jude, and Revelation. But does such early diversity imply there is no "true" message, or does it merely flow from Jesus as a controversial figure? Indeed, if even the time of the New Testament was diverse, why would we be surprised that early Christianity in the second and third centuries would be diverse?

2) *The practical historical circumstances of an unfolding canon.* Given that the twenty-seven canonical books were not lowered down from heaven in final form but written by a variety of different authors, in a variety of different time periods, and in a variety of different geographical locations, we can expect that there would be inevitable delay between the time a book is known and accepted in one portion of the Empire as opposed to another. Such a delay would have eventually led to some disagreements and discussion over various books. If God chose to deliver his books in real time and history, then such a scenario would be inevitable and natural.

3) *The reality of spiritual forces opposing the church.* One area that is regularly overlooked (or dismissed) is the role of spiritual forces seeking to disrupt and destroy the church of Christ (Rev. 12:13–17). Given the presumption of naturalism by many modern scholars, such a factor is rarely considered. Nonetheless, both the Old and New Testaments attest to such realities, and their existence gives us greater reason to expect there would be controversy, opposition, and heresy in early Christianity.

Where do these considerations leave us? They demonstrate that we have no reason to be alarmed or surprised at diversity within early Christianity and battles being waged over the cause of truth. The remarkable fact about the development of the canon, then, is not the disagreements or diversity— some of this is to be expected. The remarkable fact is the impressively early *agreement* about the core books of the canon. The fundamental unity around the four Gospels and the majority of Paul's epistles at such an early time, and in the midst of such turmoil and dissension, is the fact of the canon that deserves mention and emphasis. Because the Bauer thesis presents diversity and truth as mutually exclusive options, this fact is never allowed to receive the attention that it deserves.

Apocryphal Books in Early Christianity

As seen from the above discussion, the core value of the Bauer thesis is that all early Christian writings—apocryphal and canonical—must be seen as inherently equal with one another and that any distinctions between these writings are merely the result of later (fourth-century) prejudicial political maneuverings by the victorious party. Implied in this approach is that canonical and apocryphal writings are not distinguishable on other grounds, neither in regard to their historical merits nor in regard to their acceptance by the fathers at the earliest stages of the church's development. But can such a thesis be maintained? Can the success of the canonical books be summed up so simplistically as "some books have all the luck"?

Of course, this topic is far too vast to adequately cover here. For this reason we will restrict ourselves to the apocryphal books that Ehrman cited in the quote above alongside the canonical books: the letters of Ptolemy and Barnabas, and the gospels of Thomas, Philip, Mary, and Nicodemus.

Apocryphal Epistles
Ptolemy's Epistle to Flora

Ptolemy was a second-century Gnostic and disciple of Valentinus. He was committed to the Valentinian system of Gnosticism and wrote a number of works promoting its core beliefs. Most significant in this regard is Ptolemy's *Letter to Flora* preserved in its entirety by the fourth-century writer Epiphanius.[16] In this letter, Ptolemy lays forth the standard Valentinian understanding of the Old Testament, namely that it was not from the one true God, or from the Devil, but from an intermediate deity, the "Demiurge." Thus, by rejecting much of the Old Testament (or at least key portions thereof), Ptolemy lays the foundation for the rather bizarre Valentinian myth of creation with its complex layers of "aeons" that emanate from God.[17]

According to Ehrman, and the Bauer thesis, we are to believe that such a letter has an *equal* claim to representing authentic Christianity as any other letter in the early church. However, the problematic nature of this claim becomes clear when the historical issues are examined. This letter is dated somewhere in the middle of the second century, probably between AD 150 and 170, not remotely close to the time of the first century when the Pauline epistles were written.[18] Moreover, it was not written by someone who claims to be an original follower of Jesus or even a companion of an original follower of Jesus. The vast historical distance between this letter

---

[16]*Pan.* 33.3.1–33.7.10. For discussion of this epistle see Ehrman, *Lost Christianities*, 129–31; and Bentley Layton, *The Gnostic Scriptures* (New York: Doubleday, 1987), 306–15.

[17]A fuller version of Ptolemy's views of creation can be found in his commentary on John's prologue preserved in Irenaeus, *Haer.* 1.8.5. See also discussion in Robert M. Grant, *Heresy and Criticism: The Search for Authenticity in Early Christian Literature* (Louisville, KY: Westminster, 1993), 49–58.

[18]Many modern scholars doubt whether Paul wrote certain letters (e.g., 1 and 2 Timothy, Titus, Ephesians), but other scholars have defended the traditional authorship. For basic surveys see D. A. Carson and Douglas J. Moo, *An Introduction to the New Testament*, 2d ed. (Grand Rapids: Zondervan, 2005); and Andreas J. Köstenberger, L. Scott Kellum, and Charles L. Quarles, *The Cradle, the Cross, and the Crown: An Introduction to the New Testament* (Nashville: Broadman, 2009). However, even if one acknowledges only the seven epistles of Paul which are widely considered authentic, these still vastly predate the *Letter to Flora* and also present a radically different theology from Valentinian Gnosticism.

and the time of Christ and his apostles presents insurmountable problems for its claim to represent "authentic" Christianity.

The *Letter to Flora* also runs into problems on a theological level, since the Valentinian Gnosticism contained in this letter, and its esoteric teachings about multiple deities and the origins of the world, did not develop until the time of the second century.[19] Moreover, as noted above, such Gnostic teaching would have contradicted the canonical books early Christians were already committed to: the Old Testament. It is no surprise, therefore, that the *Letter to Flora* had been roundly rejected by all the major figures in the early church, including Justin Martyr, Irenaeus, Clement of Alexandria, Origen, Tertullian, Hippolytus, and others.[20] Thus, the letter never figured significantly into any of the early discussions of the canon, it never found its way into any of the canonical lists, nor does it appear in any of the early manuscript collections of Christian Scripture. Such a broad and unified coalition against Valentinian Gnosticism, and thus against this letter, cannot simply be dismissed as the political maneuverings of the theological "winners." Not only do these church fathers represent different geographical regions within early Christianity, but they all significantly predate the fourth-century councils that are supposedly the time when the orthodox were crowned the victors.

When one considers the vivid lack of historical credibility for this letter, it makes one wonder why Ehrman would even mention it alongside the epistles of Paul and Peter. The answer becomes clear when we observe how Ehrman goes to extra lengths to remind the reader that the author of this letter was "earnest" and "sincere" and that he "understood his views to be those of the apostles."[21] In other words, we cannot reject Ptolemy's letter because, after all, Ptolemy *himself* sincerely believed he held orthodox doctrines, and who are we to say otherwise? It is here that we, again, see Ehrman's underlying postmodern philosophical commitments rise to the surface. No matter how overwhelming the historical evidence may be, we can never say another group is wrong if that group is "sincere" and "passionate" in their belief that they are right. Put differently, the sheer *existence*

---

[19]Edwin A. Yamauchi, *Pre-Christian Gnosticism: A Survey of the Proposed Evidences* (Grand Rapids: Eerdmans, 1983); Philip Jenkins, *Hidden Gospels* (Oxford: Oxford University Press, 2001), 115–16. There may well be some aspects of Gnosticism that can be traced into the late first century (a proto-Gnosticism of sorts), but not the full-blown Valentinian version found in *Flora*.

[20]Paul Allen Mirecki, "Valentinus," *ABD* 6:784.

[21]Ehrman, *Lost Christianities*, 131.

of disagreement among early Christians requires that we declare no one view to be right. Thus, from Ehrman's perspective, one must merely demonstrate that some group during the New Testament era disagreed with "orthodox" Christians about any given topic—and instead thought they were "orthodox" themselves —and then we are all obligated to agree that distinctions between heresy and orthodoxy are meaningless.

But Ehrman's reasoning here is beset by all kinds of problems. Why is the "sincerity" or "passion" of a group a test for historical authenticity? One can be sincere and passionate and still be entirely wrong. Just because a group claims to be an authentic "Christian" group does not make it one. Moreover, if the existence of disagreement amongst two groups (that are both sincere) means that no one position can be considered true, then, on Ehrman's reasoning, we could never affirm any historical truth unless there was virtually *zero* disagreement about it. And it seems this is precisely the way Ehrman wants it to be. If he can slip such an unattainable standard into the debate without anyone realizing it, then he can prove his case just by trotting out example after example of divergent Christian groups. However, such an exercise only proves compelling to those already committed to the "no-one-view-is-the-right-view" principle from the outset.

The Epistle of Barnabas

The *Epistle of Barnabas* was a theological treatise written as a letter in the second century (c. AD 130) that proved to be quite popular within some early Christian circles. Much of the epistle is concerned with how the Jews have misunderstood their own books and how Christ fulfilled the sacrificial portions of the Old Testament. Although the letter is attributed to the Barnabas who was a companion of Paul, it was in fact written by a second-century author whose identity remains unknown.[22]

Although *Barnabas* was a popular writing—used by Clement of Alexandria, Origen, and others—this is not a sufficient basis for suggesting that it bears equal claim to a place in the canon as the letters of Paul and Peter. Early Christians cited many different writings that they deemed useful and edifying but did not necessarily regard as part of canonical Scripture (just as we are able to make the same distinction today in our libraries). Origen does not include *Barnabas* in his list of canonical books, nor does he write

---

[22]For more on Barnabas see James Carleton Paget, *The Epistle of Barnabas: Outlook and Background* (Tübingen: Mohr Siebeck, 1994); and Jay Curry Treat, "Epistle of Barnabas," *ABD* 1:611–14.

any commentary or homily on it.[23] Although Irenaeus and Tertullian comment extensively on canonical books, they show no interest in *Barnabas*. The book is absent from our earliest canonical list, the Muratorian Canon, and Eusebius even puts the epistle into the category of "spurious" books.[24] In addition to all these problems, *Barnabas* lacks the historical credentials of the other New Testament letters, being a second-century production written well after the time of the apostles. There is no evidence that it represents early, authoritative, and authentic teachings of Christianity that were simply suppressed by the political machinations of the later theological "winners." As a result, it is hard to take it seriously as a contender for a place in the canon.

In discussions of *Barnabas*, it is often argued that the epistle must have been considered "Scripture" because it was included (along with the *Shepherd of Hermas*) in Codex Sinaiticus, a codex that contained the books of the Old and New Testaments.[25] However, it is important to note the position of *Barnabas* within the codex—it was not listed alongside the other New Testament epistles but was tacked onto the end of the codex along with the *Shepherd*. As William Horbury has pointed out, there was a widespread practice in the church of listing the received books first and then, at the end, mentioning the "disputed" books or other books which were useful for the church but not regarded as canonical.[26] This pattern is borne out in the Muratorian Canon, the canonical list in codex Claromontanus, Epiphanius, Eusebius, and other codices such as Alexandrinus (which included *1–2 Clement* at the end).[27] Thus the inclusion of *Barnabas* in Codex Sinaiticus is evidence of its popularity and usefulness to early Christians but not necessarily of its canonicity.

Apocryphal Gospels
Ehrman also mentions four apocryphal gospels that supposedly have equal claim to represent authentic Christianity. We will now address each of these, albeit briefly due to the limits of space.

[23]*Hom. in Jos.* 7.1.
[24]*Hist. eccl.* 3.25.4.
[25]E.g., Bart D. Ehrman, *The Apostolic Fathers*, vol. 2, LCL (Cambridge, MA: Harvard University Press, 2003), 3.
[26]William Horbury, "The Wisdom of Solomon in the Muratorian Fragment," *JTS* 45 (1994): 149–59.
[27]Ibid., 152–56.

The Gospel of Thomas

Doubtless *Thomas* is the best-known apocryphal gospel to modern readers and the modern scholarly works on the subject are too numerous to mention.[28] Part of the now well-known cache of documents discovered at Nag Hammadi in 1945, *Thomas* contains 114 sayings of Jesus, many of which are rather cryptic and esoteric, and others which bear a closer affinity to the canonical Jesus.[29] Most infamous is its final line: "Jesus said . . . 'For every woman who makes herself male will enter the kingdom of heaven.'" In addition, *Thomas* lacks the narrative structure so common to the canonical Gospels, leaving out any account of the birth, death, and resurrection of Jesus.

Despite the efforts of more radical scholars,[30] the broad consensus is that *Thomas* was written in the middle of the second century by an unknown author (certainly not the apostle Thomas).[31] Not only is this substantially later than our canonical Gospels (which are all first-century), but *Thomas* also appears to be derivative from and dependent upon the canonical material.[32] In addition, the book has a strong Gnostic flavor throughout, advocating a Jesus less concerned with showing that he is divine and more concerned with teaching us to find the divine spark within ourselves.[33] As

---

[28] A broad survey of the scholarly literature can be found in Francis T. Fallon and Ron Cameron, "*The Gospel of Thomas*: A *Forschungsbericht* and Analysis," *ANRW* 2.25.6 (1988): 4195–251. A helpful overview of some of the key modern works is provided in Nicholas Perrin, *Thomas: The Other Gospel* (Louisville, KY: Westminster, 2007). See also the bibliography in J. K. Elliott, *The Apocryphal New Testament* (Oxford: Clarendon, 1993), 126–27.

[29] For a general introduction to the Nag Hammadi material see Christopher Tuckett, *Nag Hammadi and the Gospel Tradition* (Edinburgh: T&T Clark, 1986). A fragmentary version of Thomas was known through the earlier discoveries of P.Oxy. 1, P.Oxy. 654, and P.Oxy. 655. For more on these papyri see Joseph A. Fitzmyer, "The Oxyrhynchus Logoi of Jesus and the Coptic Gospel According to Thomas," *TS* 20 (1959): 505–60.

[30] Stephen J. Patterson, *The Gospel of Thomas and Jesus* (Sonoma: Polebridge, 1993); Elaine Pagels, *Beyond Belief*; J. D. Crossan, *Four Other Gospels: Shadows on the Contours of Canon* (New York: Seabury, 1985).

[31] Elliott, *Apocryphal New Testament*, 124.

[32] E.g., John P. Meier, *A Marginal Jew: Rethinking the Historical Jesus*, vol. 1 (New York: Doubleday, 1991), 123–39; Christopher M. Tuckett, "Thomas and the Synoptics," *NovT* 30 (1988): 132–57; Hurtado, *Lord Jesus Christ*, 473–74; Klyne R. Snodgrass, "The Gospel of Thomas: A Secondary Gospel," *SecCent* 7 (1989–1990): 19–38; and Raymond E. Brown, "The Gospel of Thomas and St. John's Gospel," *NTS* 9 (1962–1963): 155–77. More recently, Nicholas Perrin, *Thomas: The Other Gospel*, has suggested that Thomas is dependent on Tatian's *Diatessaron*.

[33] *Gospel of Thomas* 70; Pagels, *Beyond Belief*, 30–73; idem, *The Gnostic Gospels*. On the Gnostic or non-Gnostic nature of this gospel see Robert M. Grant, *The Secret Sayings of Jesus* (Garden City, NY: Doubleday, 1960), 186; A. J. B. Higgins, "The non-Gnostic Sayings in the Gospel of Thomas," *NovT* 4 (1960): 30–47; William K. Grobel, "How Gnostic Is the Gospel of

John Meier notes, this Gnostic tendency also indicates a second-century date for *Thomas*:

> Since a gnostic world view of this sort [in *Thomas*] was not employed to reinterpret Christianity in such a thoroughgoing way before sometime in the second century AD, there can be no question of the *Gospel of Thomas* . . . being a reliable reflection of the historical Jesus or of the earliest sources of 1st-century Christianity.[34]

It is not surprising, then, that *Thomas* is never mentioned in any early canonical list, is not found in any of our New Testament manuscript collections, never figured prominently in canonical discussions, and often was condemned outright by a variety of church fathers. Thus, if *Thomas* does represent authentic, original Christianity, then it has left very little historical evidence of that fact.

The Gospel of Philip

This gospel, like *Thomas*, was also part of the collection of Gnostic literature found at Nag Hammadi in 1945.[35] Whether it should be called a "gospel" at all is questionable due to the fact that it is less a historical narrative of the life and teachings of Jesus and more a theological catechism of sorts, which highlights a variety of Gnostic teachings on the sacraments (and other topics). It, too, contains rather unusual stories and aphorisms, including the idea that Joseph the father of Jesus grew a tree that later provided the cross on which Jesus was hung, and statements such as, "Some say Mary conceived by the Holy Spirit: they are mistaken. . . . When did a female ever conceive by a female?"[36]

As far as its historical credentials are concerned, it is also hard to overemphasize the paucity of evidence in favor of this gospel as representing authentic Christianity. Likely a third-century composition, *Philip* was written long after the time of Jesus and his apostles, shows obvious dependence upon the canonical material, and is clearly designed to promote the strange world

Thomas?" *NTS* 8 (1962): 367–73. For a theory of two versions of Thomas see Gilles Quispel, *Makarius, das Thomasevangelium und das Lied von der Perle* (Leiden: Brill, 1967).
[34]Meier, *Marginal Jew*, 127.
[35]For brief introductions see Hans-Martin Schenke, "The Gospel of Philip," in Wilhelm Schneemelcher, *New Testament Apocrypha*, trans. R. McL. Wilson, vol. 1 (Louisville, KY: Westminster, 1991), 179–87; Wesley W. Isenberg, "The Gospel of Philip," in *The Nag Hammadi Library*, ed. James M. Robinson (San Francisco: Harper Collins, 1990), 139–41; and Layton, *Gnostic Scriptures*, 325–28.
[36]73.8–15; 55.23.

of Gnostic (and likely Valentinian) theology.[37] As already noted above, such theology was clearly a development of the second and third centuries and at odds with the picture of Christianity derived from our earliest sources. We have only a solitary manuscript of *Philip*, compared to thousands of manuscripts of the canonical Gospels, and no evidence it was ever viewed as part of the New Testament collection. It never made it on any New Testament list, nor did it play any role in early canonical discussions. In short, it was roundly rejected as an authentic witness to the original teachings of Jesus and may be among our least reliable apocryphal gospels.

The Gospel of Mary

Although not part of the Nag Hammadi collection, the *Gospel of Mary* is another Gnostic gospel like *Philip* and *Thomas*.[38] Its fragmentary remains reveal that it is composed of two parts: (1) a dialogue between the risen Jesus and his disciples (very similar to other Gnostic texts—e.g., *Sophia of Jesus Christ* and the *Dialogue of the Savior*—that give post-resurrection teachings of Jesus); and (2) a conversation between Mary and the disciples where Mary shares a vision she has received from Jesus, describing a Gnostic view of the "aeons" (similar to the *Apocryphon of John*).[39]

Similar to *Philip*, there are very few reasons (if any) to think that *Mary* is representative of authentic Jesus tradition. It is clearly a second-century composition with no credible claim to be an eyewitness account, has been substantially influenced by the canonical Gospels, and is evidently a further development of traditional canonical material.[40] Tuckett declares, "It seems likely that the *Gospel of Mary* is primarily a witness to the later, developing tradition generated by these [canonical] texts and does not provide independent witness to early Jesus tradition itself."[41] Moreover, the substantial Gnostic theology—theology roundly condemned by the early church—also suggests this gospel is a later development with no connection

---

[37] Isenberg, "Gospel of Philip," 139.

[38] For a brief introduction see Henri-Charles Puech, "The Gospel of Mary," in Wilhelm Schneemelcher, *New Testament Apocrypha*, trans. R. Mcl. Wilson, vol. 1 (Louisville, KY: Westminster, 1991), 391–95; and for a full-length work see Christopher Tuckett, *The Gospel of Mary* (Oxford: Oxford University Press, 2007).

[39] *Gospel of Mary* 17.6.

[40] Tuckett, *Gospel of Mary*, 11–12. Some have made a compelling argument for a date late in the second century: A. Pasquier, "L'eschatologie dans L'Évangile selon Marie," in *Colloque international sur les textes de Nag Hammadi* (Québec, 22–25 août 1978), ed. B. Barc (Québec: Les Presses de L'Université Laval, 1981), 390–404.

[41] Tuckett, *Gospel of Mary*, 74.

to original Christianity.[42] As a result, *Mary* was so removed from the flow of early Christianity that it was never mentioned by *any* church father—not in their discussions of canon, nor even in their discussions of apocryphal gospels. Indeed, we would not have known of the gospel if not for the original manuscript discovery at the end of the nineteenth century.[43] Thus we are hard pressed to think this gospel can compete with the canonical four regarding authentic Jesus tradition.

The Gospel of Nicodemus
We have already seen that the gospels of Thomas, Philip, and Mary offer little hope of providing authentic Jesus tradition. The situation does not improve as we turn to the *Gospel of Nicodemus*.[44] Again, the term "gospel" is rather misleading for this apocryphal book since it is really composed of two other works: the first portion is called "The Acts of Pilate," a legendary and fictional interaction between Jesus and Pontius Pilate, and the second portion is called "The Descent into Hell," which catalogs the activities of Jesus in "hell" between his death and resurrection. The title "Gospel of Nicodemus"—which was not given to this document until the Middle Ages—is likely due to the fact that Nicodemus is supposedly the one who recorded the things contained within it.[45] The composition of *Nicodemus* dates likely to the fifth or sixth century, although some portions may date back to the fourth century.[46] It is filled with clearly embellished stories of Jesus, which Elliott calls "fanciful and legendary."[47] For example, when Jesus enters into the praetorium to be examined by Pilate, one of Pilate's Roman

---

[42]Some in recent years have attempted to challenge the Gnostic content of Mary simply by challenging the viability of Gnosticism in general. See Karen L. King, *What Is Gnosticism?* (Cambridge, MA: Harvard University Press, 2003); and M. A. Williams, *Rethinking 'Gnosticism': An Argument for Dismantling a Dubious Category* (Princeton, NJ: Princeton University Press, 1996). However, this idea has been rejected by B. A. Pearson, "Gnosticism as a Religion," in *Gnosticism and Christianity in Roman and Coptic Egypt* (London: T&T Clark, 2004), 201–23.

[43]Tuckett, *Gospel of Mary*, 3. In addition to the original discovery of the Coptic text, there are also two other Greek manuscripts, P.Oxy. 3525 and P.Ryl. 463, discovered at a later date.

[44]For an introduction see Elliott, *Apocryphal New Testament*, 164–69; and Felix Scheidweiler, "The Gospel of Nicodemus," in Wilhelm Schneemelcher, *New Testament Apocrypha*, trans. R. McL. Wilson, vol. 1 (Louisville, KY: Westminster, 1991), 501–5.

[45]Elliott, *Apocryphal New Testament*, 164.

[46]Although Justin Martyr refers to some account of Pilate and Jesus (*1 Apol.* 35), the scholarly consensus is that it is unlikely the same document as the "Acts of Pilate" found here in Nicodemus. Rather, it seems the "Acts of Pilate" here is a likely response to an anti-Christian Acts of Pilate published in the early fourth century (Eusebius, *Hist. eccl.* 9.5.1). See F. F. Bruce, *The New Testament Documents: Are They Reliable?* (Leicester, UK: Inter-Varsity, 1988), 116–17.

[47]Elliott, *Apocryphal New Testament*, 165.

servants cries out in praise, and even the images on the Roman standards bow down and worship Jesus.

Given the nature and date of this "gospel," we are not surprised to discover it played no role whatsoever in canonical discussions within early Christianity. It is never mentioned as a canonical book, nor does it make it into any canonical list. Indeed, the height of the book's popularity was not until the Middle Ages. Elliott comments, "The Pilate legends became very popular in the Middle Ages and are the inspiration behind many of the legends concerning Joseph of Arimathea, the Holy Grail, and the Harrowing of Hell."[48] Thus there are absolutely no historical reasons to think that this book represents genuine and authentic tradition about Jesus.

Summary

We have seen that these apocryphal epistles and apocryphal gospels simply do not share the historical credentials of the canonical books. With that in mind, lining them up side by side with the canonical materials as historical equals proves to be shockingly unhistorical. It is, in effect, a demand that we reject our *earliest and best* Christian sources—the books of the New Testament—and replace them with *later and secondary* sources like the ones discussed above. It is clear that such a demand is not driven by historical considerations at all but rather by a prior commitment to the Bauer model and a quest to make sure every view is equally "right." At this point, it simply will not do for the advocates of the Bauer thesis to argue that the reason for the lack of historical attestation of these apocryphal writings is that it has been suppressed by the "orthodox" party.[49] This creates an all-too-convenient scenario where the universal patristic witness against these books is simply swept under the rug of "the-winners-write-the-history." Such an approach allows apocryphal material to be entirely immune from historical arguments—the *lack* of evidence in their favor not only ceases to be a problem but can actually be viewed as proof of the Bauer thesis. As the above discussion shows, apart from the lack of historical attestation of these works, the contents speak for themselves, and the quality of material falls dramatically short of the standard set by the canonical Gospels.

---

[48]Ibid.

[49]Ehrman says as much when he declares that "the victorious party *rewrote* the history of the controversy making it appear that there had not been much of a conflict at all" (*Lost Christianities*, 4; emphasis added).

The Closing of the Canon in Early Christianity

As noted above, supporters of the Bauer thesis are fond of claiming that the canon was not "closed" until well into the fourth century, implying that the canon was "open"—wide open—before the fourth century, with no concern to draw boundaries, limits, or restrictions. Geoffrey Hahneman declares, "Not until the fourth century did the church appear to define and restrict that New Testament collection."[50] Such a conception of an "open" canon is central to the Bauer thesis because it suggests that it was not until the orthodox exerted political pressure that the canon was finally limited in some fashion.

However, this understanding of the closing of the canon proves to be rather one-dimensional. Although there were still discussions and disagreements about some books even into the fourth century, it is a mischaracterization to suggest the early Christians had no concern to limit and restrict the canon prior to this time period. Thus, we need a broader conception of what is meant by a "closed" canon.

The Definition of "Closed"

In the midst of modern scholarly discussions on canon, little attention is given to what is meant by the idea of a "closed" canon. Although the term is most commonly used to refer to fourth-century ecclesiastical decisions, there is a real sense in which the canon, in principle, was "closed" long before that time. In the Muratorian Fragment of the second century, the very popular *Shepherd of Hermas* is mentioned as a book that can be read by the church but is rejected as canonical. The grounds for this rejection are due to the fact that it was written "very recently, in our own times."[51] In other words, the author of the fragment reflects the conviction that early Christians were not willing to accept books written in the second century or later but had restricted themselves to books from the apostolic time period.[52] They seemed to have understood that the apostolic phase of redemptive history was uniquely the time when canonical books were produced.

Thus, from this perspective, the canon was "closed" by the beginning of the second century. After this time (and long before Athanasius), the

---

[50]Hahneman, *Muratorian Fragment*, 129.

[51]Muratorian Canon 74. The meaning of this phrase has recently been disputed by Hahneman, *Muratorian Fragment*, 34–72. But see the compelling response by Charles E. Hill, "The Debate over the Muratorian Fragment and the Development of the Canon," 437–52.

[52]Bruce, *Canon of Scripture*, 166. It is noteworthy that Tertullian also rejects the *Shepherd of Hermas* on very similar grounds, calling it "apocryphal and false" (*Pud.* 10).

church was not "open" to more books, but instead was engaged in discussions about which books God had *already given*. In other words, due to the theological convictions of early Christians about the foundational role of the apostles, there was a built-in sense that the canon was "closed" after the apostolic time period had ended. It is precisely for this reason that books produced at later points in the history of the church, such as the *Shepherd of Hermas* (or the *Letter to Flora* or the *Gospel of Nicodemus*) never had a genuine chance to be considered canonical. They were nonstarters from the very outset. Ridderbos comments:

> When understood in terms of the history of redemption, the canon cannot be open; in principle it must be closed. That follows directly from the unique and exclusive nature of the power the apostles received from Christ and from the commission he gave them to be witnesses to what they had seen and heard of the salvation he had brought. The result of this power and commission is the foundation of the church and the creation of the canon, and therefore these are naturally unrepeatable and exclusive in character.[53]

This understanding of a "closed" canon is an essential corrective to much of canonical studies today. Images of early Christianity as a wide-open contest between books of every kind and from every place—a primitive writing competition of sorts—simply does not square with the convictions of early believers. In their understanding, there was something inherently closed about the canon from the very beginning, even in the midst of ongoing discussions. And this fact reveals that long before the fourth century there was a fundamental trend toward limitation and restriction, not invitation and expansion.

In the end, one's definition of "closed" depends on whether one views the canon from a merely *human* perspective (whatever is finally decided by the fourth-century Christians) or from a *divine* perspective (books that God gave to his people during the apostolic time period). By myopically focusing only on the human element, the Bauer thesis cannot allow a "closed" canon, in any sense, until the fourth century.

Attitudes toward Limiting the Canon

If we are correct that Christians had such a theological category of a "closed" canon prior to fourth-century ecclesiastical declarations, then,

---

[53]Herman N. Ridderbos, *Redemptive History and the New Testament Scriptures* (Phillipsburg, NJ: P&R, 1988), 25.

contrary to Hahneman's above-cited statement, we should see further evidence, beyond the Muratorian Fragment, that Christians sought to limit and restrict the canon in various ways prior to that time period. In fact, we do see evidence for such a trend, although we can only mention a sampling of it here.

Irenaeus

As noted above, Irenaeus in the late second century did not have an "open" canon with no concern to draw limits or boundaries. At least as it pertains to the four Gospels, he was keen to draw very firm lines: "It is not possible that the gospels can be either more or fewer than the number they are."[54] For Irenaeus, the gospel canon was "closed." His unwillingness to consider newly produced gospels as potentially part of the canon was not an innovation he foisted on the church, but likely represents a trend amongst second-century Christians that long preceded him.[55] Of course, one could suggest that Irenaeus, and other early Christians, may have *mistakenly* considered some books as originating from the apostolic time period, when in fact they did not. However, aside from the fact that Irenaeus was unlikely to be duped by a recent forgery (after all, it was the historical pedigree of the canonical Gospels that was so compelling), this objection misses the point. Regardless of whether Irenaeus *correctly* limited the canon, the noteworthy point here is that he *did* limit the canon and thus reveals that such attitudes of limitation and restriction were not reserved for the fourth century.

Origen

Despite the claims of some that Athanasius in the fourth century is the first to list all twenty-seven books of the New Testament, Origen, in the early third century, lists the New Testament books in one of his homilies and seems to include all twenty-seven of them.[56] Although Origen acknowledges elsewhere in his writings that some have expressed doubts about some of these books,[57] he seems confident enough in the list to mention it in a sermon to those ordinary churchgoers in the pew.[58] Moreover, he gives no indication in his homily that the contents of his list would have been regarded as

---

[54]*Haer.* 3.11.8.

[55]Stanton, "The Fourfold Gospel," 317–46.

[56]*Hom. in Jos.* 7.1. See discussion in Metzger, *Canon of the New Testament*, 39.

[57]Eusebius, *Hist. Eccl.* 6.25.3–14. Some have even suggested the text in Origen has been altered, though there is no certainty this is the case; see Lee M. McDonald, *The Formation of the Christian Biblical Canon* (Peabody, MA: Hendrickson, 1995), 110.

[58]See the discussion in Metzger, *Canon of the New Testament*, 140.

controversial or unexpected to his hearers. Regardless of whether Origen was overconfident in his assessment of the canon's boundaries, he reveals a profound degree of comfort with such boundaries at quite an early time period.

Dionysius of Corinth

Dionysius was the bishop of Corinth and as such wrote a number of letters to the churches under his care. Around the middle of the second century, he goes to great lengths to distinguish his letters from the "Scriptures of the Lord," lest anyone think he was writing new canonical books. He even refers to his own letters as "inferior."[59] Such a distinction makes it clear that at least in the eyes of this bishop, the Scriptures were a "closed" entity and no new letters would be eligible for addition—even those written by a bishop. Moreover, the term "Scriptures of the Lord" is noteworthy here, suggesting a distinguishable body of writings about the Lord Jesus Christ, separate from the Old Testament books.[60] Although Dionysius does not enumerate which books he includes in the "Scriptures of the Lord," he mentions these in a manner that assumes his readers would readily know the books to which he was referring. Such a casual reference to this collection of books suggests that by the middle of the second century there was a collection of New Testament Scriptures that would have been not only broadly recognized but also (in principle) closed, at least in the eyes of many, to new literary productions.

Gaius

Eusebius records a debate that occurred at the beginning of the third century between a certain Gaius from Rome and Montanist heretics.[61] The debate with the Montanists had very much to do with the development of the canon, since their claim to receive ongoing "revelations" from God suggested the possibility of new canonical books. Eusebius mentions that Gaius affirmed a thirteen-letter collection of Paul—the same number affirmed by the Muratorian Canon—and that Gaius chided his Montanist opponents

---

[59]Eusebius, *Hist. eccl.* 4.23.12.

[60]Hill, "Debate over the Muratorian Fragment," 450. Curiously, Bart D. Ehrman, *The Orthodox Corruption of Scripture* (New York: Oxford University Press, 1993), uses this reference to Dionysius to argue that scribes (whether heretical or orthodox) were changing the text of the New Testament, showing that he, at least, views "Scriptures of the Lord" as referring to New Testament writings (p. 26).

[61]For further discussion on Gaius, the Montanists, and John's writings, see Charles E. Hill, *The Johannine Corpus in the Early Church* (Oxford: Oxford University Press, 2004), 172–204.

for their "recklessness and audacity . . . in composing new Scriptures."[62] Not only is it noteworthy here that Gaius has drawn up a "closed" list of Pauline letters but at least as remarkable is the fact that he proceeds to register his opposition to *anyone* producing new scriptural books. Why, if the Bauer advocates are correct that the canon was wide open at this juncture, would Gaius be so upset at the production of more books? It seems that Gaius did not have an "open" canon at all but is yet another example of how early Christians viewed the canon, in principle, as closed.

Summary

The above examples are merely a sampling of pre-fourth-century attitudes toward the extent of the canon. They reveal that the early stages of the canon were not a wide-open affair, where newly produced apocryphal literature could easily have found a welcome home, but were marked by concern only to affirm books from the apostolic time period. We should not be surprised, therefore, by this obvious but often overlooked fact: *the very books eventually affirmed by early Christians are those which the majority of modern scholars would agree derive from the apostolic time period; and those books rejected by early Christians are the ones the majority of modern scholars agree are late and secondary.* It appears that the early Christians were quite perceptive after all as to which books represented authentic Christianity and which did not.

Conclusion

It has been the goal of this chapter to deal with the question of the boundaries of the New Testament canon and the challenges presented by the abundance and variety of apocryphal literature within early Christianity. Although one chapter is not adequate to cover such an enormous topic, clarity about a number of important topics has emerged.

First, the sheer existence of diversity within early Christianity—the favorite topic of the Bauer adherents—does not itself constitute an argument against the possibility that an authentic version of Christianity did exist and can be known. Only if one enters the historical investigations with a commitment to diversity at all costs can such a conclusion be reached.

---

[62]*Hist. eccl.* 6.20.3. Gaius is well known for his rejection of John's Gospel, though doubts have been raised about the certainty of that fact (Hill, *Johannine Corpus*, 172–204). Nevertheless, even if Gaius rejected John's Gospel, this would not change the point being made here. Whether Gaius was correct in his limitations of the canon does not change the fact that he understood there to be limitations to the canon, and at quite an early date.

Second, despite the claim that apocryphal writings should be viewed as coequals with (or even superior to) the canonical books, the historical realities suggest otherwise. Taking a cue from Ehrman's own list, we examined the letters of Ptolemy and Barnabas, and the gospels of Thomas, Philip, Mary, and Nicodemus, concluding that all of these are post-canonical productions (some even dating into the Middle Ages) and often show dependence on the canonical materials.

Third, over against claims that the canon was "open" to all sorts of writings until the fourth century and beyond, we argued that the theological convictions of early Christians pointed toward a canon that was restricted to books from the apostolic time period and thus, in principle, "closed" at the very outset.

In the end, we have no reason to think that the plethora of apocryphal literature in early Christianity threatened the integrity of the New Testament canon. The historical evidence suggests that under the guidance of God's providential hand and through the work of the Holy Spirit, early Christians rightly recognized these twenty-seven books as the books that had been given to them as the final and authoritative deposit of the Christian faith.

PART 3

CHANGING THE STORY

Manuscripts, Scribes, and Textual Transmission

7

Keepers of the Text

How Were Texts Copied and Circulated in the Ancient World?

Thus far in our study we have examined the nature of Walter Bauer's model of heresy and orthodoxy and how it has impacted scholarly approaches to the development of the New Testament canon. As we now enter into the third and final section of the book, we see that Bauer's model is more far-reaching than we may have ever realized, even impacting the way some scholars view the *transmission* of the New Testament text. If early Christianity was a veritable battleground of competing theological positions—none of which had any more claim to originality than any other—then surely, it is argued, this battleground would also have affected the way these texts were copied. After all, early Christian scribes were not automatons, slavishly and mechanically copying texts while immune to the debates over heresy and orthodoxy raging all around them. Would not scribes, in the cause of battling "heretics" and defending truth, have been willing to change a difficult text to make it "say" what it was already thought to "mean"? Could the diversity evident in early Christianity be visible even in the type of textual changes that we see in our manuscripts?

179

Indeed, this is the very argument made by Bart Ehrman in his book *The Orthodox Corruption of Scripture*.[1] Armed with Bauer's hypothesis, Ehrman argues that these conflicts between heresy and orthodoxy led early Christian scribes to intentionally change the text to fit their own theological agenda. Thus, we see the effects of the Bauer thesis spreading into new territory, now challenging the integrity and reliability of the New Testament text itself. No longer does the Bauer thesis merely challenge Christianity by asking, "How do you know you have the right *books*?" It now challenges Christianity even more fundamentally by asking, "How do you know you have the right *text*?"

Now, it needs to be noted at the outset that issues related to the transmission of the New Testament text are notoriously complex, especially when they are covered within a brief amount of space as we are trying to do here. So, it is helpful if we divide the question into two parts. First, we need to ask whether there was an adequate scribal infrastructure within early Christianity to give us reason to think the New Testament text could have been passed down accurately. Who were the people who copied early Christian writings? And what sort of network existed for such writings to be "published" and disseminated throughout the Mediterranean world? In other words, was the *process* of book production amongst early Christians something that would produce reliable copies? This first set of questions will be the subject of the present chapter. Second, we need to ask about the quality of the manuscripts in our possession. How different are they? Do the textual variations they contain call into question their reliability? And did scribes intentionally change the text for theological reasons? Put differently, we not only want to examine the process of early Christian copying but also the *outcome* of early Christian copying—that is, we want to examine the state of the text handed down to us. This second set of questions will be taken up in the following chapter.

The Bookish Nature of Early Christianity

At its core, early Christianity was a religion concerned with books. From the very beginning, Christians were committed to the books of the Hebrew Scriptures and saw them as paradigmatic for understanding the life and ministry of Jesus of Nazareth. The apostle Paul was so immersed in the Old Testament writings that he even conceived of the resurrection of Jesus

---

[1]Bart D. Ehrman, *The Orthodox Corruption of Scripture* (New York: Oxford University Press, 1993).

as "in accordance with the Scriptures" (1 Cor. 15:3–4).[2] The Pauline use of
books (particularly Old Testament books) in the course of his ministry is
borne out by passages such as 2 Timothy 4:13 where Timothy is urged to
"bring . . . the books, and above all the parchments."[3] Moreover, Gospel
accounts such as those of Matthew and John, as well as books such as
James and Hebrews, exhibit similar indebtedness to the Old Testament,
often citing from it directly and extensively. Such intimate connections
between the earliest Christian movement and the Old Testament writings
led Harry Gamble to declare, "Indeed it is almost impossible to imagine
an early Christianity that was not constructed upon the foundations of
Jewish Scripture."[4]

Of course, it was not only the Old Testament books that mattered to
early Christianity. At a very early point, Christians also began to produce
their own writings—gospels, letters, sermons, prophetic literature, and
more—some of which eventually began to be viewed as (and used as)
Scripture.[5] Indeed, Christianity was distinguished from the surrounding
religions in the Greco-Roman world precisely by its prolific production
of literature and its commitment to an authoritative body of Scripture as

[2]For more on Paul and the Old Testament see Richard B. Hays, *Echoes of Scripture in the Letters of Paul* (New Haven, CT: Yale, 1989); and Francis Watson, *Paul and the Hermeneutics of Faith* (London: T&T Clark, 2004).

[3]See discussion in T. C. Skeat, "'Especially the Parchments': A Note on 2 Timothy iv.13," *JTS* 30 (1979): 173–77.

[4]Harry Gamble, "Literacy, Liturgy, and the Shaping of the New Testament Canon," in *The Earliest Gospels*, ed. Charles Horton (London: T&T Clark, 2004), 28. A fuller discussion of the origins of the Old Testament canon can be found in Roger T. Beckwith, *The Old Testament Canon of the New Testament Church, and Its Background in Early Judaism* (Grand Rapids: Eerdmans, 1986); and more recently in Lee Martin McDonald and James A. Sanders, eds., *The Canon Debate* (Peabody, MA: Hendrickson, 2002), 21–263.

[5]Some have argued that Christianity was primarily an oral religion at the beginning with little interest in texts until a much later time; e.g., Helmut Koester, "Written Gospels or Oral Tradition?" *JBL* 113 (1994): 293–97; Werner Kelber, *The Oral and Written Gospel: The Hermeneutics of Speaking and Writing in the Synoptic Tradition, Mark, Paul, and Q* (Philadelphia: Fortress, 1983). However, there is no need to consider the oral and written modes of Christianity as mutually exclusive. See helpful discussions on this point in Harry Y. Gamble, *Books and Readers in the Early Church* (New Haven, CT: Yale University Press, 1995), 28–32; Graham Stanton, "Form Criticism Revisited," in *What about the New Testament?* ed. Morna D. Hooker and Colin J. A. Hickling (London: SCM, 1975), 13–27; Graham Stanton, "The Fourfold Gospel," *NTS* 43 (1997): 317–46, esp. 340; Loveday Alexander, "The Living Voice: Skepticism toward the Written Word in Early Christian and Graeco-Roman Texts," in *The Bible in Three Dimensions*, ed. D. J. A. Clines, S. E. Fowl, and S. E. Porter (Sheffield: JSOT, 1990), 221–47; and Richard Bauckham, *Jesus and the Eyewitnesses: The Gospels as Eyewitness Testimony* (Grand Rapids: Eerdmans, 2006), esp. chaps. 2, 10, and 11.

its foundation.[6] As noted above, even by the end of the second century, a core collection of "New Testament" books was functioning as Scripture within early Christianity and was being read in public worship alongside the Old Testament writings.[7] So prominent were these scriptural books for Christians that even their pagan critics noted the Christian predilection for writing (and using) books and thus were forced to reckon with these books in their anti-Christian attacks.[8] All of these factors indicate that the emerging Christian movement, like its Jewish counterpart, would be defined and shaped for generations to come by the same means: the production and use of books.

The fact that Christianity was so fundamentally shaped by a vivid textual culture allows us to anticipate that early Christians would have been capable of establishing a reliable means to copy and disseminate these texts. Part of being a "bookish" movement is to understand how books were produced, transmitted, and circulated in the ancient world. Indeed, Loveday Alexander notes:

> It is clear that we are dealing with a group [early Christians] that used books intensively and professionally from very early on in its existence. The evidence of the papyri from the second century onwards suggests . . . the early development of a technically sophisticated and distinctive book technology.[9]

However, despite the assessment of scholars such as Alexander, Ehrman insists that we should *not* believe Christians could reliably transmit their

---

[6]William V. Harris, *Ancient Literacy* (Cambridge, MA: Harvard University Press, 1989); A. K. Bowman and G. Wolf, eds., *Literacy and Power in the Ancient World* (Cambridge: Cambridge University Press, 1994).

[7]Justin Martyr, *1 Apol.* 67.3; John Barton, *The Spirit and the Letter: Studies in the Biblical Canon* (London: SPCK, 1997), 18; Bruce M. Metzger, *The Canon of the New Testament: Its Origin, Development, and Significance* (Oxford: Clarendon, 1987), 254.

[8]Lucian, *Peregr.* 11–12; Origen, *Cels.* 1.34–40; A. Meredith, "Porphyry and Julian against the Christians," *ANRW* II.23.2 (1980): 1119–49. For more on pagan critiques of Christianity see the helpful overview in Wayne C. Kannaday, *Apologetic Discourse and the Scribal Tradition: Evidence of the Influence of Apologetic Interests on the Text of the Canonical Gospels* (Atlanta: Society of Biblical Literature, 2004), 24–57; Stephen Benko, "Pagan Criticism of Christianity during the First Two Centuries A.D.," *ANRW* II.23.2 (1980): 1055–118; Robert L. Wilken, *Christians as the Romans Saw Them* (New Haven, CT: Yale University Press, 1984); and Robert L. Wilken, "Pagan Criticism of Christianity: Greek Religions and Christian Faith," in *Early Christian Literature and the Classical Intellectual Tradition: In Honorem Robert M. Grant*, ed. William R. Schoedel and Robert L. Wilken (Paris: Editions Beauchesne, 1979), 117–34.

[9]Loveday Alexander, "Ancient Book Production and the Circulation of the Gospels," in *The Gospels for All Christians: Rethinking the Gospel Audiences*, ed. Richard Bauckham (Grand Rapids: Eerdmans, 1998), 71–111.

writings because, at the very least, Christians were decidedly less educated and illiterate than the broader Greco-Roman world around them.[10] He appeals not only to the oft-cited passage from Acts 4:13 where Peter and John are referred to as "uneducated" (*agrammatoi*) but also appeals to the writings of the pagan critic Celsus who accused early Christians of being "ignorant lower-class people."[11] Thus, Ehrman declares, "Christians came from the ranks of the illiterate."[12]

So, what are we to make of these claims concerning the nature of the early Christian movement? A number of factors warrant closer examination.

First, it is important to note from the outset that the literacy rate in the broader Greco-Roman world during the first century was only about 10–15 percent of the population.[13] So, in this sense, most people in the ancient world (Christian *and* non-Christian) were illiterate. Gamble notes, "We must assume, then, that the large majority of Christians in the early centuries of the church were illiterate, not because they were unique but because they were in this respect typical."[14] Thus, the fact that most Christians were illiterate is not at all unusual and certainly not grounds for being suspicious of whether they really placed a high value on texts. Contrary to the assumptions of our modern Western mindset, it was possible for groups, such as early Christians, to be largely illiterate and yet still have quite a sophisticated textual culture. The majority of Christians would have been exposed regularly to texts through public readings and recitations, teaching and preaching, and intensive catechetical instruction.[15] Thus illiteracy was not a barrier to being immersed in Christian writings.

Second, closely connected to the issue of literacy is the issue of social class. Ehrman argues that Christians must have been more illiterate because they were predominantly composed of lower-class people. However, the idea that early Christianity is primarily composed of the destitute "proletariat" of the Roman Empire has been rejected by scholars for many years.[16] More

[10]Bart D. Ehrman, *Misquoting Jesus: The Story Behind Who Changed the Bible and Why* (San Francisco: Harper Collins, 2005), 39–41.
[11]Ibid., 40.
[12]Ibid., 39.
[13]The standard work on literacy in the ancient world is Harris, *Ancient Literacy*. Although Harris is generally accepted amongst scholars, a helpful supplement can be found in Alan Millard, *Reading and Writing in the Time of Jesus* (New York: New York University Press, 2000).
[14]Gamble, *Books and Readers*, 6.
[15]2 Cor. 10:9; Col. 4:16; 1 Thess. 5:27; 1 Tim. 3:13; Justin Martyr, *1 Apol.* 67.3.
[16]Older studies arguing that Christianity was primarily a lower-class religion include Adolf Deissmann, *Light from the Ancient East*, trans. Lionel R. M. Strachan (New York: George H.

recent studies have shown that the social makeup of early Christianity was not substantially different from the surrounding culture and covered a typical cross-section of society.[17] Meeks declares, "The social level of Paul and at least some members of his congregations was a good bit higher than has commonly been assumed."[18] Gamble adds, "The most typical members of the Christian groups . . . had attained a measure of affluence, owned houses and slaves, had the resources to travel, and were socially mobile."[19] Thus, Ehrman's claim that the earliest followers of Jesus were "simple peasants" stands in direct contrast to the consensus of modern scholarship.[20] What is more, beyond this fact, one cannot assume that literacy was always directly correlated with social status, as Ehrman has erroneously done. Indeed, most notably, ancient scribes themselves were most often found among slaves—who had no physical possessions at all—or among the lower or middle class.[21] Members of the wealthy upper class would often not read or write themselves (even though they may have had the ability), but would employ lower-class slaves or scribes to do it for them.[22]

Third, even more to the point, it is clear that a number of early Christians—particularly the leaders—were very capable readers and writers of texts. This fact is borne out by the nature of our earliest Christian writings, the New Testament documents themselves. Not only are they clearly written by authors who were literate, and written to congregations that were literate enough to have the books publicly read and copied, but they show a remarkable engagement with *earlier written texts*, namely the Jewish Scriptures. Thus, our most primitive Christian traditions reveal that the earliest stages of the faith were decidedly oriented to literary and textual matters as Christians

Doran, 1927); and Karl Kautsky, *Foundations of Christianity* (New York: International Publishers, 1925).

[17]Wayne A. Meeks, *The First Urban Christians: The Social World of the Apostle Paul* (New Haven, CT: Yale University Press, 1983); Abraham J. Malherbe, *Social Aspects of Early Christianity* (Philadelphia: Fortress, 1983); E. A. Judge, *The Social Pattern of Christian Groups in the First Century* (London: Tyndale, 1960); Robert M. Grant, *Early Christianity and Society: Seven Studies* (New York: Harper & Row, 1977); and Floyd V. Filson, "The Significance of the Early House Churches," *JBL* 58 (1939): 109–12.

[18]Meeks, *First Urban Christians*, 52.

[19]Gamble, *Books and Readers*, 5.

[20]Ehrman, *Misquoting Jesus*, 39. In fact, in contrast to Ehrman's claim regarding the earliest Christians being "simple peasants," Meeks flatly declares that "there is also no specific evidence of people [in early Christianity] who are destitute . . . the poorest of the poor, peasants" (*First Urban Christians*, 73).

[21]Kim Haines-Eitzen, *Guardians of Letters: Literacy, Power, and the Transmitters of Early Christian Literature* (Oxford: Oxford University Press, 2000), 7.

[22]Ibid.

studied, interpreted, and applied Old Testament passages. Gamble comments, "From the beginning Christianity was deeply engaged in the interpretation and appropriation of texts. That activity presupposed not only a mature literacy but also *sophisticated scribal and exegetical skills.*"[23]

Fourth, in light of early Christianity's proficiency in textual study, Ehrman's appeal to Acts 4:13 seems less than compelling. The context of this passage suggests that the Greek term *agrammatoi* is best translated not as "illiterate" but simply as "uneducated"—that is, in respect to formal rabbinical training.[24] Peter and John were before the Jewish council, composed of formally trained priests and scribes (Acts 4:5), and the court was impressed that these two men could engage so forcefully in theological debates even though they were just commoners. When the reader notes that Acts 4:5 uses the term *grammateis* ("scribes") to describe the Jewish council, it is clear that there is a contrast being made when the council describes Peter and John with a term that is nearly its opposite: *agrammatoi*. The contrast is not about who is literate or illiterate in the formal sense of the terms, but about who has rabbinic training in the Scriptures and who is a mere layman. Given the fact that Peter and John grew up as Jews, we would expect they would have had some basic education as would have been common for Jewish boys.[25] Even Jesus was considered uneducated (John 7:15) but yet was able to step into the synagogue and read from the scroll, apparently with a substantial degree of proficiency (Luke 4:17–20). Moreover, Peter and John were certainly not "poor" in any manner that would have prevented their learning to read and write; they owned what seemed to be several boats (Luke 5:2, 7) and John's father even had numerous hired men (Mark 1:20).

Fifth, as for the derogatory comments about Christians from the pagan critic Celsus, it is difficult to believe that these should be received an accurate representation of the state of early Christianity. Elsewhere, Ehrman is eager to chide early Christian writers for misrepresenting their heterodox opponents as being perverse and morally corrupt, but, at the same time, he seems entirely unconcerned that Celsus might be misrepresenting his opponents.[26] Even though Celsus regularly overstates his case with sensationalistic language—according to him, all Christians are "ignorant,"

---

[23]Gamble, *Books and Readers*, 27 (emphasis added).

[24]F. F. Bruce, *The Book of the Acts* (Grand Rapids: Eerdmans, 1988), 95.

[25]Philo, *Legat.* 210; Josephus, *C. Ap.* 2.178; see discussion in Millard, *Reading and Writing in the Time of Jesus*, 157–58.

[26]Bart D. Ehrman, *Lost Christianities: The Battles for Scripture and the Faiths We Never Knew* (New York: Oxford University Press, 2002), 197–202.

"stupid," "bucolic yokels"—apparently Ehrman wants us to take his words at face value.[27] Although Origen acknowledges in his reply to Celsus that "some" Christians were uneducated,[28] this should not be regarded as some embarrassing concession, because large portions of *all* of society were uneducated. Since Christianity represented a typical cross-section of society, this should hardly come as a surprise. At the same time, Origen also argues that some Christians *are* educated, wise, and able to teach.[29] Thus, Origen's counterpoint against Celsus is a simple one: Christianity is not restricted to the elite of society but is composed of *both* educated and uneducated.

In the end, the consensus of scholarship is clear. We have little reason to think that early Christianity was a movement of illiterate peasants that would have been unable to reliably transmit their own writings. Instead, Christianity was a movement that was economically and socially average—representing a variety of different classes—and had a relatively sophisticated literary culture that was committed from its earliest days to the texts of the Jewish scripture as it sought to produce and copy texts of its own.

The Scribal Infrastructure of Early Christianity

Now that we have an appreciation for the "bookish" nature of early Christianity, we shift our attention to whether Christians possessed an infrastructure that allowed them to reliably copy and transmit these books. Who copied Christian writings in the earliest centuries? And what indications do we have of the level of organization and sophistication amongst these Christian scribes? To these questions we now turn.

Christian Scribes

We have very little direct testimony about the scribes who copied Christian texts in the earliest centuries (second and third) of the Christian movement.[30] Thus, our primary evidence regarding the capability and

---

[27] *Cels.* 3.44, 56.

[28] Ibid., 3.44.

[29] Ibid., 3.48.

[30] Haines-Eitzen, *Guardians of Letters*, 68. For other general works on scribes in the ancient world see E. Randolph Richards, *The Secretary in the Letters of Paul* (Tübingen: Mohr, 1991); L. D. Reynolds and N. G. Wilson, *Scribes and Scholars: A Guide to the Transmission of Greek and Latin Literature* (Oxford: Clarendon, 1968); Elaine Fantham, *Roman Literary Culture from Cicero to Apuleius* (Baltimore, MD: Johns Hopkins University Press, 1996); E. G. Turner, "Scribes and Scholars," in *Oxyrhynchus: A City and Its Texts*, ed. A. K. Bowman et al. (London: Egypt Exploration Society, 2007), 256–61; E. G. Turner, "Roman Oxyrhynchus," *JEA* 38 (1952): 78–93; Peter Parsons, "Copyists of Oxyrhynchus," in *Oxyrhynchus: A City and*

training of early Christian scribes comes from the New Testament manuscripts themselves. In the ancient world, there were two distinctive styles of handwriting. *Bookhand* refers to the style of writing that was more formal and elegant and typically used to produce literary works such as the writings of Aristotle, Herodotus, and Plutarch. The other style is known as *documentary hand* and was a more informal, rapidly written script used for ordinary documents such as letters, bills of sale, contracts, and other legal documents. The earliest Christian papyri (second and third centuries) were characterized by a style of handwriting that was somewhat of a mix of these two. Although this style did not share the elegance and artistry of the typical literary script, it was not as rough and rapidly written as most documentary papyri. It was marked by a more plain hand that could be called "informal uncial" or even "reformed documentary."[31] The practical and no-frills hand of early Christian scribes simply "suggests an interest in the *content* of the text that is more or less indifferent to its appearance."[32]

However, lest one construe the early stages of Christian handwriting as unprofessional, Roberts is quick to point out that "a degree of regularity and clarity is aimed at and achieved."[33] Although early Christian papyri certainly exhibit a mix of literary and documentary features, Haines-Eitzen acknowledges that early Christian papyri "appear toward the literary end

---

Its Texts, 262–70; and William A. Johnson, *Bookrolls and Scribes in Oxyrhynchus* (Toronto: University of Toronto Press, 2004).

[31]Colin H. Roberts, *Manuscript, Society and Belief in Early Christian Egypt: The Schweich Lectures of the British Academy 1977* (London: Oxford University Press, 1979), 14. It is important to note that some literary papyri of classical works were also written in a rather plain, unadorned, and non-calligraphic hand (e.g., P.Oxy. 1809, 2076, 2288). However, E. G. Turner does not necessarily consider this as an indication of low scribal quality; indeed, he declares that "'calligraphic' hands are suspect. . . . It is not uncommon for the finest looking hands to be marred by gross carelessness in transcription" ("Scribes and Scholars," 258–59).

[32]Gamble, *Books and Readers*, 71 (emphasis added). William Johnson points out that much of the elegance of the literary manuscripts in the Greco-Roman world was due to the fact that "the literary roll exemplifies high culture not just in the demonstration that the owner is 'literate' and educated, but by means of aesthetics the bookroll also points to the refinement of the owner. . . . In ancient society, that reading was largely an elitist phenomenon was accepted as a matter of course" ("Towards a Sociology of Reading in Classical Antiquity," *AJP* 121 [2000]: 613, 615). It is possible, then, that early Christians, concerned not with establishing their own elite status but reaching to the common man, would have (initially) constructed their manuscripts not as objects of art or indicators of status, but in a manner primarily concerned with content and accessibility.

[33]Roberts, *Manuscript*, 14.

of the spectrum."[34] Moreover, the fact that a number of early Christian manuscripts contained an impressive amount of punctuation and readers' aids—which are rare even in literary papyri—suggests that early Christian scribes were more in tune with professional book production than often realized. In addition, it cannot be overlooked that many early Christian texts do exhibit a more refined hand and literary style, such as a late second-/early third-century text of Irenaeus's *Against Heresies* (P.Oxy. 405), which has a "handsome professional hand,"[35] a late second-century text of Matthew (P.Oxy. 2683), which has an "elegant hand,"[36] a late second-century copy of Paul's epistles ($\mathfrak{P}^{46}$), which has a hand with "style and elegance,"[37] a late second-early third-century copy of Luke and Matthew ($\mathfrak{P}^{4}$-$\mathfrak{P}^{64}$-$\mathfrak{P}^{67}$), which has a "handsome script" that is "incontrovertibly literary in style,"[38] and a late second-century copy of John ($\mathfrak{P}^{66}$), which has calligraphy of "such high quality" that it may "indicate the work of a scriptorium."[39] By the fourth century and beyond, this more refined bookhand had become the norm for Christian texts.

Now, what does the handwriting of these early Christian manuscripts tell us about the scribes that produced them? It appears that the earliest Christian scribes were not necessarily trained solely in the art of copying literary texts (though some Christian scribes were), but were often "multifunctional scribes" who were used to copying *both* documentary and literary texts.[40] These were professional scribes to be sure—meaning this

---

[34]Haines-Eitzen, *Guardians of Letters*, 65. The general distinction between "literary" and "documentary" papyri has come under criticism as some scholars have challenged the sharp dichotomy that is often drawn between the two. For more on this point see E. G. Turner, *Greek Papyri: An Introduction* (Oxford: Clarendon Press, 1968), vi–vii; Roger A. Pack, *The Greek and Latin Literary Texts from Greco-Roman Egypt*, 2d ed. (Ann Arbor, MI: University of Michigan Press, 1967), 1; and Eldon Jay Epp, "New Testament Papyrus Manuscripts and Letter Carrying in Greco-Roman Times," in *The Future of Early Christianity: Essays in Honor of Helmut Koester*, ed. B. A. Pearson et al. (Minneapolis: Fortress, 1991), 39–40.

[35]E.g., P.Mich. 130 (*Shepherd of Hermas*; third century) and P.Ryl. 1.1 (Deuteronomy; third/fourth century) contain a surprising number of accents and other lectional aids. Such features indicated that many early Christian books were written for public reading; for more on this see Gamble, *Books and Readers*, 203–30, and Roberts, *Manuscript*, 23.

[36]Ibid.

[37]F. G. Kenyon, *The Chester Beatty Biblical Papyri: Descriptions and Texts of Twelve Manuscripts on Papyrus of the Greek Bible* (London: Emery Walker, 1933–37), vol. 3/1, ix.

[38]Roberts, *Manuscript*, 23. For a discussion on dating these fragments see T. C. Skeat, "The Oldest Manuscript of the Four Gospels?" *NTS* 43 (1997): 26–31.

[39]Gordon D. Fee, *Papyrus Bodmer II ($\mathfrak{P}^{66}$): Its Textual Relationships and Scribal Characteristics* (Salt Lake City, UT: University of Utah Press, 1968), 82 n.20.

[40]Haines-Eitzen, *Guardians of Letters*, 39. We have evidence from practice exercises preserved on Greco-Roman papyri that a single scribe was often capable of writing in very contrasting

was the occupation in which they were primarily engaged—and most knew their craft well, but they typically would not have been literary copyists who were employed in the commercial book trade.[41] Instead, it appears these early Christian scribes were often the type that were employed privately by individuals who may have varying needs, such as taking letters by dictation, producing administrative documents, or the copying of letters or formal literary pieces.

Such multifunctional (and largely private) scribes were common in the Greco-Roman world and their names were often expressly mentioned by their employers.[42] One of the earliest Christian instances of such a scribe can be seen in Paul's use of an amanuensis (secretary), Tertius, who also is identified by name in Romans 16:22: "I Tertius, who wrote this letter, greet you all in the Lord."[43] Thus, there are reasons to think Christians would have had ready access to professional scribal assistance, either by way of hiring scribes to do work, by using slaves who were scribes and owned by well-to-do Christians, or by using scribes who had converted to Christianity and were willing to provide secretarial assistance. Haines-Eitzen observes, "There is no reason to suppose that literate Christians who wished for copies of literature had substantially different resources from those of other literate folk in the empire."[44] As for whether private (as opposed to commercial) copying would necessitate a drop in quality, Gamble declares, "There is no reason to think that commercially produced books were of higher quality than privately made copies. Indeed, frequent complaints suggest they were

---

styles, ranging from formal bookhand to informal cursive (e.g., P.Oxy. 4669, P. Koln IV 175). We should be careful, therefore, not to assume the hand of a particular manuscript tells us everything about the training/ability of the scribe. For more see Parsons, "Copyists of Oxyrhynchus," 269–70.

[41]Haines-Eitzen, *Guardians of Letters*, 68. Of course, this is not to suggest that every Christian manuscript was copied by a professional scribe. Undoubtedly, there would have been instances where a nonprofessional scribe would have undertaken the task of copying a manuscript; e.g. $\mathfrak{P}^{72}$, a codex containing 1 and 2 Peter, amongst various other works, is clearly copied by a nonprofessional scribe.

[42]A certain clerk secretary, Chariton of Aphrodisias, did administrative work for a lawyer named Athenagoras and at the same time copied literary texts such as *Chaereas and Callirhoe* (Haines-Eitzen, *Guardians of Letters*, 32). Also, Cicero employed scribes who not only received dictated letters and copied letters, but also copied various literary works; and the scribes were often mentioned by name (*Att.* 4.16; 12.14; 13.25).

[43]In several other places, Paul mentions that portions of the letter are in his own hand (1 Cor. 16:21; Gal. 5:11; Col. 4:18; 2 Thess. 3:17), showing that the prior portions were written by a scribe (Richards, *The Secretary in the Letters of Paul*, 172–75).

[44]Haines-Eitzen, *Guardians of Letters*, 40.

often worse."[45] He goes on to note, "The *private* copyists . . . were as a rule more skilled than those employed by booksellers."[46]

Remarkably, in spite of these considerations, Ehrman insists that "early Christian texts were *not being copied by professional scribes . . .* but simply educated members of the congregation who could do the job and were willing to do so."[47] Therefore, he argues, "we can expect that in the earliest copies, especially, mistakes were commonly made in transcription."[48] However, not only does Ehrman's contention ignore the evidence adduced above, but it stands in direct contradiction to Haines-Eitzen's work on early Christian scribes where she declares, "The earliest copyists of Christian literature were *trained professional scribes.*"[49] How, then, does Ehrman reach such a conclusion? He appeals to the isolated example from the second-century *Shepherd of Hermas*, where Hermas claims to see a vision of an elderly woman who is holding a book and reading aloud from it. In the story, Hermas copies the book on site (so that he can remember its content) and declares, "I copied the whole thing, letter by letter, for I could not distinguish between the syllables" (2.1.4). So, here we have an example of someone copying a book who seemed to be a nonprofessional scribe with poor reading skills. However, what conclusions can we really draw from this story? After all, no one doubts that, on occasion, nonprofessionals made copies of Scripture.[50] Indeed, this same practice also occurred from time to time in the Greco-Roman world. Thus Atticus mentions a scribe that he uses on occasion who cannot follow whole sentences but where words must be given "syllable by syllable" (*Att.* 13.25).

The real question, then, is whether larger implications about Christian scribal practice can be derived from such a story. Should a mystical vision in a prophetical book like the *Shepherd* be regarded as typical of early Christian practice? Ehrman offers no reason why it should. It is difficult to believe that one is being fair with the evidence when this single story is used to bolster the dubious claim that early Christian literature was routinely copied by people who could not read.

---

[45]Gamble, *Books and Readers*, 91.
[46]Ibid., 93 (emphasis added).
[47]Ehrman, *Misquoting Jesus*, 51 (emphasis added).
[48]Ibid.
[49]Haines-Eitzen, *Guardians of Letters*, 68 (emphasis added).
[50]See n. 42 above.

Nomina Sacra

A particularly important inscriptional feature of early Christian manuscripts—which reveals much about the scribal environment in which they were written—was the use of the nomina sacra. The nomina sacra are certain words that were written in a special abbreviated form in Christian documents in order to set them apart as sacred.[51] The most common words abbreviated in this manner are the Greek words for *Jesus*, *Christ*, *Lord*, and *God*.[52] Although the origin of the nomina sacra is unclear and still being debated,[53] their significance lies in the fact that they not only appear in the very earliest extant Greek manuscripts, but their appearance is remarkably widespread across regions and languages—almost without exception.[54] Indeed, so distinctive was the use of nomina sacra that in many ways it identified a manuscript as being Christian in its origins. Consequently, there are good reasons to think that these abbreviations were not concerned with saving space but functioned as a textual way to show Christian reverence and devotion to Christ alongside of God—

---

[51]They usually appeared as a contraction (and occasionally by suspension) with a horizontal line over the top. Studies on the nomina sacra include Ludwig Traube, *Nomina Sacra: Versuch einer Geschichte der christlichen Kürzung* (Munich: Beck, 1907); A. H. R. E. Paap, *Nomina Sacra in the Greek Papyri of the First Five Centuries* (Leiden: Brill, 1959); Jose O'Callaghan, *Nomina Sacra in Papyrus Graecis Saeculi III Neotestamentariis* (Rome: Biblical Institute Press, 1970); S. Brown, "Concerning the Origin of the Nomina Sacra," *SPap* 9 (1970): 7–19; G. Howard, "The Tetragram and the New Testament," *JBL* 96 (1977): 63–83; Roberts, *Manuscript*, 26–48; Larry W. Hurtado, "The Origin of the Nomina Sacra: A Proposal," *JBL* 117 (1998): 655–73; C. M. Tuckett, "'Nomina Sacra': Yes and No?" in *The Biblical Canons*, ed. J. M. Auwers and H. J. de Jonge (Leuven: Leuven University Press, 2003), 431–58.

[52]Although these four are the most common, scribes occasionally experimented with new/different words as nomina sacra. Examples of such variants can be found in P.Egerton 2 and P.Oxy. 1008 ($\mathfrak{P}^{15}$). For other examples of variants of nomina sacra see Kurt Aland, ed., *Repertorium der griechischen christlichen Papyri, I, Biblische Papyri* (Berlin: de Gruyter, 1976), 420–28, and Bruce M. Metzger, *Manuscripts of the Bible: An Introduction to Greek Palaeography* (New York: Oxford University Press, 1981), 36–37.

[53]For various approaches see Kurt Treu, "Die Bedeutung des Griechischen für die Juden im römischen Reich," *Kairós* 15 (1973): 123–144; Robert A. Kraft, "The 'Textual Mechanics' of Early Jewish LXX/OG Papyri and Fragments," in *The Bible as Book: The Transmission of the Greek Text*, ed. Scot McKendrick and Orlaith O'Sullivan (London: British Library, 2003), 51–72; Trobisch, *The First Edition of the New Testament*, 11–19; Hurtado, "The Origin of the Nomina Sacra," 655–73; Brown, "Concerning the Origin of the Nomina Sacra," 7–19.

[54]Most notably, it appears the nomina sacra are found in our earliest New Testament fragment, $\mathfrak{P}^{52}$. This has been challenged by Christopher M. Tuckett, "$\mathfrak{P}^{52}$ and the Nomina Sacra," *NTS* 47 (2001): 544–48; for responses to Tuckett see Charles E. Hill, "Did the Scribe of $\mathfrak{P}^{52}$ Use the Nomina Sacra? Another Look," *NTS* 48 (2002): 587–92, and Larry W. Hurtado, "$\mathfrak{P}^{52}$ (P.Rylands Gk. 457) and the Nomina Sacra: Method and Probability," *TynBul* 54 (2003): 1–14. Nomina sacra are found not only in Greek MSS, but also in Latin, Coptic, Slavonic, and Armenian ones. For more detail see Roberts, *Manuscript*, 27.

particularly given that the earliest terms of the nomina sacra were *Jesus, Christ, Lord,* and *God.*[55]

Such an early and dominant scribal convention suggests an emerging Christian scribal culture that was not as individualistic and decentralized as is often supposed.[56] T. C. Skeat argues that the *nomina sacra* "indicate a degree of organization, of conscious planning, and uniformity of practice among the Christian communities which we have hitherto had little reason to suspect."[57] Epp agrees: "[Churches] were perhaps not as loosely organized as has been assumed, and, therefore, they were also not as isolated from one another as has been affirmed. Indeed, at least one 'program of standardization'—the nomina sacra—was certainly functioning with obvious precision and care."[58] Thus, the nomina sacra provide confirmation of what we already learned in the prior section, namely that early Christian scribes maintained an impressive amount of literary sophistication and organizational structure that would have allowed them to reliably copy Christian texts.

The Codex

In addition to the nomina sacra, another notable feature of the early Christian book—which also reveals much about early Christian scribal

---

[55]Tuckett, "Nomina Sacra," 431–58, challenges this conception of the nomina sacra. But see the rebuttal by Larry W. Hurtado, *The Earliest Christian Artifacts: Manuscripts and Christian Origins* (Grand Rapids, MI: Eerdmans, 2006), 122–33.

[56]Haines-Eitzen downplays the significance of the nomina sacra in this regard, arguing that it does not provide any evidence for organization and structure amongst early Christian scribes (*Guardians of Letters*, 92–94). She bases this argument on the fact that scribes were not always consistent in the words they abbreviated. However, she overplays the amount of disparity in regard to the way nomina sacra were employed. To be sure, there were differences amongst various scribes, but the overall pattern is still intact (particularly as it pertains to the four main epithets: *iēsous, Christos, kyrios,* and *theos*). Moreover, even if one were to grant that scribes were routinely inconsistent in the way they used the nomina sacra, one still has to explain its early and dominant appearance. The scribal convention demands an explanation even if it is inconsistently applied. With this in mind, Haines-Eitzen's explanation that the nomina sacra originated from (and were disseminated through) only haphazard scribal relationships seems inadequate. If this were the case, one would expect the adoption of the nomina sacra to be gradual and slow—precisely the opposite of what we find.

[57]T. C. Skeat, "Early Christian Book-Production," in *The Cambridge History of the Bible*, vol. 2 (Cambridge: Cambridge University Press, 1969) 73.

[58]Eldon Jay Epp, "The Significance of the Papyri for Determining the Nature of the New Testament Text in the Second Century: A Dynamic View of Textual Transmission," in Eldon Jay Epp and Gordon D. Fee, *Studies in the Theory and Method of New Testament Textual Criticism* (Grand Rapids: Eerdmans, 1993), 288.

activity—was that it was almost always in the form of a codex.[59] The primary form of a book in the broader Greco-Roman world was the scroll (or roll), which was made from sheets of papyrus or parchment pasted together (end to end) in a long strip and rolled up.[60] Writing was done only on the inside of the scroll, so that when it was rolled up the words were protected.[61] The codex, in contrast, was created by taking a stack of papyrus or parchment leaves, folding them in half, and binding them at the spine. This format allowed for the traditional leaf book with writing on both sides of each page. It is now well established among modern scholars that early Christians not only preferred the codex instead of the roll, but they did so at a remarkably early point. Various manuscript discoveries indicate that the codex was the widely established Christian practice by the early second century, if not late in the first.[62] So dominant was the

---

[59]Relevant works on the codex include A. Blanchard, ed., *Les débuts du codex* (Turnhout: Brepols, 1989); C. H. Roberts and T. C. Skeat, *The Birth of the Codex* (London: Oxford University Press, 1987); E. G. Turner, *The Typology of the Early Codex* (Philadelphia: University of Pennsylvania Press, 1977); T. C. Skeat, "The Origin of the Christian Codex," *ZPE* 102 (1994): 263–68; H. A. Sanders, "The Beginnings of the Modern Book," *University of Michigan Quarterly Review* 44, no. 15 (1938): 95–111; C. C. McCown, "Codex and Roll in the New Testament," *HTR* 34 (1941): 219–50; Larry W. Hurtado, "The Earliest Evidence of an Emerging Christian Material and Visual Culture: The Codex, the Nomina Sacra, and the Staurogram," in *Text and Artifact in the Religions of Mediterranean Antiquity: Essays in Honour of Peter Richardson*, ed. Stephen G. Wilson and Michael Desjardins (Waterloo, ON: Wilfrid Laurier University Press, 2000), 271–88; S. R. Llewelyn, "The Development of the Codex," in *New Documents Illustrating Early Christianity*, vol. 7: *A Review of the Greek Inscriptions and Papyri Published in 1982–83*, ed. S. R. Llewelyn and R. A. Kearsley (North Ryde, NSW: Macquarie University Ancient History Documentary Research Center, 1994), 249–56; Graham N. Stanton, "Why Were Early Christians Addicted to the Codex?" in *Jesus and Gospel* (Cambridge: Cambridge University Press, 2004), 165–91; Eldon J. Epp, "The Codex and Literacy in early Christianity at Oxyrhynchus: Issues Raised by Harry Y. Gamble's Books and Readers in the Early Church," in *Critical Review of Books in Religion* 1997, ed. Charles Prebish (Atlanta: American Academy of Religion and Society of Biblical Literature, 1997), 15–37.

[60]A helpful discussion of scrolls is found in Gamble, *Books and Readers*, 43–48; and more recently in William A. Johnson, *Bookrolls and Scribes in Oxyrhynchus* (Toronto: University of Toronto Press, 2004).

[61]Occasionally, scrolls were reused and writing was done also on the backside (or outside) of the parchment or papyrus. Such a scroll, known as an opisthograph, is likely referred to by Pliny the Younger (*Ep.* 3.5.17).

[62]Roberts and Skeat confirmed the early dominance of the codex by showing how it was the format of choice for Christians from the very beginning of Christian book production (The *Birth of the Codex*, 38–44). This early date has been challenged by J. van Haelst, "Les origines du codex," in *Les débuts du codex*, 13–36, where he argues for a later date for some of these manuscripts. E. G. Turner, *Greek Papyri: An Introduction* (Oxford: Clarendon Press, 1968), 10, also cautions against excessively early dates. However, T. C. Skeat, "Early Christian

Christian preference for the codex, in the face of a broader Greco-Roman world that continued to use the roll for centuries to come,[63] that some have even suggested that the codex may have been a Christian invention.[64] It was not until the fourth century and beyond that the rest of the ancient world began to prefer the codex to the roll, something Christians had done centuries earlier.[65]

With these considerations in mind, the key historical question is this: What led early Christians to adopt the codex so early and so universally when the rest of the Greco-Roman world (as well as Judaism) still preferred scrolls? Suggestions that the codex was chosen for practical advantages (convenience, size, cost) or for socioeconomic reasons (the lack of education among Christians made the informal codex more palatable) have been largely considered inadequate.[66] Although such factors may have played some role, they would only allow an incremental and gradual transition to the codex over many years and thus cannot account for the fact that the transition to the codex was rather abrupt, early, and widespread.[67] A more foundational and influential cause is needed to explain the transition. Consequently, the most plausible suggestions are those that link the codex with the early development of the New Testament canon. Skeat has suggested the codex was chosen because it, and it alone, could hold all four Gospels in one volume and thus set a precedent for early Christian book

---

Book-Production," 54–79, and C. H. Roberts, "P Yale 1 and the Early Christian Book," *AsTP1* (1966): 25–28, maintain an early date by appealing to the discovery of P.Yale 1, the papyrus codex containing Genesis and dates from AD 80–100. Moreover, recent manuscript discoveries continue to confirm the dominance of the codex. Between 1997 and 1999, a number of early manuscripts from Oxyrhynchus were discovered and were all on codices: P.Oxy. 4403–4404 (Matthew); P.Oxy 4445–4448 (John); and P.Oxy 4494–4500 (fragments of Matthew, Luke, Acts, Romans, Hebrews, and Revelation).

[63]See statistics offered by Hurtado, *Earliest Christian Artifacts*, 44–53.

[64]Skeat, "Early Christian Book-Production," 68. See discussion in McCown, "Codex and Roll in the New Testament," 219–221. Of course, now it is well accepted that the codex was likely a Roman invention (see Roberts and Skeat, *Birth of the Codex*, 15–23).

[65]Roberts and Skeat, *Birth of the Codex*, 35–37.

[66]Ibid., 45–53; Hurtado, *Earliest Christian Artifacts*, 63–69; T. C. Skeat, "The Length of the Standard Papyrus Roll and the Cost Advantage of the Codex," *ZPE* 45 (1982): 169–75.

[67]Other theories about the origin of the codex suffer from some of the same problems. For example, Epp ("Codex and Literacy," 15–37) and Michael McCormick, "The Birth of the Codex and the Apostolic Life-Style," *Scriptorium* 39 (1985): 150–58, suggest the codex was established by its use in the travels of itinerant missionaries; and Stanton, "Why Were Early Christians Addicted to the Codex?" 181–91, suggests that it was early Christian uses of primitive "notebooks" (e.g., wax, wooden, and parchment tablets) for recording sayings of Jesus or Old Testament prooftexts that led to the wholesale adoption of the codex.

production.[68] In a similar vein, Gamble has suggested that the codex was chosen because it could hold all of Paul's epistles in one volume and allow easy access to individual letters.[69] Regardless of which of these theories proves to be more plausible—and each has its strengths and weaknesses—it seems that the significance of the codex lies in its role in the development of the corpus of New Testament books. As J. K. Elliott observed, "Canon and codex go hand in hand in the sense that the adoption of a fixed canon could be more easily controlled and promulgated when the codex was the means of gathering together originally separate compositions."[70]

The link between codex and canon sheds some much-needed light on the nature of early Christian book production. If the codex was widely adopted at an early point (likely by the end of the first century), and was adopted because the early church desired to establish boundaries to the canon (or portions thereof), then we have strong historical evidence that the establishment of the New Testament canon was well underway by the turn of the century—long before Marcion and before most critical scholars have allowed. Indeed, David Trobisch, in his work *The First Edition of the New Testament*, has even argued that the use of the codex, along with the use of the nomina sacra, are good reasons to think that the *entire* New Testament was formed as a completed edition by the early second century.[71] Whether or not one finds all of Trobisch's conclusions compelling, he has rightly identified the significance of the codex: it tells us that the canon was not a later, after-the-fact development within early Christianity but was present at a very early point (thus confirming what we already learned in previous chapters). Moreover, the dominant use of the codex, like the nomina sacra, reveals a Christian scribal culture that is quite unified, organized, and able to forge a new literary path by employing a revolutionary book technology that would eventually come to dominate the entire Greco-Roman world.[72]

---

[68]Skeat, "Origin of the Christian Codex," 263–68. One is also reminded of the comments of Frederick Kenyon: "When, therefore, Irenaeus at the end of the second century writes of the four Gospels as the divinely provided evidence of Christianity, and the number four as almost axiomatic, it is now possible to believe that he may have been accustomed to the sight of volumes in which all four [Gospels] were contained" (F. G. Kenyon, *The Chester Beatty Biblical Papyri* 1:13).

[69]Gamble, *Books and Readers*, 58–66; Hurtado, *Earliest Christian Artifacts*, 69–83.

[70]J. K. Elliott, "Manuscripts, the Codex, and the Canon," *JSNT* 63 (1996): 111.

[71]Trobisch, *The First Edition*.

[72]The fact that early manuscripts like 𝔓66 (late second-century) used the even more sophisticated "multiple-quire" codex suggests this technology may have been used by Christian scribes much earlier in the second century. This is particularly true if one adopts a date for 𝔓66 in the first

The Publication of Books within Early Christianity

The prior section established the nature of early Christian scribal activity. Contrary to the claims of Ehrman, we have good historical reasons to think Christian scribes were professionals who were quite capable as transmitters and copiers of Christian literature. But there still remains the question of how books were actually "published" or circulated within the early Christian faith. Did Christians have a system for disseminating their literature from place to place, and what does this tell us about whether Christian book production can be considered a reliable enterprise? The concept of "private" copying, as discussed above, can give the impression that all instances of Christian book production were performed on a small scale and done separately and disconnected from each other—as if all scribal activity in early Christianity was a random, haphazard affair. Although we do not have clear evidence that there were established "scriptoriums" in the second and third centuries, it would be misleading to suggest there were no instances during this time where copying happened on a larger scale or within a more highly organized network. Indeed, the early and dominant use of the codex and nomina sacra (as discussed above) already inclines us to suspect that early Christian book production (and distribution) may have had a more integrated and collaborative structure than we might otherwise have assumed. Let us consider a number of other factors that support this contention.

First, even within the letters of Paul, we witness a remarkably well-structured network for the copying and dissemination of early Christian writings. Paul sent his letters through friends or associates to be delivered to the various churches under his care (e.g., Rom. 16:1; Eph. 6:21; Col. 4:7) and regularly asked that they be read publicly to the church (e.g., 2 Cor. 2:9; Col. 4:16; 1 Thess. 5:27).[73] This public reading was analogous to the *recitatio* in the Greco-Roman world where a book was read aloud to groups and acquaintances as a form of "publishing" it to wider communities.[74] Moreover, it seems that Paul expected his letters to be copied and circulated amongst the churches. For example, Galatians is addressed to a *region* of churches, "the churches of Galatia," and Romans is addressed to "all those in Rome who are loved by God," which would likely

---

half of the second century; see Herbert Hunger, "Zur Datierung des Papyrus Bodmer II ($\mathfrak{P}^{66}$)," *Anzeiger der österreichischen Akademie der Wissenschaften* 4 (1960): 12–33.

[73]For discussion of reading books in early Christian worship see Martin Hengel, "The Titles of the Gospels and the Gospel of Mark," in *Studies in the Gospel of Mark* (London: SCM, 1985), 64–84. See also Justin Martyr, *1 Apol.* 67.3.

[74]Gamble, *Books and Readers*, 84.

have included many smaller churches. It is unlikely that each of these sub-churches received the *original* letter of Paul; undoubtedly copies were made. Also, Paul expressly asks that his letter to the Colossians be passed along to the Laodiceans, presumably by making copies (Col. 4:16). Such a scenario reveals a fairly impressive network of churches that would have been actively copying and distributing Paul's letters, even within Paul's own lifetime. In addition, recent studies have shown that Paul would have undoubtedly possessed copies of his own letters, as was common in the Greco-Roman world, and may have even published one of the earliest collections of his letters.[75]

A second example can be found in the *Shepherd of Hermas*. Whereas, Ehrman uses this story to argue for nonprofessional scribal activity (as mentioned above), it is actually good evidence for an intricate scribal network amongst early Christians. Hermas receives the following instructions:

> And so, you will write two little books, sending one to Clement and one to Grapte. Clement will send his to the foreign cities, for that is his commission. But, Grapte will admonish the widows and orphans. And you will read yours in the city, with the presbyters who lead the church.[76]

This passage reveals an impressively organized system for publication and distribution of Christian literature, likely by the early second century.[77] After making two copies of the revelation he has received ("two little books"), Hermas is to give those copies to two selected individuals who will then make copies for their constituencies, while Hermas takes the book to his own constituency ("the presbyters"). It is clear that Clement and Grapte are secretaries or correspondents of sorts given the special task of making sure these texts are copied and distributed ("for that is his commission").[78] In fact, Gamble refers to Clement's role here as an "*ecclesiastical publisher*,

---

[75]E. Randolph Richards, "The Codex and the Early Collection of Paul's Letters," *BBR* 8 (1998): 151–66; David Trobisch, *Paul's Letter Collection: Tracing the Origins* (Minneapolis: Fortress, 1994); Gamble, *Books and Readers*, 100–101. Cicero illumines the Greco-Roman practice of keeping copies of (and even publishing) one's own letters: "There is no collection of my letters, but Tiro has about seventy, and some can be got from you. Those I ought to see and correct, and then they may be published" (*Att.* 16.5.5). Also, as Plutarch records, after Alexander set fire to his secretary's tent he regretted the fact that all the copies of his letters were destroyed, so much so that he sent new letters to various people asking for copies of the letters he had originally sent (*Eum.* 2.2–3).

[76]2.4.3.

[77]For discussion of the date of the *Shepherd* see Bart D. Ehrman, *The Apostolic Fathers*, vol. 2, LCL (Cambridge, MA: Harvard University Press, 2003), 165–69.

[78]It is unclear whether the "Clement" here is intended to be an allusion to the writer of *1 Clement*. Regardless, it is clear that this individual is charged with the copying and distribution of

a standing provision in the Roman church for duplicating and distributing texts to Christian communities elsewhere."[79] And if Rome retained such a system for copying, publishing, and circulating Christian literature, then we might reasonably expect other major Christian centers like Jerusalem, Alexandria, and Caesarea to have similar structures.[80]

Third, we learn more about early publication and circulation practices in the early second-century letter of Polycarp, bishop of Smyrna, to the Philippians to which he attached the collected letters of Ignatius.[81] The historical details surrounding this letter from Polycarp tell us that after Ignatius had written various letters to churches (some of which he wrote from Smyrna), the following occurred within a very short frame of time:[82] (1) the Philippians sent a letter to Polycarp asking for a copy of Ignatius's letters and also sent along another letter for Polycarp to forward onto Antioch;[83] (2) next Polycarp collected the epistles of Ignatius and had them copied; (3) then Polycarp sent a letter back to the Philippians with a copy of Ignatius's letter collection; (4) and finally, at the same time, Polycarp forwarded a letter from the Philippians to Antioch—something he appeared to be doing for many churches.[84]

This dizzying amount of literary traffic raises two important points. First, Smyrna appears to have been a veritable "beehive" of activity in regard to letter writing, copying, and distribution, showing that it had not only the scribal infrastructure to handle this sort of activity, but an ecclesiastical

---

books, whether he does it himself or has scribes at his disposal who will perform the task. Either way, a well-established publishing network is visible here.

[79] Gamble, *Books and Readers*, 109 (emphasis added).

[80] The fact that these major Christian centers contained established Christian libraries makes publication and copying resources all the more likely. For example, the library at Caesarea was established by the early third century (Jerome, *Vir. ill.* 112; Eusebius, *Hist. eccl.* 7.32.25), and contained extensive resources for copying, editing, and publishing biblical manuscripts (some colophons in biblical manuscripts, like Sinaiticus, indicate manuscripts were collated and corrected there even by Pamphilus and Eusebius themselves). Jerusalem also contained a library by the early third century (*Hist. eccl.* 6.20.1) and most likely Alexandria as well (as can be seen by the extensive literary work and possible "catechetical school" in Alexandria under Pantaenus, Clement, and Origen; *Hist. eccl.* 5.10, 6.3.3). For more discussion see Gamble, *Books and Readers*, 155–59.

[81] For dating and other introductory details see Ehrman, *Apostolic Fathers*, vol. 2, 324–31.

[82] Gamble suggests no more than a couple of weeks (*Books and Readers*, 110).

[83] *Phil* 13.1–2.

[84] Ibid. Apparently, the Philippians' request to have Polycarp forward a letter to Antioch was part of a larger pattern of churches sending letters to Polycarp to forward to Antioch. These letters were being sent at the behest of Ignatius who asked that letters be sent to Antioch (*Smyrn.* 11.3).

network between churches that made such activity a necessity.[85] Second, given the short timeframe in which Polycarp was able to collect Ignatius's seven letters, it appears this could only have been done if Polycarp *already* had copies of the letters that Ignatius had sent from Smyrna when the Philippians made their request. This suggests that when Ignatius originally wrote from Smyrna, copies of his letters must have been made before they were sent out (and those copies were then stored at Smyrna).[86] Indeed, this is suggested by Polycarp's statement that he is sending not only the letters that "[Ignatius] sent to us" but *"all the others we had with us."*[87] Not only does this scenario suggest that Smyrna was somewhat of a publishing "hub," but it reflects a similar pattern to the one we saw in Paul's epistles—authors often made copies of their letters before they were sent so that later collections could be made and published.

Fourth, we continue to learn about the transmission and publication of early Christian books in the account of the scribal resources available to Origen in Alexandria in the early third century. According to Eusebius, Ambrose had supplied Origen with a well-staffed literary team including "seven shorthand-writers . . . many copyists . . . [and] girls skilled in penmanship."[88] It appears that Ambrose supplied this literary team so that Origen's work could be extensively copied, corrected, and published for the benefit of the church—which undoubtedly explains Origen's impressive level of literary production. Although it is possible that Origen's situation was entirely unique, it is not hard to imagine that similar publication "centers" would have existed elsewhere. Surely Ambrose was not the only Christian with financial means who also had an interest in seeing Christian books produced in greater quantities. It would be quite natural to think that Irenaeus, Tertullian, Cyprian, and other Christian leaders may have enjoyed similar resources.[89] Moreover, if such resources were allocated to make sure Origen's works were adequately copied, it seems reasonable

---

[85]Gamble, *Books and Readers*, 112.

[86]Ibid., 110–11.

[87]*Phil* 13.1, emphasis added.

[88]*Hist. eccl.* 6.23.2.

[89]Indeed, a number of details suggest this possibility. Irenaeus produced *Adversus haereses* in multiple stages and yet found its way around the Empire quite rapidly in its completed form, suggesting substantial scribal and publishing resources in Gaul (more on this below). The third edition of Tertullian's work, *Adversus Marcionem*, so quickly replaced the prior two editions that it must have been copied quickly and in great quantities, suggesting again that substantial publishing resources must have been available in Carthage to publish such a lengthy work in this fashion (Gamble, *Books and Readers*, 121). As for Cyprian, not only were his collected works published soon after his death—accounting for why so many survived—but

to think that similar, or even greater, levels of resources would have been employed (at least in some instances) by Christians in the copying of books they considered to be *Scripture*.[90]

These four examples—and many others could be added—point toward a publishing environment within the first three centuries of the Christian movement that, while not necessarily at the level of "scriptoria," is nevertheless quite organized, developed, and intentional. Such a reality is borne out by the early evidence for the rapid dissemination of Christian literature within these centuries. P.Oxy. 405, a copy of *Against Heresies* by Irenaeus, was discovered in Egypt and dates to only about twenty years after its initial composition in Gaul in c. AD 180. Likewise, the *Shepherd of Hermas*, which was composed in Rome in the mid-second century, was discovered in Egypt in a late second-century manuscript (P.Mich. 130).[91] An early fragment of the Gospel of John, known as $\mathfrak{P}^{52}$, was discovered in Egypt and dates to only a few years after the original composition in the late first century.[92] It is precisely this rapid dissemination that sets Christian literature apart from its Greco-Roman counterparts—Christians enjoyed an expansive and well-established network of churches, groups, and individuals that were not only interested in the copying and publication of Christian writings but apparently had the means at their disposal for this publication to take place.[93]

Conclusion

The above survey, although far too brief and limited in scope, reveals that earliest Christianity was not a religion concerned only with oral tradition or public proclamation but was also shaped by, and found its identity within, a vivid "textual culture" committed to writing, editing, copying,

---

he seemed to promote the copying and dissemination of works during his own lifetime (*Ep.* 32), again implying a degree of scribal resources at his disposal.

[90]Although the extent of the canon was not yet resolved by the end of the second century, by that time there was a core set of New Testament books that would have been highly esteemed and regarded as "Scripture" alongside the Old Testament. See Justin Martyr, *1 Apol.* 67.3; Barton, *Spirit and the Letter*, 18; Metzger, *Canon of the New Testament*, 254.

[91]For more on this text, see Campbell Bonner, "A New Fragment of the *Shepherd of Hermas*, Michigan Papyrus 44," *HTR* 20 (1927): 105–16.

[92]The rapid dissemination of $\mathfrak{P}^{52}$ becomes even more impressive if one adopts the earlier date of c. AD 100 defended by K. Aland, "Neue neutestamentliche Papyri II," *NTS* 9 (1962–63): 303–16.

[93]Gamble, *Books and Readers*, 140–41. For more on the circulation of ancient manuscripts see Epp, "New Testament Papyrus Manuscripts and Letter Carrying in Greco-Roman Times," 35–56.

and distributing Christian books, whether scriptural or otherwise. When the form and structure of these books are considered, and not just the content within, a more vivid picture of the early Christian literary culture begins to emerge.

Contrary to the claims of Ehrman and others, from a very early point Christians not only had an interest in books but had a relatively well-developed social and scribal network—as seen in conventions like the codex and nomina sacra—whereby those books could be copied, edited, and disseminated throughout the Empire. Indeed, it is just this rapid transfer of literature that set early Christians apart from their surrounding Greco-Roman world and set the early church on the path toward eventually establishing a collection of "canonical" books that would form the church's literary foundation for generations to come.

Thus, there are no good historical grounds for doubting that there were adequate means within the early Christian communities for reliably transmitting books. The only question now is whether the manuscripts themselves are so filled with errors and mistakes that we are forced to doubt their integrity. It is to this question that we now turn.

8

Tampering with the Text

Was the New Testament Text Changed Along the Way?

The only way that the New Testament books (and *any* type of writing) could be broadly circulated in the ancient world was if they were first copied by hand. A scribe would have to sit down with the original document and copy it word for word onto a piece of papyrus or parchment.[1] Of course, in our modern day, well after the time of Gutenberg's printing press, such dependence on handwritten manuscripts seems strange to us. We give little or no thought to how a book is copied and assume that whichever copy of a book we pick off the shelf will look identical to every other copy. In ancient times, however, it was quite normal (and even expected) that scribes, no matter how professional, would occasionally make mistakes.[2] These scribal

---

[1]For discussion of the posture/position of ancient scribes and whether they ever made copies without an exemplar in front of them (e.g., by dictation), see D. C. Parker, *New Testament Manuscripts and Their Texts* (Cambridge: Cambridge University Press, 2008), 154–57; T. C. Skeat, "The Use of Dictation in Ancient Book-Production," *Proceedings of the British Academy* 42 (1956): 179–208; and Bruce M. Metzger, "When Did Scribes Begin to Use Writing Desks?" in *Historical and Literary Studies, Pagan, Jewish, and Christian* (Leiden: Brill, 1968), 123–37.

[2]This does not mean that ancient writers were always content with the amount of scribal mistakes. On occasion they would complain of how a scribe (or someone else) made so many blunders that the original document was tainted. For example, Martial complains about his

variations—slips of the pen, misspellings, word order changes, etc.—were an inevitable part of literary life in a pre-Gutenberg world (and even, to a lesser degree, in a *post*-Gutenberg world). Fortunately, as seen in the previous chapter, we have good reasons to think that early Christians possessed a solid scribal infrastructure that would have minimized the impact of such variations. Nevertheless, we still need to examine the New Testament manuscripts themselves. Are these manuscripts very different from one another? Are there reasons to think the text has been substantively changed along the way? And did the early Christian battles over heresy and orthodoxy affect the transmission of the text? It is the purpose of this chapter to answer these questions.

It is important that we begin by noting that some scholars have already given an answer. Bart Ehrman would answer "yes" to all of the above questions. In his book *Misquoting Jesus*, Ehrman argues that the New Testament manuscripts are so riddled with scribal errors and mistakes (some even intentional) that there is no way to have any certainty about the words of the original authors. In essence, he argues that the New Testament text has been changed—irreparably and substantially changed in the battles over heresy and orthodoxy—so that it is no longer meaningful to discuss what Paul, or Matthew, Mark, or Luke, wrote. We simply do not know. All we have are manuscripts. And these manuscripts date hundreds of years after the time of the apostles and vary widely from one another. So, what does the "New Testament" say? It depends, says Ehrman, which manuscript you read. He declares, "What good is it to say that the autographs (i.e., the originals) were inspired? We don't *have* the originals! We have only error-ridden copies, and the vast majority of these are centuries removed from the originals and different from them . . . in thousands of ways."[3]

Although Ehrman presents his who-knows-what-the-text-originally-said approach as part of mainstream textual criticism, it actually stands in direct opposition to many of his fellow scholars in the field (and even seems to be out of sync with his own writings elsewhere). Historically speaking, the field of textual criticism has not embodied the hyper-skepticism evident in *Misquoting Jesus* but has been more optimistic concerning the recovery

---

copyist, "If any poems in these sheets, reader, seems to you either too obscure or not quite good Latin, not mine is the mistake: the copyist spoiled them in his haste" (*Epig.* 2.8).
[3]Bart D. Ehrman, *Misquoting Jesus: The Story Behind Who Changed the Bible and Why* (San Francisco: Harper Collins, 2005), 7 (emphasis in original).

of the original text (or at least something *very* close to it).[4] In response to Ehrman, therefore, this chapter will put forward four theses that embody an approach that is more consistent with the kind traditionally taken in the field of textual criticism.

- We have good reasons to think the original text is preserved (somewhere) in the overall textual tradition.
- The vast majority of scribal changes are minor and insignificant.
- Of the small portion of variations that are significant, our text-critical methodology can determine, with a reasonable degree of certainty, which is the original text.
- The remaining number of truly unresolved variants is very few and not material to the story/teaching of the New Testament.

If these four theses are valid, then we have good reasons to think that we are able to recover the New Testament text in a manner that is so very close to the original that there is no material difference between what, say, Mark and Matthew wrote and the text we have today. Although we can never have *absolute* certainty about the original text, we can have *sufficient* certainty that enables us to be confident that we possess the authentic teaching of Jesus and his apostles. Let us consider each of these theses in turn.

---

[4]One need only compare *Misquoting Jesus* to B. H. Westcott and F. J. A. Hort, *The New Testament in the Original Greek* (Cambridge: Macmillan, 1881); Kurt Aland and Barbara Aland, *The Text of the New Testament: An Introduction to the Critical Editions and to the Theory and Practice of Modern Textual Criticism*, 2d ed. (Grand Rapids: Eerdmans, 1989); and Bruce M. Metzger and Bart D. Ehrman, *The Text of the New Testament: Its Transmission, Corruption, and Restoration* (New York: Oxford University Press, 1992). The concept of an "original" text (and our ability to recover it) has been challenged in recent studies. Although there is not space here to attempt a resolution of this question, see the following for more discussion: Parker, *New Testament Manuscripts and Their Texts*, 337–38; idem, *The Living Text of the Gospels* (Cambridge: Cambridge University Press, 1997), 203–13; Eldon Jay Epp, "The Multivalence of the Term 'Original Text' in New Testament Textual Criticism," *HTR* 92 (1999): 245–81; Metzger and Ehrman, *The Text of the New Testament*, 272–74; William L. Petersen, "What Text Can New Testament Textual Criticism Ultimately Reach?" in *New Testament Textual Criticism, Exegesis, and Early Church History: A Discussion of Methods*, ed. Barbara Aland and Joel Delobel (Kampen, Netherlands: Kok Pharos, 1994), 136–52; and J. Delobel, "The Achilles' Heel of New Testament Textual Criticism," *Bijdr* 63 (2002): 3–21.

Thesis 1: The Wealth of Extant Manuscripts: we have good reasons to think the original text is preserved (somewhere) in the overall textual tradition

The first step in answering these questions about the transmission of the New Testament text is to gain a better understanding of the manuscript resources at our disposal. Discussions about whether a text has been "changed" always involve the *comparison* of manuscripts. After all, if we only possessed a single manuscript of the New Testament, there would be no discussion of scribal variations and changes—we would not know of such things unless we compared one copy with another copy to see where they differ.[5] Although such a scenario may, on the surface, seem desirable (because then we would not need to worry about debating which variants were original!), having only one manuscript would raise a substantial problem: how would we know that we possess, in this one single manuscript, the words which were originally written by the author? If this single manuscript were simply a *later copy* of the original (which is most likely the case), then there is a good chance that some scribal mistakes, errors, and other variants have slipped into the text during the copying process. With only a single manuscript in our possession there is no way to be sure that no words have been lost or altered. Therefore, as scholars seek to know how much any writing of antiquity has been changed, and, more importantly, as they seek to establish what that writing would have originally said (by tracing those changes through the manuscript tradition), the *more* manuscripts that can be compared the better. The higher the number of manuscripts, the more assurance we have that the original text was preserved somewhere in the manuscript tradition.

But it is not just the high quantity of manuscripts that is desirable for the textual critic but manuscripts that date as closely as possible to the time of the original writing of that text. The less time that passed between the original writing and our earliest copies, the less time there was for the text to be substantially corrupted, and therefore the more assured we can be that we possess what was originally written. Unfortunately, these two

---

[5] Of course, this is a general statement. There are two ways we could notice scribal variations even if we possessed only a single manuscript: (1) nonsense readings that suggest the scribe made a blunder; in such cases conjectural emendations would be necessary; and (2) corrections within the text itself from a second scribal hand could give indications of what the readings of other manuscripts may have been. For example, $\mathfrak{P}^{66}$ (second-century codex of John) has a number of scribal corrections in the text; see Gordon D. Fee, *Papyrus Bodmer II ($\mathfrak{P}^{66}$): Its Textual Relationships and Scribal Characteristics* (Salt Lake City, UT: University of Utah Press, 1968), 57–75.

components of every textual critic's wish list—numerous copies and also some with an early date—are relatively rare in the study of most documents of antiquity. As we shall see, most of our ancient historical sources are attested by few manuscripts that are often very late.

The Quantity of New Testament Manuscripts

Not surprisingly, ancient manuscripts are hard to come by. Most have perished over the ages for a variety of reasons—burned in garbage dumps, destroyed by foreign armies, rotted or decayed, damaged by insects or rodents—or have simply been lost.[6] Historians never have as many pieces of evidence as they would like. For example, the writings of Tacitus from the first century, widely recognized as one of the greatest Roman historians, survive in only three manuscripts, and not all are complete.[7] Consider also the writings of Gaius from the second century, a Roman jurist who is well known for his essential accounts of Roman law under emperors like Marcus Aurelius. Most of his writings are lost and his key work, *The Institutes*, is preserved in just three manuscripts—but the text "rests almost exclusively" on just one of them.[8] The sizable *History of Rome* by the first-century historian Velleius Paterculus, which covers large portions of Roman history, including the life of Julius Caesar, comes down to us in a single, mutilated manuscript.[9] The work *Jewish War* by Josephus, a trusted Jewish historian from the first century AD, is better attested with over fifty extant manuscripts, but the text is mainly dependent on about ten of them.[10]

By contrast, the New Testament manuscripts stand out as entirely unique in this regard. Although the exact count is always changing, currently we possess over 5,500 manuscripts (in whole or in part) of the New Testament

---

[6]Alan Millard, *Reading and Writing in the Time of Jesus* (New York: New York University Press, 2000), 33–41.

[7]L. D. Reynolds, ed., *Texts and Transmissions: A Survey of the Latin Classics* (Oxford: Clarendon, 1983), 406–11. There are numerous later Italian manuscripts of Books 11–16, all of which are based on the single earlier medieval manuscript Laurentianus 68.2 (known as the "second" Medicean). For more, see Clarence W. Mendell, *Tacitus: The Man and His Work* (London: Oxford University Press, 1957), 294–324.

[8]Reynolds, *Texts and Transmissions*, 174. The primary manuscript (Verona, Chapter Library XV) is actually a "palimpsest," which means the parchment was reused at a later date to copy another text, and the original text of *The Institutes* is only visible underneath it. The two more fragmentary manuscripts provide little new information (P.Oxy. 2103; Florence, Laur. P.S.I. 1182).

[9]Reynolds, *Texts and Transmissions*, 431–33.

[10]Josephus, *The Jewish War*, trans. H. St. J. Thackeray, LCL (Cambridge, MA: Harvard University Press, 2004), xxvii–xxxi; Heinz Schreckenberg, *Die Flavius-Josephus-Tradition in Antike und Mittelalter* (Leiden: Brill, 1972).

in Greek alone.[11] No other document of antiquity even comes close. Moreover, we possess thousands more manuscripts in other languages. The total
for just our Latin manuscripts of the New Testament exceeds ten thousand
copies, and we possess thousands more in Coptic, Syriac, Gothic, Ethiopic,
Armenian, and other languages.[12] Indeed, there is no exact number because
there are so many of these different versions that not all have been formally
catalogued. In addition to all these manuscripts, there are also a countless
number of citations of the New Testament preserved in the early church
fathers,[13] so many, in fact, that Metzger has famously declared, "So extensive
are these citations that if all other sources for our knowledge of the text of
the New Testament were destroyed, they would be sufficient alone for the
reconstruction of practically the entire New Testament."[14]

Such a scenario, from a historical perspective, is truly remarkable. As
Eldon Epp has declared, "We have, therefore, a genuine embarrassment
of riches in the quantity of manuscripts we possess. . . . The writings of
no Greek classical author are preserved on this scale."[15] If there were ever
an ancient writing that had enough extant manuscripts that we could be
reasonably assured that the original text was preserved for us in the multiplicity of copies, the New Testament would be it. Again it is Epp who notes,
"The point is that we have so many manuscripts of the NT . . . that surely
the original reading *in every case* is somewhere present in our vast store of

---

[11]The official numbers are kept at the Institut für neutestamentliche Textforschung (Institute for
New Testament Textual Research) in Münster, Germany. In personal correspondence, Daniel
B. Wallace writes that, "Although the official tally by Münster is now 5,773, and although
the CSNTM has discovered dozens of MSS not yet catalogued by Münster, there are several
MSS that have gone missing, have been doubly catalogued, or are parts of other MSS. Ulrich
Schmid told me a few months ago that the actual number weighed in at 5,555. But I think it
would be safe to say that there are over 5,600 now."

[12]For a fuller discussion of the manuscripts, see Aland and Aland, *Text of the New Testament*, 185–221.

[13]For more on texts in the fathers, see Gordon D. Fee, "The Text of John in Origen and Cyril
of Alexandria: A Contribution to Methodology in the Recovery and Analysis of Patristic
Citations," *Bib* 52 (1971): 357–73; idem, "The Use of the Greek Fathers for New Testament Textual Criticism," in *The Text of the New Testament in Contemporary Research:
Essays on the Status Quaestionis*, ed. Bart D. Ehrman and Michael W. Holmes (Eugene,
OR: Wipf & Stock, 2001), 191–207; and M. J. Suggs, "The Use of Patristic Evidence in the
Search for a Primitive New Testament Text," *NTS* 4 (1957–1958): 139–47. For examples
of attempts to extract texts from the fathers, see the Society of Biblical Literature series
edited by Michael W. Holmes, *The New Testament in the Greek Fathers, Texts and Analyses*
(1998–present).

[14]Metzger, *Text of the New Testament*, 86.

[15]Eldon Jay Epp, "Textual Criticism," in *The New Testament and Its Modern Interpreters*, ed.
Eldon Jay Epp and George W. MacRae (Atlanta: Scholars Press, 1989), 91.

material."[16] Fee concurs, "The immense amount of material available to NT textual critics . . . is their good fortune because with such an abundance of material one can be reasonably certain that the original text is to be found somewhere in it."[17] In other words, due to the vast number of manuscripts, the challenge of textual criticism is a different one than we might expect—it is not that we are *lacking* in material (as if the original words were lost), but rather we have *too much* material (the original words, plus some variations). When it comes to reconstructing the original text of the New Testament, the latter position is much preferred over the former.

It is here that the contrast between the New Testament and classical works becomes acute. Ehrman's hyper-skeptical approach should be challenged not by insisting the New Testament text should be treated in the *same* way as classical works—for he may argue that we do not know the text of the classical authors either—but by insisting that the New Testament text should be treated *differently*. After all, if we supposedly lack assurance regarding the preservation of the classical texts due to their paucity of manuscripts (although it is doubtful whether scholars really do treat classical works with such agnosticism), then how could we not have much greater assurance of the preservation of the New Testament text due to its abundance of manuscripts? This is precisely the sticking point for Ehrman's position. He wants to be skeptical of *both* sets of writings (New Testament and classical), in spite of the fact that the historical evidence for the two is vastly different. To insist that the New Testament is as unknowable as classical works is to render the historical data utterly irrelevant to the discussion at hand. Such a position, at its core, proves to be substantively unhistorical—the conclusions are the same regardless of the evidence.

It is precisely for this reason that one wonders how much textual material would be enough for Ehrman to regard a text as sufficiently knowable. Would seven thousand Greek manuscripts be enough? Ten thousand? What if we had many more manuscripts of an early date (more on this below)? Would that be enough? One gets the impression that no matter what the evidence

---

[16]Epp, "Textual Criticism," 91 (emphasis added). For a similar point, see also Eldon Jay Epp, "Textual Criticism in the Exegesis of the New Testament, with an Excursus on Canon," in *Handbook to the Exegesis of the New Testament*, ed. Stanley Porter (Leiden: Brill, 1997), 52–53.

[17]Gordon D. Fee, "Textual Criticism of the New Testament," in *Studies in the Theory and Method of New Testament Textual Criticism*, ed. Eldon Jay Epp and Gordon D. Fee (Grand Rapids: Eerdmans, 1993), 6.

is, it would not change the outcome. The bar always seems to be set just a bit higher than wherever the evidence happens to be—like the Greek myth of Sisyphus who thought he had finally done enough to push the boulder to the top of the hill only to find it rolled back down again. As we shall see, there is only one thing that would seem to satisfy Ehrman's requirements: the autographs themselves.

The Date of the New Testament Manuscripts

If manuscripts of ancient documents are (generally speaking) relatively rare, then *early* manuscripts are even more so. As noted above, the smaller the gap of time between the writing of an ancient text and our earliest copy of that text, the more assurance we have that we possess what was originally written. Unfortunately, small gaps of time are the exception and not the rule. Of the manuscripts of Tacitus, the earliest is ninth century, nearly eight hundred years after it was originally written.[18] For Josephus's *Jewish War*, virtually all of its manuscripts are from the Middle Ages, and the earliest of these is from the tenth century, nearly nine hundred years after the original time of publication. The only manuscript earlier than this is a very fragmentary papyrus from the third century that is virtually illegible.[19] The single extant manuscript of the *History of Rome* by Velleius Paterculus is dated to the eighth or ninth century—approximately eight hundred years after its initial publication—but was subsequently lost and now survives only in a sixteenth-century copy.[20] The primary manuscript for Gaius's *Institutes* fares a bit better and is dated to the fifth century, about three hundred years after the original.[21] Such gaps of time are not unusual in the manuscript traditions of many of our classical works. As Epp sums it up, "As is well known, the interval between the author and the earliest extant manuscripts for most classical writings is commonly hundreds—sometimes many hundreds—of years, and a thousand-year interval is not uncommon."[22]

However, again, the New Testament situation is entirely different. The New Testament was written approximately AD 50–90, and our earliest New Testament manuscript, $\mathfrak{P}^{52}$, preserves a portion of John's Gospel from c. AD

---

[18]MS. plut. 68.1, Codex Mediceus.

[19]Pap. Graec. Vindob. 29810.

[20]This manuscript (Basle AN II 38) is actually a copy of an earlier manuscript dating from the eighth–ninth century, which is now lost; see discussion in Metzger, *Text of the New Testament*, 34.

[21]The other two fragments date from the third (P.Oxy. 2103) and sixth centuries (Florence, Laur. P.S.I. 1182) but offer very little of the text.

[22]Epp, "Textual Criticism," 91.

125, only thirty-five years later.[23] Other early manuscripts include $\mathfrak{P}^{90}$ (John, second century), $\mathfrak{P}^{104}$ (Matthew, second century), $\mathfrak{P}^{66}$ (John, late second century[24]), $\mathfrak{P}^{98}$ (Revelation, second century), $\mathfrak{P}^{4}$–$\mathfrak{P}^{64}$–$\mathfrak{P}^{67}$ (Luke and Matthew, late second century[25]), $\mathfrak{P}^{46}$ (Pauline epistles, c. AD 200), $\mathfrak{P}^{103}$ (Matthew, c. AD 200), $\mathfrak{P}^{75}$ (Luke and John, c. AD 200–225[26]), and many others. Of course, even our major fourth-century codices, Sinaiticus (א) and Vaticanus (B), which contain nearly the entire Greek Bible (Old and New Testaments), are still quite early compared to the manuscripts of most classical works.

The brief span of time between the production of the New Testament and our earliest copies gives us access to the New Testament text at a remarkably early stage, making it very unlikely that the textual tradition could have been radically altered prior to this time period without evidence for those alterations still being visible within the manuscript tradition.[27] Put differently, if a particular manuscript of a New Testament book (say, Mark) had been changed by a scribe in the late first or early second century, it is unlikely that the change would have been able to replace the original reading quickly enough so that our third- and fourth-century copies of Mark would fail to preserve the original text at all (thus creating a situation where we would not even know the text had been changed). Frederik Wisse comments:

---

[23]C. H. Roberts, "An Unpublished Fragment of the Fourth Gospel in the John Rylands Library," *BJRL* 20 (1936): 45–55; for an even earlier date of c. AD 100, see K. Aland, "Neue neutestamentliche Papyri II," *NTS* 9 (1962–63): 303–16.

[24]A date for $\mathfrak{P}^{66}$ in the first half of the second century has been suggested by Herbert Hunger, "Zur Datierung des Papyrus Bodmer II ($\mathfrak{P}^{66}$)," *Anzeiger der österreichischen Akademie der Wissenschaften* 4 (1960): 12–33.

[25]Skeat has argued that $\mathfrak{P}^{4}$–$\mathfrak{P}^{64}$–$\mathfrak{P}^{67}$ forms the earliest four-gospel codex and dates from the late second century; see T. C. Skeat, "The Oldest Manuscripts of the Four Gospels?" *NTS* 43 (1997): 1–34. Skeat has been challenged on this point by Peter M. Head, "Is $\mathfrak{P}^{4}$, $\mathfrak{P}^{64}$, and $\mathfrak{P}^{67}$ the Oldest Manuscript of the Four Gospels? A Response to T. C. Skeat," *NTS* 51 (2005): 450–57.

[26]The original editors of $\mathfrak{P}^{75}$ proposed a date between AD 175 and 200, making this a possible second-century text, but that is debated. See V. Martin and R. Kasser, *Papyrus Bodmer XIV–XV* (Geneva: Bibliotheca Bodmeriana, 1961), 1:13.

[27]Helmut Koester, "The Text of the Synoptic Gospels in the Second Century," in *Gospel Traditions in the Second Century: Origins, Recensions, Text, and Transmission*, ed. William L. Petersen (Notre Dame: University of Notre Dame Press, 1989), 19–37, has argued that the New Testament text could have been radically changed by the time of (and during) the second century. For the opposing view see Larry W. Hurtado, "The New Testament in the Second Century: Texts, Collections, and Canon," in *Transmission and Reception: New Testament Text-Critical and Exegetical Studies*, ed. J. W. Childers and D. C. Parker (Piscataway, NJ: Gorgias, 2006), 3–17; and Frederick Wisse, "The Nature and Purpose of Redactional Changes in Early Christian Texts: The Canonical Gospels," in *Gospel Traditions of the Second Century*, ed. Petersen, 39–53.

There is no indication that the Gospels circulated in a form different from that attested in the later textual tradition. . . . If indeed the text of the Gospels had been subjected to extensive redactional change and adaption during the second century, the unanimous attestation of a relatively stable and uniform text during the following centuries in both Greek and the versions would have to be considered nothing short of a miracle.[28]

The textual tradition of the New Testament, therefore, has a stubborn quality about it. Although a scribe can change an individual manuscript (or an individual reading), changing the *overall* textual tradition is much more difficult than one might think—the fact that there are so many other copies in circulation makes this virtually impossible to do. Kurt and Barbara Aland note that "one of the characteristics of the New Testament textual tradition is *tenacity*, i.e., the stubborn resistance of readings and text types to change. . . . This is what makes it possible to retrace the original text of the New Testament through a broad range of witnesses."[29] Again they declare:

The transmission of the New Testament textual tradition is characterized by an extremely impressive degree of *tenacity*. Once a reading occurs it will persist with obstinacy. . . . It is precisely the overwhelming mass of the New Testament textual tradition which provides an assurance of certainty in establishing the original text.[30]

In other words, Aland and Aland are arguing that the multiplicity of witnesses, combined with the stubbornness of the textual tradition and the early date of our manuscripts, make it more than reasonable to presume that the original text is preserved within our overall manuscript tradition (even though any given copy would have variants[31]).

However, despite the fact that the New Testament text, again, has substantially earlier textual attestation than most any other document of antiquity, this still does not seem to satisfy Ehrman. For example, he argues that we cannot know that we possess the text of Galatians because our earliest copy ($\mathfrak{P}^{46}$)

[28]Wisse, "Nature and Purpose of Redactional Changes in Early Christian Texts," 52–53.
[29]Aland and Aland, *Text of the New Testament*, 70 (emphasis added).
[30]Ibid., 291–92 (emphasis original).
[31]It is important to note that we do have a number of manuscripts in the early centuries of Christianity whose text is rightly characterized as "free" or "loose," leading to more variants and more original readings. The classic example of this is the fifth-century Codex Bezae (D). For more on this fascinating manuscript, see D. C. Parker, *Codex Bezae: An Early Christian Manuscript and Its Text* (Cambridge: Cambridge University Press, 1992).

was written nearly 150 years after the original was composed.[32] One wonders, would Ehrman's conclusions change if, say, we had a copy of Galatians from the middle of the second century (c. AD 150) or even earlier? This seems unlikely. Elsewhere in *Misquoting Jesus*, Ehrman argues that we can never really know what Galatians says because it is possible that one of the very first copies of Galatians could have had a mistake and maybe *all* of our extant copies derive from that single faulty copy.[33] Thus, armed with this hypothesis about what might have happened in the early stages of the transmission (a hypothesis that cannot be proven), Ehrman is always able to claim we can never know the original text, *no matter how early our extant manuscripts are*. Once again, we see how Ehrman's conclusions seem impervious to the historical evidence—the date of our manuscripts does not really matter because, in principle, the text of Galatians (or any book) can never really be known.

So, in the end, Ehrman's expressed concerns over the 150-year gap of time are somewhat of a red herring; they make the discussion appear to be about the historical data when it is really about an a priori decision never to acknowledge that a text can be sufficiently known unless we have 100 percent, unequivocal, absolute certainty. In other words, we can never claim knowledge of a text unless we have the autographs themselves (or a perfect copy of them). Needless to say, if this is the standard, then it will never be met in the real world of historical investigation.

Thesis 2: The Extent of Textual Variation: the vast majority of scribal changes are minor and insignificant
Although the prior discussion has many layers of complexity, the overall point is a simple one: the impressive quantity of New Testament manuscripts, combined

---

[32]Ehrman, *Misquoting Jesus*, 60. It is interesting to note that the very impressive study of Günther Zuntz on $\mathfrak{P}^{46}$ had a much more positive conclusion: "The excellent quality of the text represented by our oldest manuscript, $\mathfrak{P}^{46}$, stands out again. . . . Once the [scribal errors] have been discarded, there remains a text of outstanding (though not absolute) purity" (Günther Zuntz, *The Text of the Epistles: A Disquisition upon the Corpus Paulinum*, Schweich Lectures [London: British Academy, 1953], 212–13). For more on the text of Galatians in $\mathfrak{P}^{46}$ and other early manuscripts see Moisés Silva, "The Text of Galatians: Evidence from the Earliest Greek Manuscripts," in *Scribes and Scripture: Essays in Honor of J. Harold Greenlee*, ed. D. A. Black (Winona Lake, IN: Eisenbrauns, 1992), 17–25.

[33]Ehrman, *Misquoting Jesus*, 59. Even if Ehrman's hypothesis about how Galatians was copied in its earliest stages were true, we can still work back to a text that is so very near the original of Galatians that it would be more than sufficient for knowing what Galatians said. In fact, Ehrman acknowledges as much: "This oldest form of the text [of Galatians] is no doubt closely (very closely) related to what the author originally wrote, and so it is the basis for our interpretation of his teaching" (p. 62, emphasis original).

with the early date of many of those manuscripts, makes it historically reasonable to conclude that we possess the original text of the New Testament within the overall textual tradition (though not necessarily in any single manuscript). Therefore, as noted above, we actually have *too much* information—we not only possess the original text but also many textual variants. With this, we transition into the next stage of the discussion. Now we are no longer dealing with the question of *whether* we have the original New Testament text in our manuscript tradition but *how* we separate the original text from the variants. Do these variants present a considerable problem? How many of these variants are there? How different are the manuscripts we possess?

One might think we could just add up all the textual variations and we would have our answer. However, as we shall see, the answer to these questions is not as simple as providing a numerical figure. All scholars agree that there are thousands of textual variants throughout our manuscripts—maybe as many as four hundred thousand—though no one knows the exact number. Ehrman seems eager to draw attention to this fact, if not to suggest even higher numbers: "Some say there are 200,000 variants known, some say 300,000, some say 400,000 or more!"[34] Indeed, numbers matter very much to Ehrman. For him, the sheer *volume* of variants is the deciding factor and sufficient, in and of itself, to conclude that the New Testament cannot be trusted. He even offers the dramatic statement, "There are more variations among our manuscripts than there are words in the New Testament."[35] However, Ehrman's statistical enthusiasm aside, mere numbers do not tell the whole story. When other factors are considered, a more balanced and full-orbed picture of the New Testament text begins to emerge.

The Nature of the Textual Changes

All textual changes are not created equal. This fact, of course, is the fundamental reason why a numbers-only approach to textual variants is simply not viable. We need to ask not only how many variants there are but what *kind* of variants there are. It is a question not simply of quantity but of quality. It is for this reason that Eldon Epp and other textual critics recognize that there are certain kinds of textual variants that can legitimately be regarded as "insignificant."[36] This term simply refers to variants that have no bear-

---

[34]Ehrman, *Misquoting Jesus*, 89.

[35]Ibid., 90.

[36]Eldon Jay Epp, "Toward the Clarification of the Term 'Textual Variant,'" in *Studies in the Theory and Method of New Testament Textual Criticism*, 57. As a point of clarification, Epp prefers to use the term "readings" to refer to insignificant changes, and reserves the

ing or no impact on "the ultimate goal of establishing the original text."[37] These are typically minor, run-of-the-mill, scribal slips that exist in any document of antiquity (New Testament or otherwise) and thus occasion no real concern for the textual scholar—and certainly are not relevant for assessing whether a document has been reliably passed down to us. And here is the key: these "insignificant" variants make up the vast, vast majority of variations within the New Testament text.[38] Categories of insignificant variants include the following:[39]

1) *Spelling (orthographical) differences.* It turns out that scribes in the ancient world often made spelling errors/changes just like writers in the modern day. Examples of this sort of change abound. (a) If certain words ended in a *nu*, that *nu* would often be dropped by the scribe if the following word started with a vowel (this is known as the moveable *nu*). But scribes were not always consistent with this practice and often differed from one another, and would even change patterns within the same manuscript. (b) Scribes used a variety of different abbreviations, and not all were identical. For example, if the last word in a line ended with *nu*, sometimes scribes would abbreviate it by dropping the *nu* and putting a horizontal line in its place.[40] (c) Scribes would often interchange *i* and *ie* (or *ei*) in the spelling of words, which was often a form of phonetical spelling rather than a formal scribal error.[41] And on it goes. The variety of spelling differences in manuscripts seems endless and every one of them counts as a scribal variation.[42]

term "variant" for changes that are significant or meaningful. Although such a distinction is helpful, we are using the term "variant" here in both senses: to speak of insignificant and significant changes.

[37]Epp, "Toward the Clarification of the Term 'Textual Variant,'" 57.

[38]No one knows the exact numbers. Wallace estimates that insignificant variants (as I have defined them here) would constitute approximately 80–90 percent of known textual changes (though this number is inexact because we use different categories). See J. Ed Komoszewski, M. James Sawyer, and Daniel B. Wallace, *Reinventing Jesus, How Contemporary Skeptics Miss the Real Jesus and Mislead Popular Culture* (Grand Rapids: Kregel, 2006), 63.

[39]Categories 1 to 3 below are included by Epp in his definition of "insignificant" readings (Epp, "Toward the Clarification of the Term 'Textual Variant,'" 57), and I have added categories 4 and 5.

[40]E.g., John 1:4 in 𝔓[66] drops the *nu* at the end of *anthrōpōn*.

[41]Francis T. Gignac, *A Grammar of the Greek Papyri of the Roman and Byzantine Periods, vol. 1: Phonology* (Milan: Istituto Editoriale Cisalpino-La Goliardica, 1976), 189–91. Examples of such a practice abound in Codex Sinaiticus; e.g., *tapinos* for *tapeinos*, *kreinai* for *krinai*, and *dynami* for *dynamei*. Skeat and others have suggested such phonetical spelling can be evidence a manuscript has been produced by dictation. See Skeat, "Use of Dictation in Ancient Book-Production," 179–208.

[42]It is important to note that the type of changes in view here are the ones that are merely orthographic. On occasion, a spelling error may produce a new word and affect the meaning

215

2) *Nonsense readings.* Occasionally scribes would make a mistake that would render a verse nonsensical and thus the mistake can be quickly identified as not being the original reading of the text. For example, sometimes scribes would accidentally skip a line in their copying (called *haplography*), and this would create incoherent readings. A well-known example is found in John 17:15 of Codex Vaticanus (B), where the scribe skipped a line and left out the bracketed portion: "I do not ask that you take them from the [world, but that you keep them from the] evil one." Needless to say, this produces a nonsensical reading that is clearly not original! Such mistakes may tell us about habits of a particular scribe, but they have no bearing on our ability to recovery the original text.

3) *Singular readings.* Sometimes a certain reading exists in only one Greek manuscript and no other. Such singular readings—and there are thousands of them—have little claim to be the original text and therefore are irrelevant in assessing the reliability of the manuscript tradition. For example, $\mathfrak{P}^{66*}$ is the only (known) manuscript where John 17:12 has Jesus declare to the Father in his high priestly prayer, "I kept them in *my* (*mou*) name, which you have given me." All other manuscripts read, "I kept them in *your* (*sou*) name, which you have given me."

4) *Meaningless word order changes.* One of the most common scribal changes involves word order (known as *transposition*). Unlike English, Greek nouns are inflected and thus their function in the sentence is not determined by word order but by their case. Therefore, the vast majority of word order changes in Greek do not affect meaning at all. For example, again in $\mathfrak{P}^{66}$, John 13:1 reads *toutou tou kosmou* ("this world"), whereas the original likely read *tou kosmou toutou* ("this world")—no difference in meaning whatsoever. Another common word order change, especially in the Pauline epistles, is "Jesus Christ" for "Christ Jesus," or vice versa. Every word order change (and every various possible combination) counts as a variant.

5) *Definite articles on proper nouns.* Unlike English, Greek can include articles in front of proper nouns: "the Jesus," "the John," or "the Andrew." However, there is no consistency in this practice among early Christian scribes and the presence or absence of the article before proper nouns rarely affects the meaning.[43] For example, a number of manuscripts (A Δ f^1 f^{13}

---

of a passage. For example, the well-known variant in Romans 5:1 could read, "We have (*echomen*) peace with God," or "Let us have (*echōmen*) peace with God."

[43]It is possible that articles before proper nouns may occasionally be anaphoric (referring to a previous referent) and thus may be translated in a slightly different manner. E.g., Acts 19:15,

1241) include the article (*tou*) in front of the name "Simon" in Mark 1:16, whereas most other manuscripts leave it out. Either way the English translation is the same: "Simon." Every time a scribe includes or omits an article in front of a proper noun, it counts as a textual variant.

Of course, this brief overview of insignificant scribal changes is not exhaustive, and other categories could be added (e.g., scribes replacing personal pronouns with their antecedents). But the overall point is clear. Even though these types of changes are quite abundant—Ehrman is correct about that—they are also quite irrelevant. Thus, simply adding up the total textual variations is not a meaningful exercise in determining the reliability of textual transmission.

Textual Changes and the Quantity of Manuscripts

The numbers-only approach to evaluating textual variants also fails to take into account another very critical piece of data: the impressive quantity of manuscripts we possess. Obviously, if we possessed only *five* Greek manuscripts of the New Testament, then we would have very few textual variations to account for. But if we have over *five thousand* Greek manuscripts of the New Testament (not to mention those in other languages), then the *overall quantity of textual variants* will dramatically increase because the overall *number of manuscripts* has dramatically increased. The more manuscripts that can be compared, the more variations can be discovered. Thus, the quantity of variations is not necessarily an indication of scribal infidelity as much as it is the natural consequence of having more manuscripts than any other historical text.

Incredibly, then, Ehrman takes what should be *positive* historical evidence for the New Testament (the high number of manuscripts) and, somehow, turns the tables to make it evidence for its tendentious character—a remarkable feat, to be sure. One wonders what Ehrman's conclusions would be if we actually *did* possess only five manuscripts of the New Testament and thereby had very few textual variants. Would the *lack* of textual variants then be regarded as positive evidence for the New Testament's reliable transmission? We suspect not. One wonders if the objection would then be that we have too *few* manuscripts. It is a losing affair either way. Thus, once again, we see a familiar pattern emerging. Regardless of the evidence—whether the manuscripts are many or few,

---

ton Paulon epistamai, can be translated, "This Paul I recognize." Either way, it is hardly a substantive difference.

whether the variants are many or few—Ehrman's conclusions would remain unchanged.

Thesis 3: The Reliability of the Text Critical Method: of the small portion of variations that are significant, our text-critical methodology can determine, with a reasonable degree of certainty, which is the original text
The above section has demonstrated that the vast majority of textual variations are insignificant and irrelevant to determining the original text of the New Testament. However, that leaves a small portion of textual variants that can be deemed "significant." The definition of this term has two aspects: (1) "significant" textual variants are simply those that are not included in the "insignificant" category discussed above; and (2) "significant" variants are those that in *some sense* affect the meaning of the passage (though the effect can range from fairly minimal to more substantial).

Even though the quantity of these significant variants is quite small in comparison to insignificant variants, some of them can still make an impact on our understanding of New Testament passages (as we shall see below). Thus one might conclude that these sorts of changes present a real challenge to the textual integrity of the New Testament. However, such a conclusion would be built upon an assumption that we have no way to determine which of these significant variants were original and which were not. Put differently, significant variants would be a problem *if* we could assume that every one of them was as equally viable as every other. The problem with such an assumption, however, is that it stands in direct contradiction to the entire history of textual criticism—indeed, to the very *existence* of the field itself—which has consistently maintained that not all textual variants are equally viable and that our methodology can determine (with a reasonable degree of certainty) which is the original text.[44] If that is the case, then these few "significant" textual variants do not materially affect the integrity of the New Testament because, put simply, we can usually spot them when they occur.

---

[44]Of course, there is not space in this short chapter to review the basic methodological principles of New Testament textual criticism. For more on that subject, see Metzger and Ehrman, *Text of the New Testament*, 300–343; Aland and Aland, *Text of the New Testament*, 280–316; Eldon Jay Epp and Gordon D. Fee, *Studies in the Theory and Method of New Testament Textual Criticism*; Ehrman and Holmes, *The Text of the New Testament in Contemporary Research*, 237–379; David Alan Black, ed., *Rethinking New Testament Textual Criticism* (Grand Rapids: Baker, 2002).

Examples of Significant Variants

It may be helpful for us to review some examples of significant variants, though we can only scratch the surface of the issue here. For instance, in Mark 1:14 we are told that Jesus came preaching the "gospel of God." However, some fifth-century (and later) manuscripts—such as Codex Alexandrinus (A) and Codex Bezae (D)—read the "gospel *of the kingdom* of God." The cause for this slight change is obvious: the phrase "kingdom of God" is quite common throughout Mark (and the other Synoptic Gospels) and the scribe was likely harmonizing 1:14 with these other passages (a very common cause of scribal variations). Is there a difference in meaning between "gospel of God" and "gospel of the kingdom of God"? Perhaps. But the difference is hardly a cause for concern. And even if the difference were substantial, it matters little because the textual evidence is clear that Mark originally wrote "gospel of God."[45] Mark 1:14 is a very typical example of a "significant" variant.

However, there are other "significant" variants that have a more substantial impact on the meaning of a text. Two examples will suffice. One of the most commonly mentioned variants is found in 1 John 5:7–8 and is known as the *Comma Johanneum.*[46] The italicized portion of the following verses is found in only a handful of manuscripts: "For there are three that testify: *in heaven: the Father, the Word, and the Holy Spirit, and these three are one. And there are three that testify on earth:* the Spirit and the water and the blood; and these three agree." Out of hundreds of Greek manuscripts, only eight contain this variant reading—and four of those have the variants added by the scribe into the margin—and the earliest of these is tenth century.[47] Moreover, the variant is attested by none of the Greek fathers and is absent from almost all our early versions. In the end, despite the fact that this variant found its way into the Textus Receptus (and thereby the King James translation), the text-critical evidence is decidedly against it being original to John's epistle. What, then, do we make of this variant? No one can doubt that it is "significant" in that it affects the theological understanding of this verse. However, it simply has no claim to originality

---

[45]Not only does "gospel of God" have solid external support ($\aleph$ B L Θ f^1 f^{13}), but the existence of the shorter reading better explains the rise of the longer one (due to harmonization), whereas the opposite scenario is quite difficult to explain.

[46]For more on this variant see Bruce M. Metzger, *A Textual Commentary on the Greek New Testament* (Stuttgart: German Bible Society, 1994), 647–48; Metzger and Ehrman, *Text of the New Testament*, 146–47.

[47]61 88[v.r.] 221[v.r.] 429[v.r.] 636[v.r.] 918 2318.

and therefore does not impact our ability to recover the original text of the New Testament.[48] Nor is our understanding of the Trinity in the slightest dependent on this verse—indeed, the orthodox conception of the Trinity can be derived from many other New Testament verses and was well in place for centuries before this variation would have been widely known.

A second example is Mark 16:9–20, known as the long ending of Mark.[49] Most modern English translations bracket off this portion of the text and note that two of our earliest manuscripts of Mark, Codex Sinaiticus (‎ℵ) and Vaticanus (B), do not contain the long ending. Moreover, the long ending was unknown in a number of early versions (including a number of Latin, Syriac, and Armenian manuscripts) and was not mentioned by prominent Greek fathers such as Clement of Alexandria and Origen. There is also the problem of non-Markan vocabulary in the long ending, as well as the awkward transition between 16:8 and 16:9. In short, most scholars agree that the long ending of Mark was not original to his Gospel. So, what is the impact of this particular variant? There is no doubt this textual change is "significant" both in regard to its scope (twelve verses) and also its content (resurrection, drinking poison, picking up snakes). But, since we can clearly see that these verses are an addition, they bear no impact on our ability to recover the original text of Mark. There may be residual questions regarding why Mark would end his Gospel in verse 8 (which we cannot enter into here), but the textual evidence is quite clear that he did not write verses 9–20.[50]

---

[48]The recent volume by Bart Ehrman, *Jesus, Interrupted: Revealing the Hidden Contradictions in the Bible* (New York: HarperOne, 2009), offers a rebuttal to many of the criticisms of *Misquoting Jesus* and continues to insist that the variant in 1 John 5:7 is important and meaningful (p. 186). But Ehrman is missing the point entirely about this text. The reason this variant does not affect the integrity of the New Testament text is not because it is insignificant (Ehrman is correct that it changes the meaning of the passage), but because the textual evidence is so clearly against it that we know it is not the original reading. If we can tell it is not the original reading, then it does not matter how meaningful the change is. Ehrman seems so unduly fixated on the impact of the change that he misses the fact that the evidence against the variant speaks compellingly against its originality.

[49]The studies on the long ending of Mark are too many to mention here; some helpful reviews of scholarship can be found in Joseph Hug, *La finale de l'evangile de Marc: Mc 16, 9–20* (Paris: Gabalda, 1978), 11–32; Paul Mirecki, "Mark 16:9–20: Composition, Tradition, and Redaction" (PhD diss., Harvard University, 1986), 1–23; Virtus E. Gideon, "The Longer Ending of Mark in Recent Study," in *New Testament Studies: Essays in Honor of Ray Summers in his Sixty-Fifth Year*, ed. H. L. Drumwright and C. Vaughan (Waco, TX: Markham Press Fund, 1975), 3–12; and James A. Kelhoffer, *Miracle and Mission: The Authentication of Missionaries and Their Message in the Longer Ending of Mark* (Tübingen: Mohr Siebeck, 2000), 5–47.

[50]For more discussion on why Mark would end his Gospel at verse 8 see Beverly Roberts Gaventa and Patrick D. Miller, eds., *The Ending of Mark and the Ends of God: Essays in Memory of Donald Harrisville Juel* (Louisville, KY: Westminster, 2005); P. W. van der Horst,

Theologically Motivated Changes

There has been a long-standing discussion in the world of textual criticism concerning the degree to which scribes intentionally altered passages of the New Testament to better conform to their own theological preferences. Ever since the well-known statement from Westcott and Hort that "there are no signs of deliberate falsification of the text for dogmatic purposes,"[51] there has been a steady chorus of scholars intending to show the opposite to be the case. The idea of theologically motivated scribal changes can be traced back to Kirsopp Lake and J. Rendel Harris and more recently to scholars like Eldon J. Epp and his well-known book *The Theological Tendency of Codex Cantabrigiensis in Acts*.[52] Ehrman joins this chorus in a number of his recent books, but most notably *The Orthodox Corruption of Scripture*, where he argues that scribes in the early church were not merely disinterested copyists who mechanically transmitted the text in front of them, but, in one sense, continued "writing" the New Testament text by changing it to adapt to the theological and social challenges of the day.[53] Thus, argues Ehrman, these scribal changes need to be understood within the context of the early church battles over heresy and orthodoxy—battles that not only affected the development of the New Testament canon but affected the development of the New Testament text itself.

Because these theologically motivated changes can affect the meaning of a passage (though just how much is in doubt), they are rightly considered to be "significant" textual variants. A few examples may be helpful. In Luke 2:33, after Simeon blesses the baby Jesus, we read, "And his father and his mother marveled at what was said about him." However, a number of later manuscripts read, "And *Joseph* and his mother marveled at what was said about him" (Κ Χ Δ Θ Α Π Ψ). Ehrman argues that this scribal change is designed to bolster the doctrine of the virgin birth—an issue that was often

"Can a Book End with a *gar*? A Note on Mark XVI.8," *JTS* 23 (1972): 121–24; K. R. Iverson, "A Further Word on Final *gar* (Mark 16:8)," *CBQ* 68 (2006): 79–94; J. Lee Magness, *Sense and Absence: Structure and Suspension in the End of Mark's Gospel* (Atlanta: Scholars Press, 1986); and David Alan Black, ed., *Perspectives on the Ending of Mark: 4 Views* (Nashville: Broadman, 2008).

[51]Westcott and Hort, *New Testament in the Original Greek*, 2:282.

[52]Kirsopp Lake, *The Influence of Textual Criticism on the Exegesis of the New Testament* (Oxford: Parker, 1904); J. Rendel Harris, "New Points of View in Textual Criticism," *Expositor* 7 (1914): 316–34; Eldon J. Epp, *The Theological Tendency of Codex Bezae Cantabrigiensis in Acts* (Cambridge: Cambridge University Press, 1966).

[53]Bart D. Ehrman, *The Orthodox Corruption of Scripture* (New York: Oxford University Press, 1993). These same arguments appear in more popularized form in *Misquoting Jesus*, 151–75.

challenged by some heretical groups like the Ebionites—by making sure no one can (mis)use this passage to argue that Jesus had a human father.[54] A second example comes from 1 Timothy 3:16 which, speaking of Christ, declares, "He was manifested in the flesh." However, other manuscripts show a scribal change which then makes the verse declare, "*God* was manifested in the flesh" (א^c A^2 C^2 D^c K L P Ψ). Ehrman again argues that this scribal change was intentional and designed to state the divinity of Christ in more explicit terms.[55] In the midst of all the Christological debates in early Christianity, scribes may have wanted to make sure this verse expressly affirmed that Christ was God come in the flesh. A third example is found in John 19:40 where Jesus' body is being prepared for burial. We are told there that "they took the body of Jesus and bound it in linen cloths." But the fifth-century codex Alexandrinus (A) reads, "So they took the body of *God* and bound it in linen cloths." This very obvious Christological change again appears to have been introduced for theological reasons—perhaps to keep Docetists from arguing that since Jesus was God he could not have had a real flesh-and-blood body.[56]

How should we assess Ehrman's arguments with regard to intentional scribal changes? Let it be said at the outset that Ehrman's detailed textual work in *The Orthodox Corruption of Scripture* is where he is at his best. Overall, this is a very impressive monograph with much to offer the scholarly community in its assessment of the history of the New Testament text. Surely Ehrman's overall thesis is correct that, on occasion, scribes did change their manuscripts for theological reasons. That being said, there are two issues that need to be raised. First, although Ehrman is correct that *some* changes are theologically motivated, it seems he too quickly passes over equally (if not more) plausible explanations that are not nearly as provocative. For example, in 1 Timothy 3:16 above, the scribal switch to "*God* was manifested in the flesh" can be naturally explained by the fact that the word for "who" (ΟΣ) is very close to the abbreviation for "God" (ΘΣ). A simple scribal slip would easily turn one word into the other. However, Ehrman still maintains that the change was theologically motivated because four of the uncial witnesses (א A C D) show that ΟΣ ("who") was actually *corrected* by the scribe to read ΘΣ ("God")—meaning the scribe did it consciously. But the fact that these four scribes did it consciously is not the same as saying they did it for *theological reasons*. These are not the

[54]Ehrman, *Orthodox Corruption of Scripture*, 55.
[55]Ibid., 77–78.
[56]Ibid., 83.

same thing. These scribes may have simply thought the prior scribe got it wrong; or maybe they simply corrected it according to what was in their exemplar. Moreover, a number of other majuscules have ΘΣ ("God") but not as part of a correction (K L P Ψ), so there is no indication that they did it intentionally. In the end, the explanation for the variant in 1 Timothy 3:16 is likely a very boring one. Simply a mistake.

A second issue with Ehrman's work has to do with the overall conclusions that can be drawn from it. Let us assume for a moment that Ehrman is correct about the motivations of the scribes in every single example he offers—they *all* changed the text for theological reasons. But how does this change our understanding of the original text of the New Testament? What is the real payoff here in terms of assessing the New Testament's integrity? Not much. Ehrman's study may be helpful to assess scribal habits or the nature of theological debates in early Christianity, but it has very little effect on our recovery of the original text because in each of the instances he describes *we can distinguish the original text from the scribal changes that have been made.* In other words, even theologically motivated changes do not threaten the integrity of the text for the simple reason that our text-critical methodology allows us to spot them when they occur.[57]

It is here that Ehrman finds himself in somewhat of a conundrum. On the one hand, in *Misquoting Jesus* he wants the "original" text of the New Testament to remain inaccessible and obscure, forcing him to argue that text-critical methodologies cannot really produce any certain conclusions. On the other hand, in *The Orthodox Corruption of Scripture* he needs to argue that text-critical methodologies are reliable and can show you what was original and what was not; otherwise he would not be able to demonstrate that changes have been made for theological reasons. Moisés Silva comments:

> There is hardly a page in [*The Orthodox Corruption of Scripture*] where Ehrman does not employ the concept of an original text. Indeed, without such a concept, and without the confidence that we can identify what the original text is, Ehrman's book is almost unimaginable, for every one of his examples depends on his ability to identify a particular reading as a scribal corruption.[58]

---

[57]In Ehrman's recent rebuttals in *Jesus, Interrupted*, this point still goes entirely unaddressed. He continues to repeat how meaningful these changes were, but the examples he picks are often changes that virtually all textual scholars acknowledge to be unoriginal; e.g., the pericope of the adulterous woman in John 7:53–8:11 (p. 188).

[58]Moisés Silva, review of D. C. Parker, *The Living Text of the Gospels*, *WTJ* 62 (2000): 301–2.

The essence of Ehrman's argument, then, seems self-defeating. He is using theologically motivated scribal changes as a reason for why we cannot know the original text, but then he must assume we can know the original text in order to prove these scribal changes. Which one is it? In the end, it seems that Ehrman wants to be able to have his text-critical cake and eat it, too. Unfortunately, it seems the agenda in *Misquoting Jesus* is forcing Ehrman not only to deny the overall reliability of the field of textual criticism—the very field to which he has committed his life's work—but to deny even his own prior scholarly works.

What, then, is driving these inconsistencies in Ehrman's text-critical approach? Inevitably, it goes back to his commitment to the Bauer thesis and, in particular, his application of the Bauer thesis to the field of textual criticism. Even though the field of textual criticism has historically argued that some variants really are more original than others, the Bauer thesis implies that, in one sense, all textual variants are inherently equal. After all, why should one form of the New Testament text be considered genuine and not another? Who is to say which text is right? Different Christians in different regions experienced different textual variants (and to them these variants *were* the word of God). It seems, then, that Ehrman is being pulled back and forth between these two competing positions—historical textual criticism that privileges one reading over another and the Bauer thesis, which suggests no reading can really be regarded as superior. The latter position seems to be prevailing when Ehrman declares, "It is by no means self-evident that [reconstructing the original text] ought to be the ultimate goal of the discipline . . . there may indeed be scant reason to privilege the 'original' text over forms of the text that developed subsequently."[59]

Thus, Ehrman's Bauer-driven approach to textual criticism is more radical than one might first realize. His claim is not simply that the battles over heresy and orthodoxy altered the original text, but he goes one step further to say that the battles over heresy and orthodoxy imply that there is no original text. Put differently, the Bauer hypothesis does not just explain the *cause* of textual variants, but it determines what our *attitude* should be towards textual variants. They are all equal. Once again, it is clear that Ehrman's conclusions are driven less by the discipline of textual criticism

---

[59]Bart D. Ehrman, "The Text as Window: New Testament Manuscripts and the Social History of Early Christianity," in *The Text of the New Testament in Contemporary Research*, 361 n.1. For a similar sentiment see Donald Wayne Riddle, "Textual Criticism as a Historical Discipline," *ATR* 18 (1936): 220–33.

and more by his prior commitment to the Bauer thesis and the pluralistic nature of early Christianity.

Thesis 4: The Impact of Unresolved Variants: the remaining number of truly unresolved variants is very few and not material to the story/ teaching of the New Testament

The prior section has argued that even "significant" variants do not present a problem for the integrity of the New Testament because our text-critical methodology allows us to determine, with a reasonable degree of certainty, which is the original text. However, a very small number of significant variants remain where our methodology is not always able to reach a certain conclusion in either direction. In such a case, we may have two (or more) different readings and not know for sure which one is the original. Although these "unresolved" variants are quite rare, they are the only legitimate places where the New Testament text is genuinely in question, and therefore they need to be addressed.

Examples of Unresolved Variants

Needless to say, the question of what constitutes an "unresolved" variant is not always easy to answer (and cannot be fully resolved here). Certainly we cannot regard a variant as "unresolved" simply because there is *some* disagreement about its originality amongst scholars—after all, it seems that some sort of argument could be made for almost *any* variant reading if someone really wanted to try. Instead, we are talking here about a situation where there are two (or more) possible readings and the evidence for each reading (whether external or internal) is relatively equal, or at least close enough that it is reasonable to think that *either* reading could have been original. Again, a few examples may help.

In Mark 3:32, the crowd sitting around Jesus said to him, "Your mother and your brothers are outside, seeking you." However, evidence from some other early Greek manuscripts (A D) and Old Latin, Old Syriac, and Gothic witnesses (combined with some strong internal considerations) suggest that the original may have been "Your mother and your brothers *and your sisters* are outside, seeking you." Even the editorial committee of the UBS Greek New Testament was divided on the question, which has prompted a number of English translations to include a footnote in this verse with the variant reading.[60] Whichever way one decides, very little is at stake here. We know

---

[60]Metzger, *Textual Commentary on the Greek New Testament*, 70.

from other passages that Jesus had sisters (Matt. 13:56), and no doubt they would have been concerned about him along with the rest of the family. Another example, Mark 7:9, reads, "And he said to them, 'You have a fine way of rejecting the commandment of God in order to establish (*stēsēte*) your tradition!'" But, a number of majuscules (א A K L X Δ Π), some of which are quite early, substitute "keep" (*tērēsēte*) for the word "establish" (*stēsēte*). Given the similar spelling and similar meaning of these words, it is quite difficult to determine which gave rise to which. However, either way, it leaves the meaning of the passage virtually unchanged.

Both of the above examples are typical "unresolved" variants—not only are they very rare, but most of the time they affect the meaning of the text very little (and thus are relatively boring). But Ehrman has suggested that there are some other hard-to-solve variants that *do* impact the meaning of the text in a substantive manner. For example, Luke 22:43–44 describes the anguish of Jesus in the garden: "And there appeared to him an angel from heaven, strengthening him. And being in an agony he prayed more earnestly; and his sweat became like great drops of blood falling down to the ground." These verses are attested by a number of important witnesses (א*,b D K L X Δ* Θ Π* Ψ *f*¹) including Justin Martyr, Irenaeus, Hippolytus, Eusebius, and other church fathers. However, these verses are also omitted by a number of important witnesses (𝔓69vid 𝔓75 אa A B T W 1071*) as well as Clement of Alexandria and Origen. Consequently, it is difficult to be sure whether the verses are original to Luke.[61] The question, then, is whether either option raises a substantial problem or changes any biblical doctrine (Christological or otherwise). We know from other passages that Jesus felt great anguish in the garden of Gethsemane (Matt. 26:37–38; Mark 14:34), and that he was a real human being that could suffer temptation and sorrow (Heb. 2:17–18). Moreover, we have other accounts where angels attended Jesus in times of great need (Mark 1:13). These realities remain unchanged whether we include or omit this reading. Thus, either option seems to be consistent and compatible with what we know about Jesus and his ministry.

---

[61]Ehrman argues that they are not original, and we would tend to agree (*Misquoting Jesus*, 138–44), though we would disagree with his assessment of the impact of this variant. See further the discussion in Metzger, *Textual Commentary on the Greek New Testament*, 151; Ehrman, *Orthodox Corruption of Scripture*, 187–94; Bart D. Ehrman and Mark A. Plunkett, "The Angel and the Agony: The Textual Problem of Luke 22:43-44," *CBQ* 45 (1983): 401–16; Jerome Neyrey, *The Passion According to Luke: A Redaction Study of Luke's Soteriology* (New York: Paulist, 1985), 55–57; and Raymond Brown, *The Death of the Messiah: From Gethsemane to the Grave* (New York: Doubleday, 1994), 179–84.

Ehrman offers another example from Mark 1:41 (NIV) where Jesus sees a leper and was "filled with compassion" (*splagchnisthei*). Though this reading has superior external support in its favor (‭א‬ A B C K L W Δ Θ Π $f^1 f^{13}$), Codex Bezae (D) and a number of Old Latin witnesses declare that when Jesus saw the leper he was "filled with anger" (*orgistheis*). Although the external evidence is in favor of "filled with compassion," a number of internal considerations (e.g., which reading would the scribe have likely changed?) suggest that the original may have been "filled with anger." In short, it is difficult to know which reading is original.[62] So, again, we ask whether either option raises a substantial problem or issue related to the teaching of the New Testament. Although "filled with anger" certainly changes our understanding of the passage—Jesus was likely expressing "righteous indignation at the ravages of sin"[63] on the world, particularly the leper—this perspective on Jesus fits quite well with the rest of the book of Mark, where he shows his anger in 3:5 in a confrontation with the Pharisees and in 10:14 as he is indignant with his disciples. But it is also consistent with the Jesus of the other Gospels. Particularly noteworthy is John 11:33 where Jesus is faced with the plight of Lazarus, and the text tells us that he was "deeply moved" (*enebrimēsato*), a term that can better be understood to mean Jesus felt "anger, outrage or indignation."[64] Was Jesus angry at Lazarus? No, the context suggests that he was angered over the ravages of sin on the world, particularly as it affected Lazarus. In John 11:33, then, we have a vivid parallel to what might be happening in Mark 1:41—both are examples of Jesus showing anger toward the effects of sin in the midst of performing a miracle of healing and restoration. In the end, whichever reading in Mark 1:41 is original, neither is out of step with the Jesus of the New Testament.

Unresolved Variants and Biblical Authority

It is here that we come to the crux of the issue regarding biblical authority. Do we need to have absolute 100 percent certainty about every single textual variant for God to speak authoritatively in the Scriptures? Not at all. When we recognize not only how few unresolved variants exist but also

---

[62]For fuller discussion see Bart Ehrman, "A Sinner in the Hands of an Angry Jesus," in *New Testament Greek and Exegesis: Essays in Honor of Gerald F. Hawthorne*, ed. Amy M. Donaldson and Timothy B. Sailors (Grand Rapids: Eerdmans, 2003), 77–98; William L. Lane, *The Gospel according to St. Mark* (Grand Rapids: Eerdmans, 1974), 84–87.

[63]Lane, *Gospel according to St. Mark*, 86.

[64]D. A. Carson, *The Gospel according to John* (Grand Rapids: Eerdmans, 1991), 415.

how little they impact the overall story of the New Testament, then we can have confidence that the message of the New Testament has been *sufficiently* preserved for the church. All the teaching of the New Testament—whether regarding the person of Jesus (divinity and humanity), the work of Jesus (his life, death, and resurrection), the application of his work to the believer (justification, sanctification, glorification), or other doctrines—are left unaffected by the remaining unresolved textual variations.[65] Belief in the inspiration of the original autographs does not require that every individual copy of the autographs be error-free. The question is simply whether the manuscript tradition *as a whole* is reliable enough to transmit the essential message of the New Testament. As we have seen above, the manuscript tradition is more than adequate. It is so very close to the originals that there is no material difference between what, say, Paul or John wrote and what we possess today.

Of course, as we have seen above, Ehrman has taken a very different approach. For him, the quest for the original text is somewhat of an "all or nothing" endeavor. Either we know the wording of the original text with absolute certainty (meaning we have the autographs, or perfect copies of the autographs), or we can have no confidence at all in the wording of the

---

[65]In *Jesus Interrupted*, Ehrman argues that whether or not a variant affects a cardinal Christian doctrine should not be relevant in determining why it matters. He declares, "It seems to me to be a very strange criterion of significance to say that textual variants ultimately don't matter because they don't affect any cardinal Christian doctrine" (p. 186). But, again, Ehrman seems to be missing the point that his evangelical critics are raising when they say these changes "don't matter." No one is suggesting that whether Jesus sweated blood in Luke 22:43–44 is completely irrelevant—of course it is important to know what the original text said and of course it is important not to say something happened when it did not in fact take place. In this sense, then, all would agree that variants such as these "matter." But if one asks whether such a variant changes the overall Christian message about Jesus, his mission, his humanity or divinity, or any other central doctrine, then the answer is clearly "no." In this sense, the variant "doesn't matter." Surely Ehrman would agree that the central doctrines of the faith "matter" more than peripheral ones. For example, an unresolved variant dealing with justification surely matters more than one pertaining to the question of whether Jesus sweated blood in one particular instance. If one were wrong about whether Jesus sweated blood, the consequences are very minimal and affect only a minor historical detail. If one were wrong about justification, on the other hand, the message of the gospel itself is at stake. Therefore, when evangelicals say these variants "don't matter," they simply mean that they do not affect the ability of the New Testament to accurately deliver the divine message of the Christian faith. The reason evangelicals insist on emphasizing this fact is because this is precisely the thing Ehrman denies in his books—he insists that these textual variants do affect the overall Christian message. For this reason it is largely due to Ehrman claiming too much for these textual variants that has led evangelicals to rebut him the way they do. But this is not to suggest that evangelicals consider comparatively insignificant variants completely unimportant or irrelevant.

original text.[66] Unfortunately, this requirement of absolute certainty sets up a false dichotomy that is foreign to the study of history. As historians, we are not forced to choose between knowing *everything* or knowing *nothing*—there are degrees of assurance that can be attained even though some things are still unknown. This false dichotomy allows Ehrman to draw conclusions that are vastly out of proportion with the actual historical evidence. Although his overall historical claim is relatively indisputable (that the New Testament manuscripts are not perfect but contain a variety of scribal variations), his sweeping conclusions simply do not follow (that the text of the New Testament is unreliable and unknowable). We can have *reliable* manuscripts without having *perfect* manuscripts. But it is precisely this distinction that Ehrman's "all or nothing" methodology does not allow him to make.

As a result, addressing the historical evidence (the nature and extent of textual variants) will not ultimately change Ehrman's conclusions about the New Testament. It will not change his conclusions because it is not the historical evidence that led to his conclusions in the first place. What, then, is driving Ehrman's conclusions? Ironically, they are being driven not by any historical consideration but by a *theological* one. At the end of *Misquoting Jesus*, Ehrman reveals the core theological premise behind his thinking: "If [God] really wanted people to have his actual words, surely he would have miraculously preserved those words, just as he miraculously inspired them in the first place."[67] In other words, if God really inspired the New Testament *there would be no scribal variations at all*. It is his commitment to this belief—a theological belief—that is driving his entire approach to textual variants. Of course, this belief has manifold problems associated with it. Most fundamentally, one might ask, where does Ehrman get this theological conviction about what inspiration requires or does not require? How does *he* know what God would "surely" do if he inspired the New Testament? His approach certainly does not reflect the historical Christian positions on

---

[66]Remember here the fundamental argument of Ehrman: "We don't have the originals! We have only error-ridden copies" (*Misquoting Jesus*, 7). It seems Ehrman is fixated on the issue of the autographs almost as if inspiration has to do with the physical artifacts themselves rather than the text they contain. However, historically speaking, inspiration has not been about the autographs as a material object but about the text they bear. Since you can have the text of Paul without having the autographs of Paul, then it is clear one does not need the autographs to have an inspired book. It would be helpful if Ehrman would distinguish between having the original text (by which he means having the autographs), and knowing the original text (which can be achieved through the study of the overall textual tradition).

[67]Ehrman, *Misquoting Jesus*, 211.

inspiration (except perhaps those in the King-James-Only camp).[68] Instead, Ehrman seems to be working with an arbitrary and self-appointed definition of inspiration which, not surprisingly, just happens to set up a standard that could never really be met. Does inspiration really require that once the books of the Bible were written that God would miraculously guarantee that no one would ever write it down incorrectly? Are we really to believe that inspiration demands that no adult, no child, no scribe, no scholar—not anyone—would *ever* write down a passage of Scripture where a word was left out for the entire course of human history? Or is God prohibited by Ehrman from giving revelation until Gutenberg and the printing press? (But there are errors there, too.)

It seems clear that Ehrman has investigated the New Testament documents with an a priori conviction that inspiration requires zero scribal variations—a standard that could never be met in the real historical world of the first century. Ironically, as much as Ehrman claims to be about real history, his private view of inspiration, by definition, prevents there from ever being a New Testament from God that would have anything to do with real history. Not surprisingly, therefore, Ehrman "concludes" that the New Testament could not be inspired. One wonders whether any other conclusion was even possible.

Conclusion

Did the battles over heresy and orthodoxy in earliest Christianity affect the transmission of the New Testament text? Yes. No doubt a variety of scribal changes are due to these early theological disputes. But do these changes affect the text in such a way that we cannot be sure what it originally said? Not at all. Since the New Testament is a historical book that has been passed down to us through normal historical means (copying manuscripts by hand), then it inevitably contains the normal kinds of scribal variations that we would expect from any document of antiquity. No doubt some of these scribal variations were intentional and motivated by the theological

---

[68]Gordon D. Fee, "The Majority Text and the Original Text of the New Testament," in *Studies in the Theory and Method*, 183–208. Fee notes that some advocates of the Majority text (e.g., Wilbur Pickering) are motivated by the fact that "contemporary NT textual criticism cannot offer us total certainty as to the original NT text" (p. 189). It seems that Ehrman and Pickering, ironically, share the same goal/requirement: total certainty. It is just that they go about solving the quest for total certainty differently. It drives Pickering to embrace the Majority text and it drives Ehrman to reject that anything can be known about the original text. See also Daniel B. Wallace, "The Majority Text Theory: History, Methods, and Critique," in *The Text of the New Testament in Contemporary Research*, 297–320.

debates of the day. However, the New Testament is different from most other ancient texts in a fundamental way: the wealth of manuscript evidence at our disposal (both in quantity and date) gives us good reasons to think that the original text has not been lost but has been preserved in the manuscript tradition as a whole. Given the fact that the vast number of textual variants is "insignificant," and given that our text-critical methodology can tell which "significant" readings are original and which are secondary, we can have confidence that the text we possess is, in essence, the text that was written in the first century.

Concluding Appeal

The Heresy of Orthodoxy in a Topsy-turvy World

The Bauer-Ehrman thesis is invalid. Earliest Christianity was not infested with a plethora of competing heresies (or "Christianities," as Ehrman and other Bauer paragons prefer to call them); it was a largely unified movement that had coalesced around the conviction that Jesus was the Messiah and exalted Lord predicted in the Old Testament. Consequently, the apostles preached Jesus crucified, buried, and risen on the third day according to the Scriptures. There were heretics, for sure, but the trajectory spanning from the Old Testament to Jesus and to the apostles provided a clear and compelling infrastructure and mechanism by which the earliest Christians could judge whether a given teaching conformed to its doctrinal christological core or whether it deviated from it.

However, debunking the Bauer-Ehrman thesis was not the main purpose of this book. Others have provided compelling refutations before us. The intriguing question is why the Bauer-Ehrman thesis commands paradigmatic stature when it has been soundly discredited in the past. The reason it does so, we suspect, is not that its handling of the data is so superior or its reasoning is so compelling. The reason is rather that Bauer's thesis, as popularized by Ehrman, Pagels, and the fellows of the Jesus Seminar, resonates profoundly with the intellectual and cultural climate in the West at the beginning of the twenty-first century.[1]

---

[1]For a fascinating discussion of this question within the larger scope of conspiracy theories and feminist and other myths of Christian origins see David R. Liefeld, "God's Word or

233

Indeed, it is contemporary culture's fascination with diversity that has largely driven the way in which our understanding of Jesus and early Christianity has been reshaped. If it can be shown that early Christianity was not as unified as commonly supposed, and if it can be suggested that the eventual rise of Christian orthodoxy was in fact the result of a conspiracy or of a power grab by the ruling political, cultural, or ecclesiastical elite, this contributes to undermining the notion of religious truth itself and paves the way for the celebration of diversity as the only "truth" that is left. And thus the tables are turned—diversity becomes the last remaining orthodoxy, and orthodoxy becomes heresy, because it violates the new orthodoxy: the gospel of diversity.

So what can we do about this? Should we stop preaching the tenets of orthodox Christianity? Should we abandon the gospel of salvation in the Lord Jesus Christ, the Messiah and exalted Lord? Should we concede that Christian orthodoxy—historic Christianity—is but one form of several "Christianities" that equally vied for orthodox status in the early centuries of the church? Should we concede the contention of postmodernism that truth is merely a function of power and that, in fact, power is the only truth there is? To use Paul's words, "By no means!" To capitulate in such a manner would be to surrender the very claim of truthfulness so powerfully exerted by the New Testament writers in the gospel.

What should we do, then? First, we must continue to preach the gospel, in season and out of season, bold and unafraid. With God's help, we must seek to make new converts to the Christian faith, disciples of Jesus who obey all that he commanded, to the glory of God. Second, we must continue to confront false gospels, including the gospel of diversity. In so doing, we must expose paradigms that tacitly and implicitly drive popular arguments and that slant one's interpretation of data in ways that propagate the underlying agenda of a given scholar, whether anti-supernatural, atheistic, agnostic, or otherwise antagonistic to the truth of the gospel.

Third, we must proceed prayerfully, recognizing that it is the god of this world who has blinded the minds of unbelievers. With God's help, we should wage spiritual warfare circumspectly and seek to demolish demonic strongholds in the minds of people. This will involve the use of rational arguments and appeals to historical and other evidence, but it will recognize that, in the end, arguments by themselves are inadequate. Did the early church pick

Male Words? Postmodern Conspiracy Culture and Feminist Myths of Christian Origins," *JETS* 48 (2006): 449–73.

234

the right books? Absolutely. Did the keepers of the text tamper with the text? Generally, there was great reverence for Scripture, though, it is true, at times scribes, usually with the best of intentions, sought to restore what they believed to be the original wording of a given passage, and occasionally they did so inappropriately. Even where they did so, however, the original text has not been lost, and we are normally able to reconstruct the original wording with little difficulty. Thus we can have every confidence that today we have, in all essentials, the very text God inspired.

In the end, God does not need anyone to defend his truth. God's truth is able to stand on its own. In this volume, perhaps we have been able to help take off some of the obstacles that prevented our readers from seeing more clearly the truth about Jesus and the origins of early Christianity. Perhaps it has become clearer now that the Jesus we worship is the same Jesus whom the early Christians proclaimed as Messiah, Savior, and Lord. Perhaps it has also been shown that truth matters and that truth does exist, as does error. In an age where heresy is increasingly viewed as orthodoxy, and orthodoxy as heresy, this would be no small accomplishment. May God have mercy on this and subsequent generations until our Lord returns.

Subject Index

237

Scripture Index